Going Places CYTA

Kevin Craik (OAM)
Jan Craik (OAM)

With Dione Shoeman

As told to:

Howard Reid

Going places - CYTA

© Mountains Education Services Trust

First published 2024

The right of Howard Reid as author and the claim of his moral rights have been asserted. The work is copyright. No part may be reproduced or transmitted by any process, in any means, electronic or mechanical or captured through any information storage system without permission. This book was developed by Howard Reid, Kevin Craik, Jan Craik and Dione Shoeman. In addition to the authors there have been more than fifty contributors who have supplied verbal and written information.

Any errors, exceptions and omissions are unintentional. The authoring team have made every effort to verify facts related to people mentioned in this publication and clarify the interests of any possible copyright holders that may relate to any part of this publication. All dates listed, spelling of names and places have been checked and confirmed as far as is possible. If an error has been made I, Howard apologise.

E. &O.E.

Editing by J.A.R. and Dione Shoeman

ISBN: 978-0-6457725-3 print book

This Book

This book is the story of the **CHRISTIAN YOUTH TRAVEL ASSOCIATION (CYTA).** One man had a vision to build a travel organisation that for a generation would allow young adults to travel in safety around Australia and across the world. The tours offered by **CYTA** were staffed by volunteer young men and young women who read from and shared the word of **GOD** found in the **HOLY BIBLE.**

GOING PLACES CYTA is dedicated to the past **TEAM MEMBERS, DIRECTORS,** staff and anyone and everyone who provided any service or assistance to **CYTA** which in turn contributed to the **Kingdom of GOD** here on Earth.

Contents

This Book	4
Preface - A word from Kevin and Jan	6
A quick word before you begin reading	9
Part 1 - The Beginnings	11
Part 2 - Buildings and so much more	27
Part 3 - The people who built CYTA	71
Part 4 - The Tours	267
Part 5 - The Music	333
Part 6 - The initiators, the stayers	403
Part 7 - My Chapters - The author	433
Acknowledgements	447
Addendum	457

Going places - CYTA

A Word From Kevin and Jan

"This book you are about to read is a small extract of the history of the involvement and dedication of hundreds of young people and others, prepared to volunteer their time to share in a ministry to other young people in the many **CHRISTIAN YOUTH TRAVEL ASSOCIATIION** *(***CYTA***) activities. If you were a team member, you would have wonderful memories of the fun and involvement you had as well as presenting the story of Jesus while travelling and in other activities of the organisation you will read about.*

In writing the history of **CYTA***, it is not possible to cover every highlight and every activity that occurred during nearly fifty years. It was a season of ministry and as Ecclesiastes 3, verses 1 to 8 tells us that for everything there is a season.* **CYTA** *was right for its time. For former team members we trust you enjoy rekindling your memories of your great times as part of the* **CYTA** *ministry and for other people who are reading about* **CYTA** *for the first time, we trust that you will find it interesting and edifying. It is the story of what a group of young people can do.*

Whilst constant mention is made in this book of Kevin and Jan Craik, we are humbled before **GOD** *for the privilege* **HE** *gave us, to have had so many hundreds of young and older people who caught the vision, shared with others and served in the ministry. We as a couple, as well as the other original directors, were privileged to be given such an opportunity.*

"For team members, tour members concert goers and musicians we trust you will enjoy rekindling your memories of your great times as part of the **CYTA** *ministry. For other people who are reading about* **CYTA** *for the first time, we trust that you will find it interesting*

and informative as to what a group of young people can do with the LORD at their side."

"This book has been the request of many. That the history of CYTA be written. I, Kevin, now well into in my eighties, I guessed it was about time to do something."

This book is a voluntary labour of love which involved hundreds if not thousands of hours of research, discussion, clarification, checking writing, editing and rewriting. This book required a writing group. Jan and I along with Howard who was a team member in the 70's were involved in **CYTA**. *Dione Shoeman first heard of CYTA through her involvement in the development of this manuscript. Dione has been a constant source of inspiration and help. You can read about Dione in the latter part of the book under* **Kevin Craik Acknowledgements.**

Kevin

    Jan

Enjoy reading about the life of **CYTA**. Now the past has been written up and has been discussed, reviewed, revised and re-written and we have a **History of CYTA**.

(A colour copy of the picture is available if requested by email.)

A quick word before you begin reading

Hi, my name is *Howard*. When you see a sentence starting with the letter I it means me, the story teller.

Before going on please:

1. **Don't necessarily start at page one of this book**. Use the detailed contents in the Addenda at the end of the book to pick out parts, chapters, or sections where your interest lies. Reminders of the use of the detailed contents appear in Chapters 1 and 2.
2. Be aware that- **A side note** – (an example appears below in point 4), are statements included in the story where there is a conversation/event with human interest which is maybe an aside to the book's main story
3. Some of the stories in this book do not carry any names. There are good reasons for some stories to be anonymous. Please do not speculate as to who the stories may be about particularly by approaching someone and saying "I think this is you". Being part of **CYTA** was a happy, adventurous and exciting time for almost everyone involved in the organisation. However, some people suffered hurt. Speculation in any form, could cause further hurt or create new hurt. However, if you assume a story is about you and you want to check whether that is the case, feel free to ask me. I will be happy to confirm or disavow your assumption. Let's not create "fake"

history by trying to attribute a statement or an event to a person or persons to whom it may not apply.

---

4. **A side note:** The letters *née* are generally used to cite the unmarried name of a woman who has taken her husband's name after marriage. *Née* is used for any situation where a woman has changed her name for any reason, marriage, divorce, by choice etc. *Née* has been used in this book.

Part One – The Beginnings

Going places - CYTA

1. 1956, Olympics, television and the inklings of CYTA

CYTA starts going places

Australia won the bid to host the 1956 Olympics games in Melbourne heralding a new age in the life of Australians. Until then Australia was a comfortable but pedestrian location with some of the most exciting food treats available being chicken in a basket and prawn cocktails or a popular chocolate bar coated in batter and cooked in boiling oil at the local fish shop.

During the late 1940s Australia was asked to take 100,000 migrants displaced after World War 2, a migration that would eventually change the country.

> **A side note:** In 1949 the immigration minister at the time, Arthur Caldwell, talked of the nation being composed of:
>
> "Coffee coloured people".

Greater Sydney finished in the west around Bankstown, a mere sixteen kilometres from the CBD.

But by 1956 most of the world was coming to us. The arrival of television in Australia, which was due to commence in late 1956, was sped up so we could watch the "Games". Those fortunate to have sets could watch the biggest sports carnival of all. The first channel on Australian television was Channel Nine and they had the rights to the games.

Going places - CYTA

1956 was not just about the Olympic Games or the advent of television. It also heralded the genesis of a movement that saw thousands of young people travel in a secure, non-threatening environment on tours led by other young people who as Christians embarked on a mission field found at home in Australia. It should be said that many of the young people who became leaders on **CYTA** tours may have not considered themselves working in a mission field or as missionaries but none the less they were.

1956 was the year a young **Kevin Craik** took a trip to the snow with two mates. One, a young man named Warren had an ancient Vauxhall. He and his car were popular mates of Kevin.

In 1956, it was not yet about Christian tours but just some mates enjoying a trip to the snow. The following year, '57, for his return to the snow, Kevin and his group of two mates drove to Canberra and joined a group from Canberra Baptist. Kevin toured the Snowy Mountains in '58 to look at the construction going on of the hydro-electricity scheme and the then almost non-existent ski fields. Thredbo at the time consisted of a petrol pump and a tin shed.

Whether he knew it or not Kevin was preparing for the adventure of a lifetime that would occupy most of his working life.

Another skiing trip was organised with friends in 1959. This was a pre-CYTA trip. This trip and other early snow tours operated under the name Christian Youth Tours

Going places - CYTA

(CYT) The initial leg of the journey to the snow was by car. No fancy coaches.

> **A side note:** The tours of CYTA were always under the name Christian Youth Tours **(CYT)**. **CYTA** as an organisation did not exist at first. It was only when the loose partnership (in law even if not registered) was registered as the company, **CYTA Pty. Ltd.**, that the name always used to brand the tours, **CYT**, was transferred to the new legal structure. The tours were always labelled **CYT**. There is more on the legal structure of **CYTA** and **CYT** later in this chapter.

Through these early trips the love of the snow for Kevin had been born. That love grew and was sustained, a love he wanted to share with fellow Christians, for many decades to come. Kevin's desire was for young people to enjoy the snow. A movement, a business, a ministry had begun that expanded into other areas of travel and took thousands of predominantly young people across Australia and across the world.

In 1960, Kevin was working on the building of the coaxial cable from Sydney to Melbourne. A significant development which took television from a regional broadcast to one that allowed programs to be potentially shown across Australia.

By 1962 weekly snow tours for the new organisation were ready to go. Tours had been planned from 1958 and started operating from 1959 but not on every weekend.

Going places - CYTA

Kevin proudly states:

> "That from 1962 till 1998 weekend snow tours ran every year, every week of the snow season."

Though the snow tours commenced in 1962, it was not till 1964 that coaches replaced car convoys. The convoy tours drove to Cooma where the **TOUR MEMBERS** loaded onto Ansett Coaches to go to the snow fields.

Kevin Craik recalled that,

> "On one occasion before we used coaches for snow tours, there were 29 cars taking 100 people to the snow (Cooma). The first weekend snow tours were car convoy tours out of Sydney started at $18.60 for weekend tours and covered all costs for the trip."

> "Over time the growing popularity of the tours saw over 50 coach groups in some weeks of a snow season. At first the fledgling organisation used the United Motel in Cooma, and then the Salvation Army Hostel for tour member accommodation. In 1969 the accommodation moved to the newly renovated **CYTA LODGE**".

Leaders were needed to staff these early tours. No **CYTA TEAM** as former **TEAM MEMBERS** knew it had been established and it was still some years away. The **initial DIRECTORS** of the new **CYTA** ministry and their spouses acted as **TOUR LEADERS** and were supported from time to time by their friends.

One more person came on board in 1962. Later the love of his life **Jan Berice Shipway** joined Kevin and his pioneering group. They married in 1966. A decade on from beginning the dream that would occupy most of Kevin's life a new adventure began for Mrs as well as Mr Craik.

These pioneers and their families were young people in their twenties, of whom some were recently married and/or buying their first home. Some of the pioneers of **CYTA** were also starting families. Selfless dedication, long hours and hard work led to the start-up and ongoing development of a travel service that allowed young people to travel to places not before thought of and to hear the message of salvation by grace through the death and resurrection of *Jesus Christ*.

The loose business basis that underpinned the early years became **CYTA**, (**Christian Youth Travel Association Ltd**). **CYTA** became the name of the legal entity (company) from 1970. **Christian Youth Tours** (**CYT**) was the enduring operating name for all tours from the beginning of the convoy tours till the closure of **CYTA**. Once **CYTA** Pty. Ltd. was established, the new company owned the **CYT** trading name.

The Ltd in **CYTA** Pty. Ltd is an abbreviation of the word Limited, which in corporation law, (company law) means limited liability. **CYTA** was a not for profit company limited by guarantee. Limited by guarantee means that in the case of business failure, the **DIRECTORS** and other **members** of the company (friends of the business who undertook to be financially liable in the case of business failure) were obliged to pay a pre-determined amount from their personal funds to fund any debts owed, should the business cease trading.

Going places - CYTA

The initial **DIRECTORS** and **company members** but were prepared to underwrite the guarantee were:

> Colleen Barrington, Victor Barrington, David Collins, Mary Collins, Joy Craik, John Craik, Robin Craik, Kevin Craik, Janet Craik, Graham Drayton, Suzanne Drayton, Graham Thorburn, , Jennifer Thorburn, Leslie Shakespeare, and Rosalind Shakespeare.

More will be heard of many of these people in the pages to come

As the ministry expanded, a number of **TEAM MEMBERS** became company members

There were six initial directors and 11 other company members who were providing guarantees against the new venture. Fortunately, the business traded at a profit from day one till the day it closed.

The tour itinerary for the organisation's 1959 commencement featured a weekend Snowy-Mountains tours. It was a full day in the snow after the overnight trip down from Sydney in car convoys.

The trip down from Sydney was only interrupted by hot chocolate and raison toast at the old "Paragon Café" in Goulburn. It was a supper stop. The chocolate was hot, the toilets crowded and the "Bill of Fare" sometimes went beyond raisin toast.

Going places - CYTA

> **A side note**: The owners of the Paragon Café in Goulburn are said to have sponsored people emigrating from Greece to Australia. It is believed that these new arrivals were trained in Goulburn and then sent off to establish their own Paragon Café. If you are in a Paragon Café it just **may** have an historical link back to the original café in Goulburn.

Once these very early groups left Goulburn, the next stop was Cooma with breakfast at the Alpine Café. Breakfast over, the cars left behind, the next stop for the tour members who were now in coaches, was the snow for a day of skiing with accommodation back in Cooma at the United Motel.

Sunday morning after breakfast back into the cars with the first stop Canberra Baptist Church for the morning service followed by lunch. The afternoon tour of Canberra seemingly never changed from these first tours.

Years later the Goulburn stop switched to "The Celebrity" a French café in Goulburn for the Friday night suppers. The tour members and their leaders went into the upstairs' room where the **tour** groups were fed and provided with hot chocolate. The owner of the café would on occasion bring out "delicacies", such as canned eel and canned caviar. Food such as this can be regularly found in Sushi and other dishes today but was often a new taste sometimes reluctantly enjoyed by the tour leaders, who chose to taste the foods first.

Going places - CYTA

When the tours returned to "The Celebrity" on the Sunday the owners Peter and Palsa Salvi, allowed the tours to take up the whole restaurant.

> **A side note**: When Kevin and David Collins (a founding **DIRECTOR**) approached the owners of "The Celebrity" café, Peter and Palsa wanted to be assured that the tours were not from a football club. Football clubs were banned following several rowdy encounters. The café took the bookings which provided good service to each tour group over many years.

Sunday was a trip home, via the Cooma "Clog Shop" where the proprietor always finished his talk with:

> "In a minute or three you'll walk away in a tree."

> **A side note**: *Keith and Elisabeth Jarret*, **TEAM MEMBERS** who met and married while in the **TEAM**, in the eighties purchased the machinery from the Cooma Clog Cabin. A memento of another time

On the way home from the snow, dinner was in Goulburn on Sunday and then back to Strathfield. Seven-day snow trips as well as weekend trips were offered. Skiing was at Perisher Valley.

Tasmania was an early non-snow trip. Today, "Tassie" is an easy place to get to. It was a little over an hour's flight from Sydney by the 1970's. But up till then it was largely unknown to many people living in NSW.

Media at the time was comprised of regional newspapers, which carried little news other than that of the region they serviced and some national political news.

Going places - CYTA

The Sydney newspapers of the time, Sydney Morning Herald the Daily Telegraph, The Daily Mirror, and, The Sun, as well as Sydney television stations were very much more locally based than the networks of today. Many people in NSW had never seen an AFL match.

Tasmania provided a ready market for **CYTA** in the early days. It was like going overseas without going overseas. A trip to Tasmania was a great precursor to overseas trips away.

Long weekend tours over Easter, June and October long weekends featured a variety of itineraries. Trips to Lightening Ridge, Buchan Caves in Victoria and the Gold Coast were always available plus "special tours" such as an extended tour to the 1988 Brisbane Expo. Trips to Coffs Harbour included white-water rafting.

Canowindra included the gentle pursuit of ballooning, while a weekend trip to Lake Macquarie included house-boating. There were numerous tours to "Mystery Destinations" which booked out, as dates were released. No two of these mystery tours were ever the same.

Longer tours including trips to the Red Centre and numerous overseas tours such as to Japan, New Zealand, Fiji, and a trip to Nepal were established on the heels of those early snow trips. You could travel around the Pacific to New Zealand, Fiji along with a three-country tour to Fiji, Samoa and Tonga as well as further afield to the United States of America and Canada. The most adventurous tour was to Kathmandu.

Going places - CYTA

CYTA built up relationships with overseas carriers that allowed the organisation to offer their tour within another tour. A discrete group of **CYTA** travellers operated within the confines of another tour operator. This arrangement worked well for the 90 day (sometimes a little longer or shorter) overland trip from Sydney to London.

Along with providing an extensive list of generally safe and well-resourced, well-planned tours, **CYTA** ensured that everything they did was of the highest quality. Promoting recognition of **CYTA** and the CYT tours was not just achieved through the offer of touring in a comfortable Christian environment but also maintaining integrity and honesty in all that **CYTA** did.

CYTA led the way in tours for young people and demonstrated forward business thinking in many ways such as the use of a trust account to hold tour **MEMBER'S** payments till the tour had been commenced. This was long before such a requirement was legislated. Using a trust account to hold travellers funds became a mandatory requirement following legislation for travel agency licencing.

Only once did the finances of **CYTA** just escape a possible catastrophe. One time, the **DIRECTORS** decided to earn an additional return on the cash held by **CYTA** by placing it with a short-term money market dealer. These short term deposits could be for as little as two days. The return for such deposits, are far more attractive than a short term fixed deposit at a bank. The transaction occurred without any problems. The dealer company though went into insolvency a few weeks later.

Going places - CYTA

This was the first and last short-term money market deposit by **CYTA**.

As time went on, when Kevin had a new idea for the direction of **CYTA**, he would float the idea with several trusted **TEAM MEMBERS** for feedback. I can say I was asked once about pricing of tickets for an international touring band, which proved to be **André Crouch and the Disciples**. I was only asked to provide advice once. I think that having had my opinion once was enough for Kevin.

Kevin along with Jan was the driving force that built the **CYTA/CYT** and later the **AUSTRALIAN CHRISTIAN MUSIC FOUNDATION (ACMS)** brands.

> For information on **ACMS** check the chapter details in the extended contents page in the Appendices at the end of the book.

Though, Kevin seemed to be endlessly involved in the development of **CYTA**, he was at the same time involved in a state wide service to youth through the Baptist Youth Fellowship (BYF). He continued in his role with BYF till 1971. In his taking on a long term role with BYF, clearly he was not busy enough with a full time job, **CYTA** and during the latter portion of those early years, a young family.

Jan reflected on the approach **CYTA DIRECTORS** developed and used from its early days towards decision making:

> ""Being central to the decision making of the Board on all things I knew how and why

decisions were made. I was there when decisions were made. There was much prayer in regard to anything we went ahead with. We always believed that anything we went ahead with was through the prompting of the Holy Spirit".

A kindred spirit

You wonder if **CYTA** was unique.

Andrew Drylie a long term active **TEAM MEMBER** thought so.

"**CYTA** *was unique. There will never be anything like it again*"

Fletch Wylie the trumpeter in **André Crouch** and the **Disciples** who has stayed in touch with Kevin since their first Australian tour more than forty years ago said to Kevin in relation the development of the **AUSTRALIAN CHRISTIAN MUSIC FOUNDATION**

"*I have travelled the world and I have not seen a concept like the* **ACMS.** *This is a unique* **Australian** *– based youth imitative*

Certainly in Australia **CYTA** with its collection of activities was unique and seems to have been unique in the Southern Hemisphere. There are Christian music festivals in other counties but **Fletch Wylie**'s comment speaks to the uniqueness of the **ACMS**

Kevin in his travels discovered an organisation in England which had similar evangelical goals to those of **CYTA** offering tours, (which the organisation calls expeditions). This was **Oak Hall**. This company owned a

Going places - CYTA

lodge equivalent to **CYTA LODGE**. They had bought an old mansion and named it **Otford Manor**. The programs offered by Oak Hall, carried the same evangelical thrust into their travel operations through Europe and into the world beyond as did **CYTA**.

Oak Hall still operates today offering exciting weekends away and expeditions to Europe and the near East. Expeditions are also available to, Canada, Iceland, Ireland, France, Switzerland and Spain. In advertising for Oak Hall, stays at the manor included such things as:

> "Dangerous Camping - Faith in Kids. – Fire – Woodland – Burgers – Activities with their Dad and their friends. Jesus Christ. Everything your children love!"

CYTA TEAM MEMBERS, who visited Oak Hall England and were keen to work there, were given ongoing employment by Oak Hall in recognition of their training with **CYTA. Paul Cleasby a TEAM MEMBER** who you will read about in later chapters was given a job as a Coach Captain when working at Oak Hall.

> Check the chapter details on the **CYTA TEAM** in the extended contents page in the Appendices at the end of the book.

It's good to know that there were at least two organisations on either side of the globe, winning people for Christ through the medium of travel.

Going places - CYTA

Part Two - Buildings, so much to manage

Going places - CYTA

2. CYTA LODGE

Question: What do worker dormitories and huts have to do with CYTA?

Answer: CYTA LODGE.

The Snowy Mountains scheme was and still is one of the biggest, most complex construction projects ever undertaken in Australia. The "Snowy" project was to irrigate farmland and provide hydro-electric power to south east Australia. The scheme began in October 1949 and was officially completed in 1974, though the extended development of the scheme continues to this day with the early stages of "Snowy 2" under way.

In chapter one of this book we read that Australia was asked to take one hundred thousand refugees. Europeans displaced by World War 2 and its aftermath of ruined towns and industries. Around sixty-thousand of the refugees accepted by Australia worked on the Snowy Mountains scheme.

With thousands of workers, most of whom were unmarried, arriving for work in and around the snowy mountains, accommodation was needed. Hence the development of workers camps, most in the nearest substantial town to the scheme which was Cooma, a dormant town with some tourism but little industry until the Snowy scheme came to town.

 The erection of dormitories housing single men as well as small huts used as offices and on occasion as married quarters was carried out to house the mass of people arriving to work on the project. As the project

Going places - CYTA

neared completion, (the first time) and the number of people required to work on the project fell, some of the worker accommodation became surplus to needs.

The reduction of activity on the initial Snowy Mountains project provided a perfect opening for **CYTA** to establish a lodge. As we learned earlier the new organisation used the United Motel in Cooma, overlooking the township and also the Salvation Army Hostel as early accommodation locations. However, the possible purchase of accommodation in what had been workers camps became available.

The initial plan was to establish a lodge that would accommodate 50 to 60 **TOUR MEMBERS** and leaders at Jindabyne. However, once the workers quarters became available in what was known as "East Camp", they were reviewed by the initial **CYTA DIRECTORS**. This was a general workers camp. Consideration was given to relocating buildings from this camp. Then the **DIRECTORS** were introduced to an alternative location.

In September 1969, Kevin and Jan, 5 week old Darren, David Collins, and Graeme Thorburn travelled to Cooma to meet with the property managers of Snowy Mountains Hydro Electricity Commission (SMHEC) regarding the possibility of purchasing snowy workers huts and other buildings. Jan stayed behind in the motel, where the group was staying with baby Darren and prayed that *God* would support and lead the "boys" in their endeavours. He sure did.

Kevin's thoughts on the purchase were:

> *"Instead of acquiring buildings suitable for 50, we were offered West Camp, a place that eventually had over 300 beds, as **CTYA LODGE**. **The DIRECTORS** originally had such a small vision. Our Lord surely had a bigger vision."*

"West Camp" was built to house "SNOWY" management and office staff as well as engineers and became what most **TEAM MEMBERS** and **TOUR MEMBERS** knew as CYTA LODGE.

The **DIRECTORS** prayed. Terms offered to **CYTA** included a three-year lease period with the full purchase payment to be made at the end of the three years. They bought West Camp. It was the beginning of **CYTA LODGE**.

The day that the **CYTA DIRECTORS** took possession of "West Camp", it was just a matter of calling by the "Snowy" authority security office on as it turned out, a Good Friday, and picking up the key. It was a simple task. Payment for the purchase of the **LODGE** came from surplus funds accumulated from the operations of the ministry over the three year lease period.

The disposal manager representing the Snowy Mountains Authority had apparently taken a liking to Kevin and his "mates" and wanted them to have every chance to succeed. Once the purchase of the property was completed the disposal manager said to Kevin:

> *"I had expected to have West Camp back in my possession (the Snowy Mountains Authority) within the year."*

Going places - CYTA

Upon taking ownership of the site, the **CYTA DIRECTORS** and their families slept on the floor of what was the then block known as A Block in initial visits to the site. The first snow weekend was the June Long weekend 1970. After taking control of the site during Easter there was 9 weeks later a booking for 100 **TOUR MEMBERS** predominately from *Blakehurst Baptist*.

Merv and **Daisy Claire** who hailed from Newcastle were appointed the first **LODGE** managers. There was already accommodation on site, a unit of which became the caretaker's cottage for **CYTA**. There living space was in the original Block A. Later another building was moved to the site which then became the new Block A.

Their accommodation in the middle of the original A Block was far from ideal. The **DIRECTORS** did try to ensure the Claire's were as comfortable as possible.

> Check the chapter details for the **CYTA LODGE people** in the extended contents page in the Appendices at the end of the book.

Kevin and Jan Craik, David Collins, Graham Thorburn, Graeme Drayton and John Craik were the initial **DIRECTORS** of now growing organisation/ministry. They along with the wife of Graham Thorburn, Jenny, Graham Drayton's wife Sue and John's wife Robin tasked themselves with the day to day operations of **CYTA** as well as the management of **CYTA**. These people along with many friends/supporters played a significant role in ensuring **CYTA LODGE** was "room ready" in those initial 9 weeks of occupation of the **LODGE**

However, the **DIRECTORS** realised they would need a workforce to help build and refurbish the "West Camp" as **CYTA LODGE** and to lead the ever expanding list of tours. These initial pioneer **DIRECTORS** were soon to be joined by a very motivated group of young people who had caught the vision of developing West Camp into **CYTA LODGE**.

This was start of the **CYTA TEAM**. So important to the development of the Lodge and the development and expansion of **CYTA** were the **TEAM**. The **CYTA TEAM** warrants its own chapters which you will find in another section of this book.

> Check the chapter details for background information on the first **DIRECTORS** in the extended contents page in the Appendices at the end of the book.

Further development from the original buildings saw, **CYTA LODGE** able to accommodate over 350 young people at a single time. It reached capacity on many occasions.

In the development of the **LODGE** and of the whole organisation there was no strategic five year plan, though one Director did call for such a plan to be developed. **DIRECTORS** considered the financial position of the organisation, prayed together and either agreed by consensus to proceed and if consensus was not reached they dropped proposed changes and improvements to the **LODGE** and applied the same

Going places - CYTA

thinking and decision making to any proposed change in the operations of **CYTA**.

Amongst the people who also contributed strongly to the reinvention of "West Camp" as **CYTA LODGE** was a group known as the *Ladies Guild,* which was initially coordinated by *Carole Reece*. The group managed much of the fitout of the **LODGE** interior.

> **A side note**: Kevin once enquired of the *Ladies Guild,* as to whether they would prefer a different nomenclature. The members of the Ladies Guild insisted they were happy with their self-proclaimed title.

Among the achievements of the Ladies Guild was the provision of the red curtains and cushions in the **LODGE**. The material had been given to **CYTA** by prominent Christian business man *Alan Pederson,* on behalf of his company *Petlee*. The business he owned managed, amongst other activities, dyed material. An error was made in the dying process for a customer order. Some rolls of red fabric were not suitable for the client but fitted in perfectly as curtains for the many windows of **CYTA LODGE.**

Vic and *Colleen Barrington*, who were for some time the Queensland Managers for **CYTA**, remember the early days. They were among the friends of the foundation **DIRECTORS** who worked on the **LODGE**.

> *""Many of the originals (before the advent of the **TEAM**) of **CYTA** were singles and young couples who had never decorated a house of their own, so taking on planning, buying, sewing*

> *and decorating the **LODGE** was quite a task. But no job was too big, and we set about getting the **LODGE** together. Before the **LODGE** opened, we spent many a weekend putting the finishing touches to the amazing accommodation which would see thousands of young people from all over Australia enjoy many hours of fun and life changing experiences."*

I can say that Vic and Colleen along with the Greg and Dianne Cumberland and Ken and Dianne McGill were excellent role models to copy in the pre-**TEAM** era and in the early days of the **TEAM**. The couples were all different, but each couple had exemplary behaviours as **TOUR TEAMs** and workers for **CYTA**. It was wonderful for me as a single person to see the commitment of married couples to the organisation and in service to God.

With the purchase and fit out of what would become **CYTA LODGE** some additional capital was required. Four families, the Directors, whose existing Sydney houses were worth around $40,000 each at the time, had to put up their houses as collateral for a $10000 loan.

Kevin remembers that at time:

> *"Banks at that time required you to almost show you did not really need the loan."*

This was a different time and approach to banking than that portrayed in Banking Royal Commission of this era.

In developing the LODGE, new building works would be undertaken as the need arose. For instance on one weekend the entrance to the female toilet which at one stage faced into the main Lodge area was moved while the weekend snow **TOUR MEMBERS** were at the snow.

Development around the **LODGE** provided work for the local community. **CYTA** had a good relationship with the local council. The council was happy to have **CYTA LODGE** succeed as it attracted people to the area at a time when the local population was declining as the Snowy Mountains Scheme came to an end.

Kevin remembers:

> *"The Council Engineer during the early years of developing the **LODGE** was a Christian. He was on side with the continuous progress made at **CYTA LODGE**."*

One activity carried out on the **LODGE** grounds was the introduction of a noise retardant to reduce the impact of **LODGE** noise on their immediate neighbours.

A copse of 4000 pine trees was planted on the hill and Lions Lookout, behind **CYTA LODGE**. The plants were gifts from the Forestry Commission. The contractors employed to plant the seedlings, planted all the plants one Sunday morning. This venture was managed by **Les Shakespeare** who was a business oriented **TEAM MEMBER** who among other jobs he held, drove coaches for Sunline managed the motel on the hill below the **LODGE** as well as for a time managed **CYTA LODGE**.

Going places - CYTA

The plants over time fulfilled their purpose by offering the required sound abatement for the locals as well as a wind shield when strong winds arose around the property. However, trees mysteriously disappeared around Christmas time. Around a dozen mature trees disappeared each year. Pine-trees, means Christmas trees.

Kevin Craik who led the refurbishment of "West Block" as **CYTA LODGE** was always astute in sourcing and purchasing not just what was needed at the LODGE but much of all the needs of **CYTA**. So astute was he that he was approached to go into business by two people who were involved in the management of **CYTA**.

The proposed business involved the purchasing of selected items, generally at auctions, and reselling of goods particularly if any proposed purchase of an item was grossly undervalued. Kevin declined the proposed business activity as he believed that such a business would put him into a conflict of interest with his work for **CYTA**. Kevin Craik, a man of principal.

Modifications and improvements at **CYTA LODE** were ongoing throughout its life. In 1974 the then Australian Government was providing grants to community organisations. **CYTA** was a recipient of a grant for $34000 which was put to good use.

Kevin recalls how the money was spent:

> "We spent the government grant well. The grant enabled us to build ten bathrooms on the back of 'Y' Block. Countless thousands of people who stayed at **CYTA LODGE** enjoyed a hot shower

Going places - CYTA

*after their return from the snow and other **LODGE** based activities "*

> Check the chapter details for the **CYTA LODGE people** in the extended contents page in the Addendum at the end of the book where **Kevin Craik** reflects on the input of **LODGE** managers who worked with local businesses to ensure the ongoing success of the **LODGE** operation.

CYTA had a strong involvement in Christian Camping International (CCI) Australia, now Christian Venues Australia. **CYTA** was briefly the NSW representative at the formation of CCI Australia in 1975. Kevin and Jan were made life members of CCI Australia in 2007.

A tribute to **CYTA** and the **LODGE** from Reverend *Ted Edwards*

> *"When I arrived in Cooma (NSW) in 1976 as the **Pastor of Cooma Baptist Church**, I never imagined the blessing that would await me there, not only in terms of the wonderful people that I would minister to and meet, but also in terms of the wonderful blessing that **CYTA LODGE** and the **AUSTALIAN CHRISTIAN MUSIC SEMINAR** (discussed in detail in later chapters in this book) would prove to be in my life.*
>
> *In January 1978 at the Dinner of the first **AUSTALIAN CHRISTIAN Music SEMINAR**, Jenny my then future wife joined me as my partner at the seminar dinner. What began that night would finally lead to our marriage at **CYTA LODGE** on 29th April 1978. The service was*

> *conducted by Jenny's father, Rev Ian Emmett. In fact, our marriage at the **LODGE** was the first marriage to have ever held there. Instrumental in the blessing of this day was **Les** and **Ros Shakespeare**, who were the managers of the **LODGE** at this time, and **Kevin Pool**, who was amazing in organising the catering as well as in many other practical ways."*

*Part 2 of this tribute to **CYTA** is found in the chapter dealing with the **AUSTALIAN CHRISTIAN MUSIC SEMINAR**.*

Ah, what a great way to finish this chapter on the **LODGE**. The all-purpose **LODGE**. No doubt there is much more to know. To paraphrase a well-known saying, if only its walls could have spoken.

A side note: From here on there is no more annoying further references to the use of the extended contents page found in the Addenda to this book. I am sure that all is clear in that if you want to read a particular story you can find it by reference to the contents list.
---

though places - CYTA

Going places - CYTA

3. SEASONS OF MINISTRY

QUESTION: What do RESERVOIR HILL – SMA WEST CAMP – CYTA LODGE – PACIFIC LODGE – JOULE RIDGE all have in common?

ANSWER: They are all the sme piece of land.

Press release by the Snowy Mountains Authority on 11/2/2021 ·

> "Construction is underway for a $19 million, 126-bed accommodation development to house Cooma-based workers for the Snowy 2.0 pumped-hydro renewable energy project. Snowy Hydro and Snowy 2.0 principal contractor Future Generation Joint Venture celebrated with a sod-turning ceremony at the site today. Known as Joule Ridge, the accommodation investment is another significant contribution by Snowy"
>
> Reference:
> https://www.snowyhydro.com.au/news/new-cooma-accommodation-development

Everything changed - the LODGE was no more.

By the 90s, the travel environment for young people had changed. Mega churches were big enough to run their own tours/camps without having to join with other church groups. Adventure travel was now the norm, with young people now confident in regard to solo travel or travelling as two or three, and financially able to travel to faraway places that were not visited by earlier generations.

Going places - CYTA

Where a previous generation would have gone on holidays as a member of an organised tour, such as those offered by **CYTA**, the demand for such tours was in decline. Demand for weekend snow tours of the type offered by **CYTA** had fallen as trends in travel changed. In fact, the demand for all coach travel apart from day trips from retirement villages had almost come to a halt

In late 1995 the demand for coach travel showed signs of weakening and this caused the then **DIRECTORS** to consider the long term future of the **LODGE**. Sale was seen as a possible watershed event in the life and mission of **CYTA**.

An unexpected, unsolicited offer for purchase of the **LODGE** property came from Pacific Hills Christian School (PHCS).Consideration of the offer and with it the future of CYTA required much prayer,

Sue Hayes,

> "It is so sad. (The Lodge has gone) *CYTA* was part of my life for at least 15 years, giving me the best memories of my life."

A decision was made by the then **CYTA** Directors to sell the **LODGE** and so ended 27 years of **CYTA** service to our *Lord* The closure of one ministry heralded the opening of another. The keys were handed over to the Pacific Hills Christian School on June 6, 1997. **CYTA** continued to use the Lodge for the **AUSTALIAN CHRISTIAN MUSIC SEMINAR (ACMS)** until the 2002 Music Seminar. The organisation was placed in a position of having to hire for five years a location they had previously owned.

Going places - CYTA

This was the end of **CYTA LODGE**, but not the end of **CYTA**. Its ministry would continue in for another decade after the handover.

Chris Watson remembers:

> "I am glad for the wonderful memories and great experiences. I was so blessed to have been involved. I have been able to serve in so many ways at the lodge. Nobody can take that away"

A side note. *The piano used in the CYTA Homebush Centre and then at* **CYTA LODGE** *was kindly donated by the parents of Chris Watson*

The sale of the **LODGE** and accompanying land to Pacific Hills Christian School was not just about money. The then **CYTA** Directors recognised that the school had a similar evangelical Christian Spirit that had driven the first Directors of **CYTA** and those Directors who followed including **MEMBERS** of the **CYTA TEAM** who became Directors. Such an evangelical spirit was a consideration in making the sale to Pacific Hills Christian School.

David Willersdorf is a professional Christian musician who recalls his times at the **CYTA LODGE** for the various music seminars in a FACEBOOK post recalls the **LODGE**:

> ""I made many lifelong friends there (the **LODGE**). I had a look on a recent tour of Australia and the buildings were mostly there. Sad to see it all go. Kevin and Jan are much appreciated!"

Going places - CYTA

The **LODGE** renamed Pacific Lodge did not get the long term intended use that was planned by PHCS. A place developed as holiday accommodation was still used in a similar way. In 2018, PHCS sold the Lodge and the related land to the Snow Mountains Hydro-Electric Scheme Authority (SMHES). The ownership of the Lodge and the accompanying land had returned to the owner from which it had been purchased.

From its sale to **CYTA** in 1970, the land and everything on it was sold back to the former owner in 2018.

Geoff Surtees posted on the **CYTA** Facebook page on seeing the picture of the now cleared land where the **CYTA LODGE**:

> *"Many, many, fond memories of the **LODGE**, work weekends, etc. The **CYTA LODGE** was a great witness to all those who passed through it. Sad to see it gone but memories live on forever."*

All buildings on the old **CYTA** site excluding what is known as the "manse" have been bulldozed to provide a green-field site for developers of the land. The site has now become a housing estate for a new generation of Snowy Mountains Scheme workers, housing people working on "Snowy 2." The site is now called Joule Ridge.

Christine Pegram writes

> *"At least the memories remain! These were great times with lots of fun and laughter. I am blessed to have made longstanding friendships from those days. Especially have wonderful memories*

> *of working with Kevin Pool. King of Cooma - he brought so much fun and presence to the* **LODGE***!"*

Nobody can take away the memories of the work done by so many during the life of **CYTA** for *God's Kingdom* here on earth. A sentiment echoed by ***Elaine Abrahams.***

> *"They may bulldoze the buildings, but the memories and the legacy of that place are alive and ongoing."*

The vibrancy and expectation and renovation work of **TEAM MEMBERS** especially from the '70s, to build and support the LODGE as a premium youth location had come to an end. The work of successive **TEAM MEMBERS** in building a holiday location, which in reality was a mission field, was gone.

Don Kinscher, who was the Lodge manager just after the turn of this century (then owned by PHCS) speaks to his sadness at the demolishing of the **LODGE**

> *"I am incredibly saddened to see it* (**CYTA LODGE**/Pacific Lodge) *gone but immeasurably grateful to God for the way in which He used the* **LODGE** *and us (along with hundreds of other willing workers) to touch the lives of thousands and turn hearts toward Himself.*
>
> *The loss of this piece of earthly history is sad but the eternal effect it had on so many of us will be felt for many years to come."*

Sue Hayes was saddened.

Going places - CYTA

> *"It is so sad the **LODGE** has gone. CYTA was part of my life for at least 15 years, giving me the best memories of my life."*

However, before the complete demise of the buildings that was once **CYTA LODGE** created on final local news story.

The Monaro Post November 28. 2019 at 5:43 PM

Huge fire at CYTA LODGE

> *A grass fire broke out behind the Snow Season Motor Inn (previously the Marlborough Motor Inn) on the corner of the Monaro Hwy and Solomon. (The) fire threatened to spread*
>
> *At approximately 12:15pm last Friday 29 November, a grass fire broke out behind the Snow Season Motor Inn (previously the Marlborough Motor Inn) on the corner of the Monaro Hwy and Solomon Lane in Cooma, resulting in the total destruction of two disused buildings and further damages to surrounding buildings*
>
> *Many looked on as the flames climbed trees and jumped across the Monaro Highway, threatening to spread. Firefighters brought the blaze under control, with no one harmed in the incident.*

The fire heralded the end for ever of what was **CYTA LODGE**.

Going places - CYTA

When **CYTA** had sold the **LODGE**, had the **LODGE** served its purpose? Only *God* knows whether it served its full purpose. But it was certainly right for its time.

Greg Oates, who only came to the **LODGE** for the **ACMS (the music** seminars), recalls the LODGE.

> *"This place was the launch pad of many great artists who today are still making Jesus known through the music God laid on their hearts to write."*

However, **CYTA LODGE** was the central piece of a ministry that did not proclaim itself as a ministry. For half a century the **HOLY SPIRIT** had used the **CYTA LODGE,** which became Pacific Lodge mightily, through their ministries to win people for Christ as well as bring about the renewal in the faith of many people who may have fallen away.

A side note: A longggg… one **CYTA LODGE PATCH** – It's very own mystery tour!

He spotted an old memory one day that he had to get hold off. This is the story as told by **Kevin**.

*"**Kevin Pool**, among other duties operated the **LODGE** souvenir shop. The **CYTA LODGE** clothing patch was one of the items sold in the shop which sold out in double quick time. The Sydney CYTA office didn't retain a sample of the patch.*

*On 30 October 2021, I opened the eBay website and unexpectedly the screen read **CYTA LODGE PATCH** available in Salt Lake City for $9.99 USD. This excited* me and I started to process the details to buy the patch into the computer, but then saw "Does not post to Australia"

Not to be outdone, I called my friend **Perry Morgan** (whose story is told in the chapter dealing with music) in California – to see if I could buy the patch and have it sent to his address. Perry could then forward it on to me Perry agreed. I paid for the patch, and it arrived at Perry's address. Perry then posted it on to Australia on Monday 18 November, using regular Air Mail with correct address details.

It didn't arrive.

Perry said he believed it would turn up. He believes in prayer to the Almighty. December, January, February, March, then. April 17th, 2022, it turned up back in Perry's letter box in California! You can imagine the excitement this caused on both sides of the Pacific!

On April 30th, Perry posted it again, this time by signature required, address double checked and it arrived for signature in the Village Office on Tuesday 3 May 2022.

What was lost is now found. I was rejoicing I that I had received the patch. It now holds pride of place on my desk. Our prayers were answered.

Do you have a **CYTA LODGE PATCH**? If so, then please let Kevin know by email kevjan@hotmail.com he would value knowing how many people still have the patch.

Going places - CYTA

(A colour copy of the patch is available if requested by email)

(A colour copy of the patch is available if requested by email)

Going places - CYTA

4. Even CYTA needs an office, storage

Offices and training facilities

The early camping equipment used by **CYT** (not **CYTA** at that stage) had to go somewhere. There needed to be an office set up so bookings could be accepted and processed. An office was needed so that potential **TOUR MEMBERS** could visit and ask questions and pay for trips.

Online payments did not exist when **CYT** was in its formative years. Bookings were made in person, over the phone or by "snail mail". An office as well as training facilities were needed for **CYT**.

Kevin Craik established the first **CYT** office on a small table in the lounge room of his parent's Marrickville house. The table was spread with travel brochure proofs, bookings, tour schedules etc. This was a situation that needed to change.

A small office in Knight Street Homebush was rented for $8 per week. The space was so small that if three people were in the space, one would have to stand.

Kevin's friends as well as family members were involved in in the emerging travel organisation. A small office was not enough. A place for meetings was needed.

Carole Reece one the very early **CYT/CYTA** supporters and **TEAM MEMBER** remembers attending the very early **CYT** meetings.

> The early meetings of the initial **DIRECTORS** and other people involved at the start were at the home of **Mr and Mrs Craik Senior** held in an informal seating. I remember **DIRECTORS** such as *"Thorbie" (Graham Thorburn)*, and *"Drayt" (Graham Drayton)* sitting around relaxing in the lounge room

Larger meetings were held at a house at 135 Wentworth Rd. **Carole Reece** (as well as Kevin) remembers the house. The following is a combined reflection from them on the house.

> "The house was the headquarters of the **Australian Inland mission (A.I.M.)**. The parents of **David Collins's** (One of the original **DIRECTORS**) were missionaries with the Aboriginal Inland Mission and had served many years ministering to the Indigenous people of Australia in many areas of Australia but especially in Darwin.
>
> It was a very large home and had a large lounge room with a great fireplace. It was a very suitable for large gathering. When **CYT** started getting larger than just the directors we needed a place to meet informally to hold so called "committee and training/discussion meetings". It was in the lounge room that in 1968 we prepared our first 11 minute promotional audio /visual – a "slide show!" It was premiered at the end of year function in the Grace Bros Auditorium. The house at 135 was where David Collins commenced his **Christian Sound** business,

Going places - CYTA

> *135 Wentworth was the base in Sydney for AIM staff. Helpers and other people involved with A.I.M. travelling through Sydney received hospitality at the house. Mr and Mrs Collins were very gracious and welcoming people hosting AIM meetings as well as other organisation's not the least **CYT**.*
>
> *A fire damaged the building around mid-year 2021.after we and every other group using the house were well gone. We met at 135 Wentworth till the organisation set up an office and **TEAM** space at 21 Everton Road Strathfield in 1971"*

From the hole in the wall office **CYT** moved to a shop in **Everton Road Strathfield**. The move to Everton Road became available when a real estate business vacated the space. With an office in the front and a small amount of storage space in the back this was a significant step up for the organisation. The shop space was big enough to hold information nights and **TEAM** training with everyone sitting on camp stools used on tours.

However, Thursday training nights soon migrated to **Homebush Baptist Church**. The numbers in the **TEAM** had grown to the point that a large building seating at least eighty plus was needed on each training night.

The break-through in office accommodation and storage of camping equipment came when a building became available that could hold an office, storage of equipment and training sessions for the **TEAM**. **Homebush, 16 The Crescent**, was an old service station complete with bowsers and service bays. Sections of the building were partitioned off to provide office space, an equipment storage area and a training area for **TEAM** training nights.

The building was purchased by **CYTA**. Offices occupied by **CYTA** up to this point had been rentals. Homebush was purchased and belonged to **CYTA**. It provided enough space to do anything and everything.

Over time the priorities of **CYTA** changed. Homebush provided space for everything but was in a residential area, so noise abatement was always on the mind of the **DIRECTORS** of the organisation.

DIRECTORS meetings were held at Homebush. An administration office and **TEAM** meeting areas were easily accommodated. Some parking was available for tour staff going on weekend tours. However, Kevin was always looking ahead.

> *A side note:* Such dedication **TEAM MEMEBERS** had. I can assure you *Kevin* tells the following story with much pride. *"There was much work to be carried out to fit out the Homebush Centre. Kevin Craik who barely stayed away from the place came in one Saturday Afternoon to find **Shayne Standen (Née Henderson), Bev Carruthers and Linda Web (Née Sykes)** scraping paint of the former workshop walls. What a great find to lift his spirits?*

Kevin was always quick to grab a bargain he thought might be useful to CYTA. It was as true of the fit out of the Lodge as it was in any of the **CYTA** offices. One of the latter **CYTA** office staff commented:

Going places - CYTA

> "Don't go to lunch if you like the typewriter you have."

Kevin admits that the joke about typewriters is a true one. He said

> "Our office was ahead of its time. In 1983, I walked into an auction, just as they were auctioning an IBM word processor for $5400. I thought it was a personal desktop computer. Later in discussion with the IBM salespeople, I was informed that the previous owner paid $35 000 for the equipment less than 12 months before. IBM advised that the sale contract still had training courses for 8 staff, so our office-staff were well-trained in the use of the word processor"

With ownership of the new Homebush all-purpose space increasingly **CYTA** was involved in a music ministry. The seventies and the eighties were a time that many Christian bands sprung up at the behest of Churches to play in services though the members of those same churches were not keen on bands practicing in the church. Some of these bands played as commercial bands during the week or at regular weekend bookings as well as playing a different set of songs at Christian venues. The mixture of what traditionalist might call secular and Christian music performances was a balance between ministry and ensuring finances to sustain the band.

The biggest problem with **CYTA** supporting Christian bands was finding somewhere for a band to practice.

Going places - CYTA

Homebush did provide enough space but with nearby neighbours, echoing sound and cement floors, it was not the ideal location.

The fostering of bands including the need for rehearsal and performance space was not new. The need to support bands through providing rehearsal space had been suggested and to some extent pushed on many occasions by myself, while charged with booking bands for each snow weekend and managing the concert schedule for local bands.

After some time of corporate and individual prayer by each of the **DIRECTORS** a decision was made to step forward in faith. Homebush was sold and the search for a more suitable venue for the requirements of operating coach tours, given there was limited parking space for coaches (a problem not solved by the Homebush move that had occurred at the two previous offices) as well as providing rehearsal and performance space for Christian musicians had begun.

A secondary concern which impacted the sale of Homebush was that Kevin felt some people wanting to book a **TRAVELWAYS** tour (the commercial arm of **CYTA,** which merits is own chapter) were somewhat "frightened" by the word "Christian" on entering the **CYTA** office.

It was a return to now expanded offices in **Rochester Street, Homebush** that held Travelways Australia when it first commenced business. The **TEAM** began to meet on Thursday nights in the local primary school. This could not last too long.

Going places - CYTA

Kevin always looked ahead to the next location. Kevin took tours of **TEAM MEMBERS** to possible new locations. Such tours included de-licensed club premises in Homebush and finished with the leasing by **CYTA** of a Silverwater de-licenced club which from then on carried the name **CYTA CENTRE Silverwater.**

In 1988, the Bicentennial year for Australia the *CYTA Centre at Silverwater* became the offices and **TEAM** meeting area of **CYTA**. The premises were still set up as a club which **CYTA** used as a venue for functions and concerts. There was sufficient off street parking for **TEAM MEMBERS** for Thursday night **TEAM** meetings, and alternatively room to load a full weekend of coaches. The Silverwater premises were leased by **CYTA** from 1988 till 1999.

Time at Silverwater was not without incident. One night shortly after opening the new venue, flooding of part of the building occurred and over $39,000 of new carpet had to be replaced.

On another occasion, someone stole copper piping installed in the roof for the air conditioning drainage system. A kind supportive plumber, ***Bruce Kesby*** replaced the copper piping, a gift from Bruce to **CYTA**. The gift saved hundreds of dollars of expenditure. A thief's prize was a small setback for **CYTA**.

However, Silverwater offered what previous venues could not. The building had an auditorium with a seating capacity of 400, which allowed **CYTA** to offer a location to Christian musicians, especially the more "rocky" groups to practice. No more upset for church **MEMBERS** or church neighbours.

> **A side note:** A Saturday night music event was tried at Silverwater. It was named in the first Instance **True Colours** and later as **The Voice**. A separate chapter in **Part 4 – The music** explores this venture.

An established sound desk was set up in the auditorium with a hidden duct, which allowed cables to be passed along from the desk to the stage, without any safety concerns for the audience. (It was still not the time of radio microphones.) Short curtaining and a lighting rig were in place when **CYTA** took over the lease.

CYTA took over the established bar area but the new serving area did not carry alcoholic drinks. However, the absence of alcohol during the years **CYTA** occupied the building for a short time turned out not to be the case.

Kevin recalls that he was given 5 days by a licensing officer to remove the poker machines left behind by the previous users of the premises:

> *"I was told by a licensing inspector to get rid of them or I will charge you with having controlled gambling items in unlicensed premises."*

> **A side note:** A popular drink among non-alcoholic drinkers was Lemon, Lime and Bitters (LLB) (or Soda Lime and Bitters for those wanting the drink sugar free.) Now if you are reading this you may already know that the bitters do have a small alcoholic content. Not enough, after one drink to register a reading of any significance on a roadside breath test but any product containing even a small amount of alcohol is under

Going places - CYTA

legislation deemed to be a controlled substance. A bank manager, representing the bank financing **CYTA**, conducting a regulation audit of the centre noticed the bitters and alerted Kevin. Further enquiries revealed that there had been an inadvertent breach of the liquor laws. Kevin was quick to remove the offending bottles LLB became Lemon Squash.

*Several **TEAM MEMBERS** held their wedding reception at the centre in which **TEAM MEMBERS** and professional caterers were involved.*

Silverwater also had an independent church operating within its walls on a Sunday for several years. A local Sydney Christian City Church, which is generally known as a C3 began at the **CYTA CENTRE**. The church now operates in a different area of Silverwater Road. The church that started its life in the **CYTA CENTRE at SILVERWATER** has gone from strength to strength.

Storage of all that gear

Storage at first was in Kevin and Jan's garage. From the **TEAM**, a group of people mostly but not always composed of men met on a Tuesday night in Kevin's driveway, to sort, clean and refurbish equipment. If the chores were done early, then there was time for pancakes.

Equipment began to be stored away from Kevin and Jan's when **CYTA** took up the lease at Everton Road. Storage space was still limited and much of the catering equipment stayed in the Craik's garage. It was only when the later move to Homebush occurred did the Craik's get to use their garage, though Kevin always held onto a few things, just in case. His bower bird

Going places - CYTA

approach of collecting and holding onto things, just in case, has persisted throughout his life.

A space for everything and everything had a place. Space was not an issue at the **CYTA CENTRE Silverwater**. The building was 100 feet by 100 feet, 10,000 square feet, which equates to approximately 93 square metres. It had established office space, reception areas, change rooms as well as shower facilities. Anything you might expect in what was once a licensed club.

The **CYTA CENTRE Silverwater** offered parking for around one hundred cars. The space for parking when devoid of cars made moving coaches in and out easier, than previous road side pick-ups and drop-offs in other locations. It allowed the **TEAM**, to park their cars when coaches were not in residence to park without fear of receiving a traffic infringement. **CYTA** could carry on all of its normal activities at Silverwater as well as add new activities.

More space to work in. More space to work for Christ.

5. Other ventures – Nothing Ventured, No Gain

Kiah Ridge

Kevin and the rest of the **CYTA** Board were not just on the lookout for new space for the central operation of the ministry. There were other endeavours in which the organisation wanted to become involved.

In 1988 operations for **CYTA** moved to the new premises at Silverwater but it was also the year that Kiah Ridge was purchased at auction.

The Tahmoor NSW property at the time of sale was known as the Willows. It had eight motel type rooms plus two houses. There was a large reception area and meeting area (auditorium.) The accommodation was to be expanded if **CYTA** took possession.

Also on the property was a large pool and the lay out for an 18 hole golf course with tees, greens and fairways positioned but unfinished. What became known as Kiah Ridge was situated on 170 acres of which about one third of which was mowed primarily for the golf course, with a dam and a jetty in Tahmoor NSW.

Jan described Kiah Ridge.

> "It was overall a gorgeous property."

Kevin had heard, (through his seemingly infinite knowledge of what was happening almost everywhere through his contacts on almost anything and everything), on a Thursday about the auctioning of the property, which was previously a rehabilitation/health farm owned by a doctor who fell on "hard times" and was subsequently deregistered. Kevin was informed of the availability of the property by the same friend of the **TEAM** who later donated a Nissan Urvan to **CYTA**. (Check the detailed contents page for the chapter on the **TEAM**.)

After inspecting the property, on the Saturday, two days after hearing about its impending sale, Kevin had the rest of the Board drive out to look at the property on the Sunday but only after they had attended church.

After praying, and reviewing the proposed ministry opportunity and an informed discussion was held by the Board a decision was made to attempt to purchase the property and a limit was set on how much could be bid at auction. **CYTA** bought the property at auction inside the limit set, with $2500 to spare.

This new location was to be adapted and used as a new lodge. Informed calculations were made and the break-even point (where total cash outflows, on a project, equates to total cash inflows on the project) with a bank interest estimated at 14% for this investment, was set at three years.

Though, the cost was small compared to today's valuations, the interest rates were high. **CYTA** throughout its existence always paid all its bills, though money was always tight. At the time Kiah Ridge was purchased and work began on fitting out the property, interest rates on the bank loans increased, hitting a high of 22.5%. This occurred at a time when Australia was last in recession before the COVID downturn.

Going places - CYTA

Small groups of **TEAM MEMBERS**, up to 14 at a time, went out and worked on the property on weekends. Over 12 months was spent working on the "new **LODGE**" without any revenue generation. The objective was to bring the property up to the highest standards that could be afforded at the time. It was not known as a camp but as a conference centre. It was to be known as the Kiah Ridge Christian Conference Centre.

Purchases were made from various opportunistic sources to keep renovation and fit out costs to the lowest level possible including carpets and chairs from the original Sydney Exhibition and Convention Centre. Much of the kitchen equipment was sourced from the Pizza Hut store within the shops attached to the convention centre. From the Dungeon night club in the basement of the AMP building a variety of items were purchased which were put to good use both at **KIAH RIDGE** and **CYTA LODGE.** Quality catering and kitchen equipment was obtained by a strip out and refit of a restaurant at the historic heritage listed Campbelltown Town Hall. Procuring the various items at auction saved thousands of dollars on buying them new.

As interest rates rose to 22.5% the property became unsustainable for **CYTA** to continue the fit out. The property was "burning" up cash, without a reliable prospect of opening for customers in a short period of time following its purchase.

The interest bill was being funded from the company overdraft. An overdraft is generally used for paying for operational activities in expectation of generating known income that will be earned and received in a short period of time. Overdrafts are for operational activities such as preparation for tours till the commencement of each tour and the release of travellers' funds from a trust account. Mortgage loans are designed to fund capital purchases (major assets).

The Board met again in regard to **KIAH RIDGE** but with a different purpose to the meeting from when they decided to attempt to acquire the property. Board members prayed individually before the meeting and prayed corporately at the meeting. The Board as a whole considered the financial position of the organisation and whether there was scope for continuing the development of **KIAH RIDGE**. The Board decided that funding the ongoing work on **KIAH RIDGE** could not continue (though there was considerable heartache attached to the decision).

The Board of **CYTA** worked on consensus agreement. A Director who was charged with managing the development of the **KIAH RIDGE** property disagreed with other Board members on the future of the property and chose to leave the meeting. The remaining Board members reached a consensus decision without that person. Sell, **KIAH RIDGE.**

The Director involved in the sudden departure from the Board meeting subsequently resigned from the Board, (though the person remained as a company member). A twenty five year working relationship with Kevin was broken in a minute.

It is difficult when different people believe *God*'s will is different for them than other people. Without taking sides, it is true that sometimes even in the most harmonious organisations, particularly those operated by Christian's, that there will be differences of opinion between the various people involved. People are fallible. *God* is not.

There was now a search on to find a buyer for **KIAH RIDGE**. Kevin talked to the Youth Director for the Baptist Churches in NSW/ACT. The Baptist Church was looking for a facility for youth.

KIAH RIDGE was sold to the Baptist Union of NSW/ACT who is the current owner.

KIAH RIDGE could be labelled a failed project of **CYTA**. Should it have ever gone ahead? Was it spurred on by a need to replicate a past success, buoyed on by all the learning that had occurred when **CYTA LODGE** was developed?

Kevin and Jan believe, as with the many other decisions of **CYTA** that buying Kiah Ridge was guided by the Holy Spirit.

The centrality of prayer in the lives of the original and the later Directors of the organisation was I believe a key to the success of **CYTA**.

What was **KIAH RIDGE**, in its new work is today is a success story. Today this asset is serving *God*'s Kingdom on Earth and is a facility that is being used to bring people to Christ.

Maybe the role of **CYTA** in this project was to start the project and hand it over to someone else to finish. Maybe through this project **CYTA** was taking on a new role, the initiator but not the finisher. Today the property accommodates over 140 people in excellent facilities and delightful surroundings. It is a now a success story started by **CYTA**.

Stories of coaches and other vehicles
Not just property - A Hino Coach

CYTA for a while had its own mini coach. A new 19-seater HINO coach was purchased in 1981 and modified to **CYTA** requirements, including a roof rack, reclining seats, curtains etc. It was to be used for interstate tours and **TEAM** training. It was ideal for small group touring. On a December tour to Tasmania, **CYTA** was able to use a **TEAM MEMBER** as the Coach Captain.

The coach got as far as the locals describe them the - "infamous Gundagai Hills". An automatic coach with a newly licensed coach driver, new to the coach and the up and down of the hills resulted in the transmission coming apart. A dead stop.

There was the usual call to Kevin of "Help." A replacement coach was on the way. The replacement coach still made it to Melbourne at the booked time to catch the ferry to Tasmania.

The Hino coach was sold in 1985. Problems in operating the coach, the inexperience of drivers, plus the cost of maintenance and repair, meant a prayerful relooking at the need for **CYTA** to own its own coach. The Hino Coach was disposed of within four years of its purchase.

Going places - CYTA

Another Coach story- Not a coach owned by CYTA
(The beginning of an important partnership)

Les Shakespeare recalls his early connection with the bus company that would become Sunliner Coaches

> My earliest contact with a MEMBER of the Richter family was as a boy; my dad and Frank Richter were contractors, each with a tip truck on the Gosford Shire Council. In the early fifties, Frank joined his brothers Ron and George who were farmers and bought out the Riley family bus business and began the Richter Bros. Bus Service which was based at Ocean Beach (Umina) and operated bus runs between Gosford and Patonga on the Central Coat of NSW.
>
> In the late sixties, I purchased an old Reo Bus from the Richters for use by the Sunday school and Youth Group of the Green Point Baptist Church. I was also able to charter a semi-coach from the Richter boys for long distance outings, and subsequently **CYTA** was to charter their more modern coaches. In conversations with Ron Richter one day, he mentioned that the business was for sale and nominated a price.
>
> One of my close friends and co-workers in the church Youth Group was **Graham Leishman**. He and I were also involved in leading tours for **CYTA**. I spoke with him about the possibility of purchasing the Richter bus business. He in turn discussed it with his dad Alex, who was in Real

Estate at the time, and the decision was made to check out the possibility of proceeding with a purchase. I was given the task of investigating possible financing arrangements and together we discussed the ways and means of operating the business. Having thoroughly considered the financial viability and the make-up of a business arrangement, we were able to access the finance required and in mid- to late 1972 proceeded with the purchase.

*During the period of our negotiations, we had many discussions with **Kevin Craik**, CEO of **CYTA**, as we were very interested in providing charters for **CYTA**. Kevin was instrumental in encouraging us to consider the building of a 12 metre Denning Coach when such a sized vehicle was approved by NSW Transport, and an order was placed for the first 12 Metre coach in Australia.*

A new company, "Central Coast Transit Company" was formed to purchase the business and we commenced operating on 1 December 1972. On the 8 December 1972 the new coach was delivered from Brisbane and so was born the Sunliner Coach branch of the business

The significance of the Leishman family to CYTA

Whilst Kevin and his fellow directors were seen to be the face of **CYTA**, there was a body of people behind the scenes supporting the ministry in prayer and in practical

Going places - CYTA

ways. They deserve special mention for their valuable contributions.

Alex Leishman with his son Graham and friend Les Shakespeare formed a company to buy out Richter Bros Bus Service which was operating in Umina on the Central Coast of NSW, and nearby areas. This was a commercial operation. However a good reason for their purchase of the business was that it could be of assistance to **CYTA**, with the provision of coaches for the tour operations of the ministry.

Brand new coaches were purchased and operated under the Sunliner banner. Les Shakespeare, who had a long association with Richter Bros. and with the **CYTA DIRECTORS**, became the new Company Operations Manager.

These three gentlemen shared the vision of the then **CYTA** Directors and in many ways were the reason for the early success of the **CYTA** Tours. It also gave access to Christian coach captains with many of the Leishman family also being great drivers and supporters of the ministry.

Alex Leishman – a Christian businessman – saw the great potential of this fledgling ministry to the young people of Australia. His backing put **CYTA** tours equal to any tours operating at that time. Sadly, Alex passed away in 2021.

CYTA honours Alex, Graham, his son and Les Shakespeare for their commitment and support over many years.

Going places - CYTA

Other vehicles

Kevin Craik remembers with affection the "utes" as well as the coach. Their memory of their use and usefulness through is maintained through specially registered number plates.

> "Great memories of **CYT014** CYT015 **CYT016** and not forgetting the **CYTA** number plate for the Hino mini coach that **David Ohlmus** had made for the coach when passing through Adelaide when returning from a **CYTA** tour to Western Australia."

> *A side note:* Darren the son of Jan and Kevin still has the shell of the old one tonner that Kevin used and was essential n moving equipment around. Plans to refurbish the vehicle are on a permanent hold.

Part Three - The people who built CYTA

Going places - CYTA

6. The First DIRECTORS, families, commitment

The Original DIRECTORS

Who would be so bold as to follow Kevin Craik's vision? Who would be so reckless as to put their biggest asset, their house on the line for the vision?

We know who. The **founding DIRECTORS** bought the dream and many **TEAM MEMBERS** such as I have benefited from it.

The founders of **CYTA** were the first administrators, tour staff, packing group and underwriters of **CYTA**. As mentioned in an earlier chapter, they collectively borrowed $10,000 in the early days of establishing **CYTA LODGE**, putting up their homes as collateral.

The original Directors, with their spouses along with their young families made a commitment to establishing CYTA that turned into the organisation the **TEAM** knew. It is these people and their spouses, sometimes with young families in tow that were fully committed to making what became **CYTA**, (offering **CYT** tours), a reality.

Following is the story of the original **DIRECTORS**.

John Craik - Kevin's brother was there at the beginning of **CYTA**. John operated his own insurance agency, catering for general insurance. He also offered a financial planning service as part of his business portfolio. His work hours were flexible, and John did all

Going places - CYTA

the running around in the city to gather documentation to get **CYTA** Pty. Ltd. established.

John and Robin, his wife, first met at Belvoir Street Baptist Church married and built their home in Castle Hill. They were MEMBERS of Castle Hill Baptist Church for over 50 years. They have since retired to Tea Gardens on the mid- north coast of NSW, where they are heavily involved with the local St Andrews Anglican Church. They have 3 children - Matthew, Rebecca and Peter plus several grandchildren

John served as a director from the very early days of **CYTA** until 1979, He decided at that time to work part-time for 2 days a week in his business. John used the other days of the week to serve voluntarily as the initial director of Prison Fellowship of Australia. The Australian organisation was only the third one established in the world. Prison Fellowships exist today in over 100 countries.

John in 1976 visited Lorton Prison, Washington D.C., and was challenged by the power of the Gospel to change lives. John was privileged to have an entrance pass to every jail in NSW. In 2018, he was received a Commonwealth of Australia award for his many years of service to the Prison Fellowship Australia, his work in the Insurance and Superannuation Industry in Australia and for some 17 years his work as a member of the Pacific Hills Christian School board.

David Dixon Collins - **CYT,** started with regular committee/pre-**TEAM** meetings, in David's parent's home in the early 1960s.

Going places - CYTA

David was a carpenter by trade. His day work was with Lend Lease and because David was such an exemplary tradesman, he was the man that his company sent to fix up all the little faults at Kingsdene Estate at Carlingford NSW.

Jan Craik suggested that:

> *"David was really good with a hammer and nails and could put anything together. David had a quality work ethic, and everything had to be done 100% correct.*

David Collins *is quoted as saying:*

> *"If it's worth doing, it's worth doing properly."*

Much of the finished look that existed when **CYTA LODGE** got up and running came from David's skills and/or directions. He also contributed to the **CYTA** office fitouts in Strathfield, Homebush and Silverwater.

Not only was David involved in the building of the **LODGE** and the fitout of offices, David Collins was also the initial **TOUR LEADER** of the Fiji tours. The tours he took were in August 1969 and August 1970 - all girls - one with 19 and one with 21.

Who organised that?????!!!

The tour went around Fiji anti--clockwise – from Nadi to Suva and all the way back to Nadi – then the boat trip/cruise to Beachcomber Island along with the southern section of the YASAWA Islands.

David is recorded as saying:

Going places - CYTA

> *"We did not have air beds to sleep on, so we just slept on the ground."*

David was also interested in sound engineering. He provided the sound for the monthly BYF rallies, held in Scots Church, Sydney. He also provided sound for youth groups, bush dances and BYF camps. He had a great collection of vinyl Gospel Country and Western albums. He was also a great asset to the leadership Team of BYF Camps. David was a driving force for the **CYTA** sponsored after-church Sunday night concerts in Strathfield (NSW) Town Hall, where around 200 people on average attended which generally finished with as **Kevin** remembers:

> *"...a blast of a coach going past on its way home from the snow "*

"Christian Sound" was established by David. The business at first operated in an old house and then moved to what had been a service station. The company, Christian Sound Services (CS), installed many church auditorium sound systems throughout Australia and the Pacific Islands, including the new Australian Parliament House. They also designed and installed the sound system in the 2000 Olympic Stadium. In addition they provided over 80% of all sound systems required in all venues for the Sydney Olympics.

I remember, employing Christian Sound while I worked at the Wesley Central mission to install a new sound system in the now gone Lyceum Theatre which the mission then used for church. It was an excellent sound system.

Now retired, he still spends a good deal of time with others, sharing his knowledge and skills. The success of C.S. is like the story told of a little seed growing into a giant oak tree which, at the time, was not dissimilar to **CYTA**.

As much as *Graham Thorburn,* another **DIRECTOR**, was up front, David Collins was a back-room operator. He was a very particular tradesperson who wanted to ensure that all the work carried out at **CYTA LODGE** was precise and was a quality finished job.

Graham Stanley Thorburn - Graham's involvement in **CYTA** involved the extensive use of his professional skills. At that time, he was studying architecture at the old Ultimo Technical College, (now Sydney TAFE). He was very heavily involved with the youth work of the Central Baptist Church Sydney and the monthly youth rally which was separate from the monthly BYF rally, (which was also held in the Central Baptist Church).

He worked with the firm Noel, Bell, Ridley, Smith and Partners. The company held expertise in community building, which featured church design and aged care facilities throughout Australia and in New Zealand. Among their projects was the design of St Andrews House and the Hillsong Convention Centre. Graham held particular expertise in the design of prisons.

Graham's design skills along with *David Collin's* wood working skills combined to provide a significant impetus to the work carried out on **CYTA LODGE.** His input in the development of **CYTA LODGE** in Cooma was invaluable.

Going places - CYTA

Graham was the **TOUR LEADER** on the first tour to New Zealand in 1968. In 1969, he carried out a survey tour to Western Samoa, Tonga and Fiji, which was to become the South Sea Safari.

Graham's artistic and graphic design flair was on show with the early **CYTA** publicity. **CYTA** had a small printing press. Graham had skills in graphic design. He developed many of the lay outs for the early brochures and carried out the printing. The **CYTA** logo is one of Graham's creations. In the move from Everton Road to Homebush, the press was dropped. It was never to work again. The machinery was sold for parts.

Graham had an exceptional work ethic. He devoted much time to the ministry of **CYTA** and to his architectural work.

Kevin tells the story of his last visit to Graham in hospital at Royal North Shore Hospital, just before his going home to Glory.

> "Here was Graham, sitting up in bed, with plans 50mm thick, for a new aged care centre. He never gave up! Did we hear someone say he was a prolific producer?"

Graham was one of the joint **TOUR LEADER**s on the February, 1968 Gold Coast tour where there were two Jenny's as **TOUR MEMBERS.** One Jenny married *Cliff Warburton*, the coach captain for the tour/holiday, and the other one married *Graham Thorburn*.

Going places - CYTA

A trained nurse, Jenny Thorburn like all the directors' wives, was a tower of strength behind the scenes, particularly in the early days of **CYTA LODGE**

Kevin recalls:

> "Jenny Thorburn had, had a ministry with **CYTA** and RUACH Christian Community. The RUACH Community is a gathering of predominantly house churches found in the Northern Beaches area of Sydney that seeks to foster strong Christian personal relationships. Jenny and Graham had 2 children, Nolan, who lives who lives with his wife in Japan and Nerida and several grandchildren. Jenny Thorburn went home to heaven before Graham. Graham followed her in 2015."

A fitting tribute to the design work carried out by Graham Thorburn was published upon his death in the Sydney Morning Herald of September 15, 2015. It reads as follows.

> "THORBURN Graham
>
> 1943-2015
>
> The Victorian Ravehall and Hopkins Project teams are saddened by the recent death of their dear friend and colleague. Graham's passion for excellence in architecture was reflected in every aspect of his work, and he has made an outstanding contribution to prison design in Australia."

Going places - CYTA

Graham Ronald Drayton - Graham was a High school teacher, who became a subject master. He went on to be the manager of special developments in education, a District Inspector of the Riverina area of NSW, the Arts program director for schools and the Arts in School program director.

Graham injected a sense of excitement into the Board, always challenging his fellow Directors to go further. The early formation of the unincorporated organisation **CHRISTIAN YOUTH TOURS** (CYT) was the coming together of a like-minded group of "young people" who had a common interest of serving their Saviour in youth work and other activities with a strong Christian emphasis. Graham Drayton was one such person.

He was a problem solver. Graham would handle any difficult public relations problems with aplomb. He was the Mr Fix-it for the organisation. He was a great wordsmith and a "diplomat" when it needed him to be.

In addition to being a **DIRECTOR**, Graham was an enthusiastic pioneer **TOUR LEADER**, who led the first extended camping tour for **CYTA**. The tour was to Central Australia. He also pioneered tours to Central Australia as well as a double coach tour with 86 passengers for two weeks on the western coast of Canada and the USA. His wife, Sue, accompanied him as the **HOSTESS** on this tour, as well as the tour of Tasmania.

Graham Drayton as a young man was known wide and far for his accordion-playing, especially his rendition of The Holy City.

Going places - CYTA

I have to say, "Drayt" appeared to really want to be a music impresario. During his years with **CYTA** he supported and managed a group with the "big band sound", **Foundation**.

In later years Graham in his work life away from **CYTA**, took on the role of coordinating talent for the 2000 Olympics. He was the co-ordinator between SOGOC, the NSW government and the NSW Education Department, in relation to the involvement of public schools in the Sydney 2000 Olympics and the Sydney 2000 Paralympic Games.

After the Olympics, Graham moved to Wollongong, where he took over an abandoned private school and started a public performing arts high school. He was instrumental in recruiting several international artists to teach at the school and established a local community-based orchestra.

Kevin speaks of one of the fine endeavours of Graham's teaching career in the NSW Education Department.

> *"To top off his career, he had the task of reinvigorating the Wollongong Conservatorium of Music and the television station WIN-4 Wollongong Symphony Orchestra.*
>
> *He was a director of the Sydney North Ensemble, where his organisational skills came to the fore with a successful tour by the ensemble, to Columbia (South America) as a response to an invitation to take part in the Music of the Americas. Graham was highly involved with CYTA his career in education and the*

> *pursuit of music in education and in the community but with Sue had time to raise their children, Jeff, Rodney, Lauren and Philip.*
>
> *Sadly, Graham passed away in February 2018.* "

Kevin Craik - Kevin started his working life at Qantas before moving to the Postmaster General's Department, (the section where he worked we now know as the company Telstra). He worked on telephone installations as well as specialised projects such as the building of the Coaxial cable which allowed for television in one city to be shown in another. The cable stretched from Sydney to Melbourne.

Kevin was the prime mover and catalyst of what become known as the Christian Youth Travel Association (**CYTA**). He worked tirelessly during the early years, rushing into the **CYTA** office during his lunch hour, to allocate work and deal with any problems and then returning to work. It was not till 1978, that the then Board appointed Kevin on a full-time basis.

Kevin in retirement has not lost his zest for working with other people. He written on his LinkedIn page that he still "Enjoys helping others"

Jan Craik

Jan Craik, (Née **Shipway)** and Kevin married in 1966. Jan was a registered nurse and worked as a nurse educator. The role Jan played in the establishment and development of **CYTA** should never be understated. Jan's primary role as a **DIRECTOR** was to provide training to the **TEAM in** practical camping skills foundation camping skills including catering and first aid.

Kevin describes Jan's contribution to CYTA and her support for him.

> "Jan provided first aid training to the **TEAM** as well as her activity on the Board. She also became a mentor, coach and support to the many young women as they passed through the **TEAM**. This latter role she continued beyond the life of **CYTA**. At the start of **CYTA** Jan did this with a young family as well as being a sounding board for me. In all this time she was "providing 100% support to me."
>
> It was clear to me and too many young women on the team that Jan was woman who was an example of the role women would play in society, churches and families in the future. Jan always said that in her role on the Board that she was always ready to take on new ideas and become a pioneer for those ideas she supported. She has always enjoyed looking ahead to see how she can support like-minded women."

Jan and Kevin had two children, Darren and Meredith (Susie)

The changing Board
The original **CYTA DIRESTORS** founded the organisation. We should not forget the other "**MEMBERS**" of the company who backed the new venture with a financial guarantee.

Over time the Board changed. People moved onto other endeavours. But ready replacements emerged quickly, generally coming from the now older and wiser former **TEAM MEMBERS.**

One of the key differences between the **CYTA** Board and most other Boards was their approach to decision making. The **CYTA BOARD** never voted on any decision.

I reiterate the approach of the **CYTA BOARD** to decision-making. Any decision made had to be a consensus between the **BOARD MEMBERS**. Lack of consensus meant that the issue/project being discussed was held over to the next meeting or possibly, prayerfully, abandoned.

The first change of a DIRECTOR
From John Craik to Stuart Gow

In 1978, John Craik felt lead to take up the appointment as founding Director of Prison Fellowship Australia. This was a voluntary position.

Stuart Gow accepted the invitation to join the **CYTA BOARD** and took up the position as **CHAIRMAN**, a position he held for fifteen years. Stuart and his brother together owed an accounting practice. Before and during his time as **CYTA BOARD CHAIRMAN**, Stuart was also he treasurer of **Scripture Union** NSW. Stuart was a man of the utmost integrity and reliability. He was always a strong contributor to be both of the ministries in which he was involved.

Families of the original Directors

When the original Directors committed to **CYTA**, the commitment was all encompassing in that their families were "ready or not" an integral part of that commitment.

Jan Craik was a Director and number one support for Kevin in his role of Managing **DIRECTOR**. Kevin could not help but to be immersed in the ministry of **CYTA**.

As with all the DIRECTOR's wives *Jenny Thorburn* was a tower of strength. Jenny worked with Jan on the extensive shopping that was needed for each tour.

Joy Craik, (*Née Chandler*), *David Craik's* wife (Kevin and John's younger brother who later joined the BORAD) assisted Jan Craik from time to time on developing menus for tours. Graham Drayton's father *Ron Drayton* was the office manager for **CYTA** for several years. The children of the **BOARD MEMBERS** were around, especially *Darren* and **Meredith (Susie) Craik**.

Regardless of the work in which each family MEMBER was involved with **CYTA**, families faced the hours away from home for each Director as they dealt with the issues, challenges and successes of **CYTA**. Each family gave a lot in support of the spread of the Gospel.

Kevin and Jan would like to make special mention of their own parents. *Rick and May Shipway* regularly looked after Darren and Susie when either Jan and/or Kev were away for any length of time. *Mum and Dad Craik*, aka Mrs Craik or Mum and Pop Craik were tirelessly supportive of Jan and Kevin over many long

Going places - CYTA

years. Every Thursday **TEAM** night, the senior Craik's were babysitting two growing grand-children. They also weekly faithfully cleaned the **CYTA** office and **TEAM** centre for many years.

Jan often said:

> "Our kids had five grandparents" – the fifth one being "**Reecie**", who was Carole Reece's mother.

Reecie lived close to Meredith (Susie's) school, so after school, Susie would spend many hours having cooking lessons from her fifth grandparent. Reecie also treated both Susie and Darren to extended stays which she always made a highlight of their growing up. Carole's dad, **Trav. Reece**, in conjunction with David Collins, was responsible for their voluntary effort in the making of the many orange and brown boxes that made our camping tours so efficient and well-organised.

> *A side note:* I expect almost everyone will know the Craik's daughter **Meredith** was generally called **Susie**. Apparently **Darren,** when introduced to his new baby sister, was too young to get his mouth around Meredith, so it was suggested by his parents to call her "sis/sus", which translated into Susie over time.

A brave decision made by all involved on the establishment of CYTA, the **DIRECTORS** and their families risked much to start the organisation and see it through its early growth. An organisation blessed by GOD.

We might ask ourselves: **Would we have done it?**

7. The TEAM, it grows
The pre-TEAM
Before the **TEAM** a "pre-**TEAM**" developed over time. Laster there was the Ladies Guild, *Jill Heyworth* (now home in heaven), was one of the Ladies Guild, a group mentioned in an earlier chapter. *Jill Heyworth* spent many days on weekends and through the week helping set up the **LODGE** for its first occupation. She and *Daisy Clare, (*CYTA LODGE's first co-manager) had a similar sense of humour and got on famously. Jill laboured for hours readying the lodge. This was before any concept of the **TEAM** was developed.

 Jill along with others such as *Carole Reece* became the early default **TEAM**. Carol was the secretary of the **Baptist Youth Fellowship (BYF)**, chorus and orchestra. This pre-**TEAM** were friends of the **DIRECVTORS** and people who came in contact with Kevin and Jan and caught the vision for **CYTA** and the **CYTA LODGE**.

Peter Croft, *Tony Milne* and Peter's girlfriend **Margaret** (later they married) met Kevin Craik at a **BYF** camp, one of the first camps Kevin had ever managed in 1962. Tony Milne met *Joy Milne* (*Née* Cameron) on an early BYF camp. All four were studying at the Wagga Wagga Teachers College (now Charles Sturt University, Wagga Wagga) campus.

Peter lent his support to **CYTA** leading various tours including the 1969 Barrier Reef tour, snow weekends and a tour from Oberon High School (where he was a popular teacher with both the students and the parents) to Central Australia.

Tony took what is considered is the first school tour from Bass High (Bass Hill NSW) to Canberra for the day.in 1962 Tony was a Geography teacher and led student camping tours to New Zealand and Central Australia.

Colleen and **Victor (VIC) Barrington** straddled this period of "pre-**TEAM**" into the establishment of the **CYTA TEAM**. They were competent, enthusiastic **TOUR LEADER**s. **Colleen** along with **Jenny Thorburn** and **Jan Craik** shopped for tours at a large grocery warehouse, Campbells, and would pick up four cages of product, not your supermarket trolley, the type of cage that supermarket employees draw from to fill the shelves. On one occasion they bought six cages/trolleys full of goods.

Colleen remembers the three of them on the shopping trips.

> *"Planning menus and buying all the food for tours became a regular activity for Jan, Jenny and me, accompanied by our three, which soon became six children. We would pull up at the wholesale grocers and put the kids that were still in car seats on the giant trolleys. Before long, the children were buried under boxes of food. But they all survived and often slept peacefully as we as we sorted and packed multiple boxes of food to leave with tours all over the country and around the South Pacific. I remember Jenny, Jan*

> and I doing the maths for the largest quantity of coleslaw you have ever seen. This was before you could buy readymade packaged coleslaw."

Not a **CYTA TEAM** as most people would know it but genuine Christian people willing to help from the beginning of the organisation.

The TEAM – Beginnings and Growth

Around a thousand people joined, worked in and passed through **CYTA**. Some were looking for adventure, some looking to be part of something that was exciting and also Christian. Some people were looking to meet new friends, escape from dying churches, replace non-existent youth groups and lack of youth/young adult activities yet for some others for a group they might in their mind call a de-facto family. A few people sought all of these.

Glennis Craig (*Née Richarson*) remembers well with great fondness her time with **CYTA**

> "Where I grew as a young person from late teens to my mid-twenties, it was being on the **CYTA TEAM** where my real growth occurred. It was there I met such a range of people whose lives had been changed by **JESUS CHRIST**. The **TEAM** meeting nights, training weekends was a very big Fellowship for me. That time was filled with joy, laughter, sorrow with some unexpected deaths, regrets when things went wrong and the excitement of being on a coach with friends seeing Gods creation."

Going places - CYTA

The purchase, fitting out and opening of **CYTA LODGE**, was the most significant event in the growth and formalisation of the **TEAM**. The demand for leadership in the expanding tour schedule was required. The **TEAM** continued to expand to meet that demand.

All Tours needed a **TOUR LEADER**, a **HOSTESS**, and sometimes an extra assistant. The **TOUR LEADER**, a male and the **HOSTESS**, a female had the responsibility for leading the tours. **TEAM MEMBERs** generally were people who had been on a tour as a **TOUR MEMBER** joined the **CYTA TEAM** and put their hand up for service.

Two such people were *Gil and Chris Williams. Kevin* relates their story.

> "Gill and Chris were prominent in the early days of **CYTA** LODGE. As an architect, his skills were put to good use, helping Graham Thorburn in the **LODGE** architectural design and development. Gill and Chris took their first tour to Tasmania in 1972 and for the next four years, were enthusiastic **TEAM MEMBERS**, taking tours to the Barrier Reef, New Zealand and many of the long weekend tours to destinations such as Lightning Ridge and the Warrumbungles.
>
> Gil has said they had nothing but great memories of the tours they took and the friends they made – some of whom they still met many years later – and in trusting their Lord lives were impacted for the Kingdom Sadly, Chris went home to be with her Lord in early 2019."

Going places - CYTA

> **A side note**: Gill was to be the architect to add an additional floor to the club, which ultimately became the Silverwater headquarters of **CYTA** in 1988. The alterations were never completed however, to Gill's disappointment, and he moved on to another company.

The titles awarded to the leaders of a tour and their respective duties, will seem somewhat antiquated by today's standards. Today you might say that you would have a male and female **TOUR LEADER**. **CYTA** was an organisation of its time for its time. Over time there were female **TOUR LEADER**s, though the concept of the male "**HOSTESS**/cook" was only just starting in the 1960's.

However, *Kevin* did use female **TOUR LEADER**s in the sixties and seventies and has made a very clear statement as to how he selected people for roles as tour staff.

> "I chose people based purely on what I thought they can do, how they showed themselves and how they could contribute to the lives of those people who were on tour."

> **A side note**: In the above paragraph I have referred to the young women of the TEAM as females. Kevin suggested but I demur to referring to the **male** members as **"guys"** and the **females** as **"girls'**- "Girls and guys." I know it was used by music, music radio and music television in 1960's to 1990's but I don't recall it

> as common usage or commonly used at CYTA gatherings. An American inspired terminology? However, if you read men or male and want to think, "**guy**" or for women or females and want to think "**girl**" then that is fine. Maybe you remember better than I do.

The **TEAM MEMBERS** came together as "One **TEAM**" on the work weekends. There was no differentiation on task. Whether you were male or female if you wanted to help pull the antiquated out of service water heaters from the roof of the accommodation buildings, you were on the job. Men and women dug holes and painted. Men cleaned and cooked alongside women.

Hans Beilhac a **TEAM MEMBER** reflects upon his introduction to **CYTA** and his involvement in the **TEAM**

> *"My first full tour was the weeklong Ski trip in 1969 at the Valhalla Ski Lodge in Perisher Valley. There were only 5 people on the trip. We went down with a weekend ski trip one weekend then came back the next weekend. I went on the same trip then next year, 1970 with more people accompanying me. Next was the Lightning Ridge trip in October 1970, with 4 coach loads of campers.*
>
> *I had joined the **TEAM** and was involved from 1971 to 1974. Lots of work weekends, working on the renovations to the accommodation blocks and the main hall and then as a **TEAM MEMBER** on snow trips. We would go down with a group of **TOUR MEMBER's** on a Friday night,*

> but I stayed at the **LODGE** to prepare the meals and carry out work around the **LODGE**. In 1975 I led the Overland Trip from Kathmandu to London."

Kevin remembers **Hans**

> "Hans was a regular on early work weekends, getting **CYTA LODGE** up and running. He recently expressed great memories of Merv and Daisy Clare, the first and great loving managers of **CYTA LODGE**. They, with the early **TEAM**s, were largely responsible for creating the foundations of what was to become "the **CYTA TEAM**", whose efforts with the permanent **LODGE** staff was to make **CYTA LODGE**. The 1970s were a long time ago, but the memories of those times are still very real."

The **TEAM** which helped grow and sustain **CYTA** tours as well as the later **AUSTRALIAN CHRISTIAN MUSIC SEMINARS** were all voluntary young people. Most were based in Sydney, though not all.

Without the **TEAM**, **CYTA** could not have operated. At any one time there were up to 80 plus voluntary young people in Sydney, along with a later established group of up to 40 people in the Melbourne **TEAM** that maintained a vibrant and variable tour program.

So high was the demand from young people to join the **TEAM** that a limit of eighty per year was imposed on the Sydney **TEAM** as the nineteen seventies closed and the eighties had begun. The young people (and a few who

Going places - CYTA

were no so young) gave many hours of service to the **CYTA** ministry.

Margaret Quinn (*Née* **Hollier**) remembers her time in the **TEAM**,

> *"I'm so thankful for **CYTA**!!! All the nice people I met!!! The fun times!!! Good memories!!! (I) wish there was a **CYTA** for retirees."*

During and at the end of each tour the **TOUR LEADER** gave a promotional talk to encourage those people who were interested in the ministry of **CYTA** to apply to join the **TEAM**. *John Grinsell* proved to be a champion recruiter who recruited six new **TEAM MEMBERS**s following one extended New Zealand tour.

Ross Killick reflects on his time on the **CYTA TEAM**

> *"I cannot thank Kevin Craik enough for the amazing experiences I had over the three-year period I was involved in the **CYTA TEAM** and the trust Kevin put in me. I do recall struggling to meet time expectations with **TEAM** nights and gear preparation at Kevin's home in Strathfield as I was juggling work and part-time engineering study at Uni.*
>
> *I dedicated my annual leave to **CYTA** tours for three consecutive years to contribute to the January tours. At the time I thought it was a big task. But I did it willingly. Looking back now I'm overawed with the responsibility I took on. I always had a strong sense of God's presence in my life and protection but lacked the maturity*

> *that only comes with time. My **CYTA** experience gave me a strong interest in both future leadership/Christian service and world travel. Marriage to my wife Dianne in December 1973 resulted in me moving away from Sydney in 1975 and being unable to continue with **CYTA**."*

To join the **TEAM**, you would attend an information night. If after that where you were committed to joining the **TEAM** you required to make a two year commitment to the work of the ministry. That commitment involved attending two of three work weekends each year generally held over long (three day plus) holiday weekends as well as regular attendance on Thursday night training nights. Those people who agreed to join **CYTA** on those terms joined existing **TEAM MEMBERS** in a dedication service which commenced each New Year of activity.

***Anna Carr (Née Vanderloos*)** recalls the happiness and fun of the **CYTA TEAM**.

> *"I have only happy memories of my experiences with **CYTA** and all the people I met in my time as a tourist and later as a **TEAM MEMBER**. In early 1975, I joined the **CYTA TEAM** and was a **HOSTESS** on one or two or three ski and other Weekend trips. One Week end trip I remember sleeping in a farm shed with mice everywhere. I was on **TEAM** until 1977 and briefly again in 1985. We had fun and it was a warm welcoming, comforting and joyous time for me and helped me as a young Christian girl.*

Going places - CYTA

> *These were special, special times. I remember funny antics with **Jenny** and **Lyndall** and lots of other friends. I even drove the URVAN once! So thank God for **CYTA** and thank you amazing men and women who started this beautiful thing. Thanks Kevin and Jan and others whose names I can't remember. I always have you in my heart and pray for you."*

It should be noted many people started serving **CYTA** immediately upon deciding to be committed to the organisation. This was before attending a dedication service. Such was their enthusiasm. **Max Watson** was one of those people. I like Max came from our respective tour coaches directly to the following Tuesday work night.

Other team members took a circuitous route. **Steve Groves** explains.

> *"My first contact with CYTA was when I and several other guys from Castle Hill Baptist were asked in 1978 by the church music director to help out at the Christian music seminar held in Cooma. We all had a great time. We met some nice girls at the seminar and some of us went onto to date them.*
>
> *We spent our time at the seminar, singing and acting around while we helped in the LODGE kitchen, working the dishwasher and doing a variety of chores out of the kitchen such as moving furniture and sound equipment to where it was required.*

Going places - CYTA

At the last morning service I sat with my mates and the girls we had met. Communion was offered. The girls all took the communion but only one of our group, (not me), took the communion. I guess that was the beginning for me. It dawned on me that I believed what Christians believed but had not made Jesus the Lord of my life.

Over the next few months I am God interacted more than before the seminar. My family went to the Billy Graham Crusade April 29, 1979. I answered the appeal to accept Christ and went forward to join other people who wanted to know more about Jesus Christ. I grew in Christ as I read the Bible and interacted more openly with other Christians at our youth group and in church. I eve wrote a few Christian songs. I went to other music seminars throughout each year attending as many as ten seminars in some years. I remember celebrating my Birthday which was in January at Cooma with Liz Jarret who also celebrated her Birthday in January.

*I also have great memories of going with my youth group on **CYTA** snow tours. I had a ball at the **LODGE**, mucking around with friends as well as meeting and getting to know a few girls along the way.*

*Having had three head injuries I am unclear of the exact date I joined the team. It was some time in the early eighties. I went away to the Barrier Reef with **Dave Joyce**. A trip to New*

Zealand with a future girlfriend was financed by some work on my uncle's farm a year or two before where he gave me bull calf, sold it and gave me the money from the sale.

I lead three tours to New Zealand back to back in a mini bus. Though I was the **TOUR LEADER**, I was also the cook, the driver, packer and cleaner on the tour. I also drove a mini bus on a tour to Western Australia.

CYTA gave me lifelong friends, romantic and plutonic relationships, enabled me to deepen my faith, as well as aided me to share and encourage others who we served while in the **TEAM** as well as other people with whom I worked alongside. Being on the **TEAM** allowed me, along with other TEAM MEMBERS, to effect a massive multiplication of the Kingdom of God, which happened when we went back to our churches and we could disciple other people and thereby grow the Kingdom of God."

All **TEAM MEMBERS**s had something to offer. *Janet Broughton,* (now home in heaven) was on the **TEAM**. She was chosen to be part of a Central Australia **TOUR TEAM**. Janet who was a teacher at East Hills High at the time went to Kevin and said she could not use her hands fully as she had a circulation problem. **Kevin** responded to her reservations with positive reassurance that she could handle the **HOSTESS** role.

*"The job of the **HOSTESS** is not to do all the work but organise the work to be done".*

Going places - CYTA

The **TOUR MEBERS** were 100% supportive of her. The CYTA office received glowing reports of the way the leadership team performed on the tour.

There was a role for everyone.

Training Nights

TEAM training nights in Sydney were initially held in the lounge room of David Collins' home in the "pre-**TEAM**" period. At this time the attendees at training were the fiver male Director, Jan as the sixth **DIRECTOR** and close friends, who were involved in the ministry of **CYTA**.

The **TEAM** took off with the acquisition of **CYTA LODGE** and training nights were moved to the Everton Road office, (too small) and then Strathfield Baptist Church where seating was available for more than the usual **TEAM** size at that time of 80 plus people. With the acquisition of the Homebush site and then the move to the Silverwater **CYTA** Centre, training nights along with other activities were held in the one place.

In between Homebush and Silverwater the **TEAM** met in the local primary school at Homebush, while the hunt was on for what turned out to be the **CYTA Centre at Silverwater**.

*Barbara Wimble (*Née *Moore)* speaks with affection of her introduction to the **CYTA TEAM**

> *"My association with **CYTA** began when I met Robin Morris at the end of 1976. I had just returned from overseas and started teaching again in Sydney. Robyn was working in the office*

> *of **CYTA**. We led a Sunday school teachers' training course together. She suggested joining **CYTA** as a way of meeting new friends and getting involved with their camping and snow holidays. I loved their weekly meetings and training weekends at Cooma."*

Training nights covered a variety of information:

- Legal responsibilities of **CYTA** to people on tour, general information on booking and receipt of monies as well as legal responsibilities to and for other **TEAM MEMBERS**.

- Christian leadership principles based in **BIBLE** truths. There was a continuous reinforcement of the evangelical profile of **CYTA**. It was not just about travel but introducing people to the *Kingdom* of *God* and supporting the faith of existing believers. Believers and non-believers toured with **CYTA**.

- The responsibilities of **TOUR TEAM**, the safe and competent use of equipment, how to set up and break down camp as well as coach packing

- Also covered on training nights were activities being undertaken by **CYTA** such as information nights, work weekends, **TEAM** training weekends, concerts that might be scheduled, and who the team might expect as future Thursday night guest speakers.

- There was always a time for **BIBLE** Study (sometimes for the group as a whole or in small groups), which may involve a **TEAM MEMBER** delivering a **BIBLE** study, a study by a chaplain, or a guest speaker bringing alive a passage from the **BIBLE**. Such studies tended to be full-some in that they covered longer passages from the **BIBLE** than may be covered in a Sunday church sermon. I can remember covering the story of Nehemiah in one evening.

There was always time to mingle with others and meet with new people at the end of a night. Getting people to leave was always a pleasurable and time consuming task for the person in charge of the session, generally Kevin or **Geof Hyde**.

> **A side note**: As with any group of people there was always lost property. *Geoff Jay*, a **TEAM MEMBER** who often would lead the singing on **TEAM** nights, if you are reading this, as you likely know Kevin was keeping the **BIBLE** your brother gave to you a half century ago that was lost. After fifty years Kevin has sent it to you. We hope you received it.

Relationships with churches could prove difficult on occasion, as Kevin and other Directors received complaints about "flock stealing" that is taking away a **TEAM MEMBER** from church responsibilities they held at their local church.

Early in the life of the **TEAM** it was generally only personal details and church affiliation information that was taken from each person at the information night.

However, as time went on the application form to join the **TEAM** grew to four pages and three references were required. One referee had to be from the **TEAM MEMBER**'s home church pastor. It was stressed that before being accepted, that **TEAM MEMBERS** needed to show evidence of not dropping any responsibility in their home church.

Reflections of **Rick Gribble**, a TEAM MEMBER from 1972 to 1978

> *"I am forever grateful to discover Christian Youth Travel in December 1971. Earlier in the year I had set out for a ski weekend to the Snowy Mountains with a work colleague. He was driving us into Sydney to catch a commercial tour coach but en-route we collided with another vehicle. My head went through the windscreen and the underneath of my chin landed on the remaining glass. A little either way could have been more serious. This trip was definitely over and replaced with a ride in the back of an ambulance to hospital and many stitches. My brother's wisdom was:*
>
>> *'The Lord obviously has better plans for you'.*
>
> *Sometime later a friend gave me a brochure called 'Going Places with **CYTA**' – this certainly seemed like a safer way to travel! In Christian company! So, I booked on the coach tour to Tasmania for my Christmas holidays. It was amazing to be amongst young people of similar*

Christian faith as well as having young people actually leading the tour. These were young people representing the love of God to young people.

*I was particularly struck by the warmth and integrity of the **TOUR LEADER** who made each traveller feel welcome.*

*After that first tour I joined the **CYTA TEAM** and a 7 year adventure began. The weekly **TEAM** training nights were meticulous in detail and a standard of excellence applied in every way. Being on the voluntary **TEAM** brought a lot of excitement at Cooma **CYTA LODGE**. The training and work weekends prior to the snow season tours were great. Just to be on a trip with other young people was wonderful fellowship with the destination a secondary consideration.*

*To be on the **TEAM** was fulfilling enough and I certainly did not seek leadership. However, for Christmas 1972 I was allocated as **TOUR LEADER** for the New Zealand Tour with 40 young people but with the backup of an experienced assistant. We saw the Lord's hand upon the tour, but two tourists confronted me saying they would not believe*

*In summary: As a tourist on the **CYTA** Tasmania Tour it opened up a whole new world of Christian fellowship with young people for me, but with the appointment as a **TOUR LEADER** it opened up a whole new world of caring for young people.*

Going places - CYTA

My brother was right – the Lord did have better plans for me beyond that car crash in 1971 and Jeremiah 29: 11-13 became my favourite text.

I am incredibly grateful for the opportunities afforded me by Kevin Craik and for his faith placed in me and so many other young people. Kevin's unruffled nature, genuine love and Godly heart for young people have left an indelible Christian footprint on the Sydney community and beyond. As a visionary Kevin has given his whole life to young people;

Snow Tours, Weekend tours, School holiday tours, Interstate tours, tours overseas, Rhapsody in Blue Dinner concerts, Evie concerts and **André Crouch** *concerts to name but few of the projects. The Board of* **DIRECTOR's,** *all committed* **CHRISTAINS** *and all successful in their own fields of endeavour, gave quality support to Kevin. As an example, when there was not a unanimous vote on a Board issue they would defer and only proceed to adopt an agenda proposal when all directors had prayed for the Lord's direction and could vote in total agreement. Kevin together with his wife Jan have given so much of their everyday life to the Lord's work amongst young people and we all love them for it..*

A VERY BIG THANK YOU, WE HAVE BEEN BLESSED INDEED!!!"

For **John Grinsell** being in the **TEAM** became a family affair

> *"I certainly had a great time on the **CYTA TEAM**. My time on the **TEAM** during the 1980's helped me grow in my faith, develop leadership skills and gave me the opportunity to use those skills. My wife Judy also joined the **TEAM** and we enjoyed great times on **TEAM** together. We enjoyed the **TEAM** nights, training weekends, tours, concert tours and promotions. The great memories and friendships from being involved in **CYTA** continue".*

Tuesday Nights were maintenance and tour preparation as well as fun nights. If you were not working on equipment, you could be engaged in filling and addressing envelopes for regular promotional mail-outs.

Elva Harris sums up her time in **CYTA**, which I suspect represents the thoughts of many other people.

> *"A Fun time also a time of experiencing great **TEAM** togetherness and a **TEAM** that worked together. We grew in our Christian faith through input from speakers and musicians and sharing together".*

Activities for the **TEAM,** with the **TEAM** and about the **TEAM**

Coming to the TEAM as a result of conversion
Here is just one story of a **TEAM MEMBER** who met *Christ* though a **CYTA TOUR**.

Anna Carr who worked at the LODGE during the snow seasons remembers after reading about the decision of

Going places - CYTA

Cliff Warburton the moment of her accepting Christ into her life.

> "And me.......!!!!! Thank you Jesus!!!!December 31st 1974. Barrier Reef tour...at Airlie Beach....on the bus steps..."

Anna recalls what lead up to that moment

> "I was 17 in 1974 and a girlfriend from work showed us a leaflet about a June Long Weekend snow trip. We went, had loads of fun, got wet, as we didn't have proper snow gear, and couldn't ski for nuts. We were made so welcome by the **TEAM** on the Snow trip and at the **LODGE**, loved the Hot Chocolates, Roast dinner and all you could eat, yummy cooked breakfasts. And I loved the friendliness of everyone and the singing! I went on another weekend tour (Mystery) and on both bus trips. I was taken by the happiness of some of the other tourists and their singing. I'd never heard choruses before. At this stage I wasn't a Christian though I thought I was. Later in December, I took a trip to the Great Barrier Reef. They were really happy and nice people. Hey! I thought….how can I be like that? What have they got I don't? I found that out on New Year's Eve 1974 at almost midnight. MY question to one of the **TEAM** was "Is God fussy about who He lets into Heaven?" That young man led me to Jesus, Step by Step through a prayer that brought me to my Lord and Saviour Jesus Christ. My life changed forever, thank You God!"

Anna *finishes her story by remembering how special was, her time of conversion:*

> *"New Year's Eve is always so special to me! I gave my life and my heart to Jesus on New Year's Eve 1974 and He took me and made me His forever and ever and ever and ever and ever..........................and ever...............and ever"*
>
> Anna quoted a Bible Verse which epitomised her coming to Christ.
>
> 'Revelation Chapter 3: Verse 20 *"Behold, I stand at the door and knock; if anyone hears my voice and opens the door, I will come in to him and will dine with him, and he with me.'*
>
> ***"So Anna heard Him knocking and I opened that door and...Oh boy"***

It can be said with certainty that this happened on many tours. People were won by the Holy Spirit, for Christ on tour, or they gave their lives to Him soon after returning home.

Wild Weekers

Some **TEAM MEMBERS** and many other people, who volunteered, had time to give during the week. Some **TEAM MEMBERS** two or three at a time were able to volunteer a week of work at the **LODGE**. They left on the coach on a Friday night with a group of people who were on the weekend snow tours and returned to Sydney on Sunday of the following week with a returning group. These people were known as "Wild Weekers". They had a day at the snow and a full week of "cold: at Cooma where it is reported that sometimes it was:

> "Warmer in the freezer than it was in the kitchen"

A time to leave the TEAM

The Bible in Ecclesiastes 3 Verses 1 to 7 tells us that there is a time, a season for everything. There was time for people to join the **CYTA TEAM** and for **TEAM MEMBERS** to end that part of their life.

Is there a time, a season for all things in our life, in your life?

Glennis Craig recalls the end of her season with **CYTA**.

> "Around 1980, my time with **CYTA** came to an end, as I entered into Bible College but the cords of relationships from **CYTA** days continued into the next phase of life. Not by chance but through God's Guidance."

Some people remember their leaving of **CYTA** with regret, sadness or in most cases joy after having been involved in a ministry that allowed them to learn and prepare to start a new adventure. A variety of responses were to be found in **TEAM MEMBERS** as they completed their **CYTA** journey.

For some there may have been unresolved tensions with other **TEAM MEMBERS**, remembered times of joy, comradeship, even friendship and for some all-consuming human love, which manifested itself in finding a life partner for some, from being part of **CYTA**.

One More Time, 22 April 2014

It started off with a surprise mystery tour, led by *Alan* and *Janelle Hale*, with a coachload of **CYTA TEAM MEMBERS**. There was an unsuspecting knock on the door at Kevin and Jan's home.

It was a 3 hour tour of significant suburban locations that facilitated many of the **CYTA** activities. One Last Time was a great reunion of over 160 people, who were in **TEAM** or committed to the ministry.

The event was run as if it was a **TEAM** night. During the evening program, Jan asked those present if they met their life's partner in and through the ministry of **CYTA**. The best part of 80% of those present, stood. Bringing Christian women and men together as life partners is indeed a demonstration of the effectiveness of the **CYTA** ministry though not one of its key purposes.

> "But what a blessing"

The ending of every season may be happy or sad. Each season may bring a new beginning or a sad end. The sale of **CYTA LODGE** heralded the start of a new season, the beginning of the end of the **CYTA TEAM** and of the organisation.

I received a message from one former **TEAM MEMBER**.

> *"Those CYTA days were great days."*

To *God* Be the Glory for the people and work of the:

Christian Youth Travel Association

Going places - CYTA

8. L'Abri and other gifts

L'Abri

L'Abri is an evangelical organisation, which offers a place to stay, to think, to learn Bible truths and to share ideas on the Christian life. It was founded in Switzerland. L'Abri was founded by **Francis Schaeffer** and his wife **Edith Schaeffer**. Schaeffer turned his back on church modernism and followed a protestant line. He established the L'Abri community for curious travellers as a forum to discuss philosophical and religious beliefs.

Kevin and the Board decided to send a small group of **TEAM MEMBERS** to L'Abri for three months to be part of the program. The objective of such a trip was to equip **TOUR LEADER**s with spiritual authority in living out as well as speaking out about their Christian faith.

Geof Hyde who worked for some years for **CYTA** recalls his thoughts on L'Abri.

> *"I was fortunate to spend some time at L'Abri in Switzerland after leading an Overland and a Grand Europe tour. L'Abri is a place of study and reflection. I know others from* **CYTA TEAM MEMBERS**s *also spent time here and benefited from their time there both spiritually and also physically. For most of those people it has had a huge impact in their day-to-day Christian faith and continues to shape their lives."*
>
> *This was an example of expression of love that Kevin (and Jan) as well as the rest of the Board had for the* **CYTA TEAM**. *Building the* **TEAM** *was building Christian warriors. It was also*

> helping to shape **TEAM MEMBERs** lives for the long term."

David Joyce is thankful for his time at L'Abri.

> "Praise the Lord for **CYTA**'s generous 3-month sponsorship of my time in Swiss and UK L'Abri. The Christian community's input was a milestone in my Christian growth. We worked half a day and studied the other half.
>
> I remember that from some tours, some of the travellers decided to attend L'Abri after their tour had finished and enjoyed the experience."

Rick Gribble talks about the time he spent at L'Abri

> "Some weeks after I completed an Overland trip I travelled to Jerusalem for Easter included the sunrise service at the Garden Tomb, a reminder of God's salvation plan accomplished. We had met a new friend Rob when we first arrived in Israel at Tel Aviv. He had joined our small group and gone with us to the kibbutz. As we were returning to London, Rob offered to give me a lift from London to Swiss L'Abri as he planned to drive his large campervan from there on to Germany.
>
> Rob and I arrived at Swiss L'Abri and were allocated to different chalets since we had differing needs. I was assigned to a lecturer who set my study topics for books and recorded lectures and all students attended live lectures together. Rob was seeking answers to his life.

Going places - CYTA

All lecture sessions had ample opportunity for honest answers to honest questions and Rob said he had such a complicated question to resolve. To his amazement another person had unknowingly asked the exact same question and this with the resulting answer had overwhelmed Rob.

The coincidence of the question and the answers he found at L'Abri was enough for Rob to later walk out into the Alps and under the night sky give his heart to the Lord who most certainly had led him here.

I had taken funds with me for a month's stay at L'Abri. Amazingly at the end of that month I received a surprise phone call from Kevin Craik **CYTA** *Chairman saying that the Directors had met the previous night and wanted to sponsor me at L'Abri for as long as I needed to be there. This was 'out of the blue' and since I had stayed up until midnight the previous evening to list what I still needed to study I surely knew I should stay on for the full three months of my visa…God's timing and provision is perfect. Kevin's "to sponsor without strings attached" was so Godly and generous and was a lesson I have held close for my own lifetime. Having been challenged by young people on tour "to show me God then I will believe" was the reason why I needed L'Abri and after my time there I could readily share from my strengthened faith and apologetics together with the historical grounding*

> of Israel. Am ever so grateful for **CYTA** support and encouragement!!

> The conclusion of my time at L'Abri coincided with the final thawing of the snow-caps on the Dents du Midi mountain peaks across the valley that we could see from our chalet. To celebrate with several roommates we set out from Champery to climb the mountain over two days, overnighting in a stone cabin and summiting to 3,258m early the next morning. The view from the summit across the roof of Europe to Mount Blanc was stunning with snow still crowning the highest peaks attesting greatness to our God of all Creation."

Other Gifts
A pastor in training

There were other occasions when the Board reached out to supprt people. On one such time, Kevin was contacted by the *Kevin Crowther* the father of **JOHN CROWTHER** to ask:

> "Do you think that 25, is too young to be a pastor?"

Kevin asked for more information. The family had been in working in the **Ind***ependent State of Papua New Guinea*. They were about to return and **John Crowther** was considering a future calling to ministry. The **CYTA** Board appointed John as their ministry chaplain and later sponsored the first three years of John's theological training.

A great love blossomed between CYTA and many of GOD's people

9. Groups, ministries, activities
Many Groups, ministries, activities
CYTA did not just concentrate on tours and once and up and going just tours and music. CYTA started and backed financially many different groups, some ministering to TEAM MEMBERS, others ministries external to the organisation. There were activities which CYTA sponsored. There were a lot of them. Let's get going but don't be surprised if you are tired at the end of this chapter.

On Eagles Wings (Men)
The **CYTA** Board felt committed to establishing a men's ministry.

On Eagle's Wings was launched to the group of men who were on the **CYTA TEAM** and/or involved in **CYTA** activities. A launch to more than 160 men seemed to show that the need existed for a men's ministry.

John Grinsell, a former **TEAM MEMBER**, **TOUR LEADER** and **DIRECTOR** of **CYTA** laboured faithfully on the On Eagles Wings ministry. .*John* led this group. He summed up the role of Eagle's Wings,

> "It was a group of (**CYTA**) men who arranged events and camps for men after **CYTALODGE** was sold"

However, men were reluctant after the launch to join the group. There was a reluctance to get together. John said of On Eagles Wings that it had "its season". The life of the group was short lived.

Now there are many locations for men's conferences and men's **BIBLE** study groups. Social groups for men are not hard to find. However, still today men are still often reluctant to meet with other men in groups to discuss their faith.

However, at the time of launching On Eagle' Wings, not many organisations were tackling men's ministry. **CYTA** and its **DIRECTORS** always sought the direction of the **HOLY SPIRIT** through prayer as to whether they should be involved in new ministries. Though this ministry may have not been a great success, it contributed to the support of Christian and non-Christian men.

World Vision Sponsorship

CYTA as a ministry and an ever increasing number of individual **TEAM MEMBERS** were sponsoring World Vision Children. It was one ministry (**CYTA**) sponsoring another ministry (World Vision). Some of the **TEAM** formed into groups to jointly sponsor World Vision Children. Commitment to child sponsorships continued unabated through the years

At the end of year function was held in 1971, (a catered dinner, for **TEAM MEMBERS** and people who had travelled with **CYTA** that year) was held at Bankstown Town Hall. Some 300 people were in attendance. Ken McGill, (who along with his wife Diane were two of the most reliable people to send on tour and when on tour showed wonderful Christian Leadership), stepped forward with a cheque for $3000 to go to World Vision.

Going places - CYTA

The money was collected from people who did not accord with the right description of the vehicle in which they travelled. They dared to call the vehicle a "bus" rather than a "coach". Money was also collected from those people on the tour that were visiting an attraction or just shopping who failed to arrive back at the coach by the required departure time. Each time someone committed either of these heinous offences then a contribution had to be made to a tin placed at the front of the bus.

The enormity of this donation may be lost when looking at the amount in 2023. I recall that my total annual wage around that time was about $2000 per year.

Ex CYTA Friends Group
The Ex CYTA Friends group (not to be confused with the Friends of CYTA), was a group of young married an unmarried early **TEAM MEMBERS** who had moved on. The group was formed by couples who had new life priorities, new homes to set up, and new additions to the family to look after.

Such was the enduring friendships that were made in and through being a **MEMBER** of **CYTA** (many had met their spouse through **CYTA**) that although nearly 40 years have passed, the core group who were there at the beginning still meet on a regular basis, almost once a month for ten months of each year. Not young marrieds as they were but now mostly are now grandparents.

Elva Harris now keeps all informed of where the next activity is due.

> "The group has changed over time and is known simply called the **Ex CYTA Friends Group**. The group meets each year in late January or early February to put a program together. I have volunteered to type up the program and send it out and I do keep track of our Contact list. But we share the organising of each event, which is usually about each month. Usually, the person who makes a suggestion of what to do organises that event. I have volunteered to type up the program and send it out and I do keep track of our contact list. But we share the organising of each event, which is usually about each month. The total group numbers to about 35, with about 15 -23 coming to most of the monthly activities."

Elva continues.

> "My non **CYTA** sister recently asked me about the group and Ito which I responded:
>
> I love getting together with that group of friends. No one tries to compete with anyone else. We are all interested in each other. The others talk about their children and grandchildren, and I want to hear and I don't really feel left out. I sometimes talk about my nieces and nephew. But we talk about other things, besides family."

This is a wonderful outcome. The young people that many years ago decided to follow the dream of travel and ministry of **CYTA** continue to meet. This is an example of true Christian friendship that has continued through the years.

Deportment Classes

CYTA also held deportment classes. This was the brainchild of, **Karen Kearns**. Karen was the wife of **Steve Kearns** who was at the time the pastor of Burwood Church of Christ and who was also a part time chaplain with **CYTA** at Silverwater Centre.

Kevin remembers these classes.

> *"When the suggestion came up, I said, "why not?!" It was a professionally run course run over six weeks on a Saturday morning in our Silverwater Centre.*
>
> **TEAM MEMBERS** *remarked to me that the morning exercise activities were as much a confidence building exercise as deportment. As I opened and closed the Centre for these classes, from time to time I watched as the participants were coached by Karen. I knew this was a valuable exercise and another good use of the Silverwater Centre."*

CYTA sports clubs and sponsorship

CYTA looked at sponsorships of organisations as good corporate advertising, a public relations exercise, but also as a way of supporting and sustaining Christian sporting groups. Sponsorships were provided to the Baptist Senior Netball Competition and to the Northside Churches Rugby Competition. Christian life permeates all areas of human activity.

Support differs from group to group. **CYTA** supported many groups with **TEAM** shirts or uniforms and/or financial support. These were some of the groups who received supprt from **CYTA**:

- NSW Baptist Senior Girls Netball Comp
- Northern Beaches Churches Rugby Union Comp
- Campsie Baptist Netball Club
- **CYTA** – Canoe Club
- **CYTA** – Ten Pin Bowling Club

Supporting Horizons Ministries

One organisation that **CYTA** assisted was the established British charity *Horizons Missions* .They needed office space. *Cathy Sampson*, a much loved **TEAM MEMBER** at the time and a group of young women mostly from the then **CYTA TEAM** were involved with organising a support group for Horizons Missions. Cathy who now lives in Phoenix Arizona was the Australian Leader of the UK-based Horizons Missions UK.

Friends of CYTA

As people took on new jobs and/or married and/or no longer had the time to be a **TEAM MEMBER** in that they could not fulfil the training and work weekend requirements, some joined the friends of **CYTA**. The friends not only included former **TEAM MEMBERS** but for any person who had **CYTA** at heart. Some of the friends were people who may have been on tour but were unable to commit to being on **TEAM** whilst other friends were prayer warriors to uphold the ministry in prayer.

The friends of **CYTA** (not to be confused with the later established Ex-**CYTA** friends group) were invited to attend training nights once a month to stay in touch with the ministry, its changing nature and maintain friendships with other former **TEAM MEMBERS**, and develop supportive relationships with current **TEAM MEMBERS**. They were also welcome to join work weekends.

Kevin remembers the helpfulness of the "friends":

> *"On nights where there was preparation for the mailing out of publicity, the Friends of **CYTA** were a great help. They also assisted in preparation of tour equipment as well as being some who had extended winter stays at **CYTA** **LODGE** Some of the friends assisted at several Music Seminars".*

A legacy element was introduced to **CYTA**. A band of people who had served *God* through **CYTA** continued in service that allowed for the joining of the past to the future, in a continuity of Christian service. We give thanks unto our *Lord* for all the wonderful support of the Friends of **CYTA.**

Nissan is our car

The funding of a purchase of a Nissan Urvan came from a former **TEAM MEMBER**. The **TEAM MEMBER** had moved on to the **Friends of CYTA** group. The bus, (yes in this case we could call it a bus), was an eight seater. Kevin gave *Rod Hills* a **CYTA DIRECTOR** at the time responsibility for the purchase.

> *"He was charged with the purchase of the vehicle and was told to go round to the dealers*

> and get the best possible price you can and complete the purchase of the vehicle"

The benefactor of the vehicle was concerned about the use of **TEAM MEMBER's cars** for **CYTA** activities. The wear and tear on vehicles as well as the safety of **TEAM MEMBERS** and their cars concerned the funder of the purchase.

Church Promotions
For a short time **CYTA** was booked by churches to take an evening service. Small groups of **CYTA TEAM MEMBERS** went out to the churches, taking a service and distributed **CYTA** material. The **TEAM MEMBERS** also became a resource for young people at the church services to talk to about the gospel.

Fun and Frivolity
After the initial establishment and growth of the **TEAM** a highlight of serving in **TEAM** was the arranging and presentation of a musical to parents and friends of **TEAM MEMBERS**. This provided a link from **CYTA** back to the family of the young people who gave up their time in service.

Uncle Kevin's Pancakes
A popular Saturday Night event hosted by rostered **TEAM MEMBERSs** was *Uncle Kevin's Pancakes*. A social evening that was regularly held throughout the year at the Homebush Centre.

End of Year Events
Each December after the crazy build-up of getting tours ready for the summer season was the *End of Year*

Going places - CYTA

Function. End of year functions were hosted by the **CYTA** Directors and spouses. It was a "present" given in appreciation of the contribution to **CYTA TEAM MEMBERS** throughout the year. These were fun events each year in different locations.

For several years the end of year celebration involved a Hawkesbury river Cruise. The event was also held at the Meroe Conference Centre and featured the band Country Sound, who provided entertainment for the event in three of the years the end of year event was held. It was also held at the then new Bankstown Civic Centre as mentioned earlier in this chapter.

In 1968 the end of year party was held at the then Broadway Grace Bros Auditorium. This was the year of a prominent tour launch, which included an audio visual presentation that had been worked on for weeks. The supper was sandwiches and a drink which at that time cost $1.

The Grace Bros auditorium on Broadway carried a level of notoriety. The place of many high profile events held in Sydney. CYTA was moving up. The building no longer exists as it was. It has been refurbished/replaced by a shopping centre and housing.

As time progressed the catering for most of the end of year **TEAM** events was a combination of the efforts of **CYTA** and individual **TEAM MEMBERS**. **CYTA** would supply the bulk items. **TEAM MEMBER5** as they rang in to add their names to the list of those attending the end of year event, were asked to, or more likely allocated, to bring specific items.

"Can you bring a bottle of lemonade? A pineapple cut up, ready to eat? A Greek salad would be great?"

The CYTA mums and dads

Mention must be made of the Mums and Dads who drove their **TEAM MEMBER** sons and daughters to tour departure points, including airports, and upon their return, collected them at all hours of the day or night. There are many hundreds who could be called "hidden tour members".

What a list of activities. There may be more we have not found

10. Yesterday and Today

Following the sale of the **LODGE** and the down turn in tours the **TEAM** still existed but it was a **TEAM** that would need to be motivated without the incentive of travel. There were still activities happening at the **CYTA** Centre to involve the **TEAM** but no prospect of travel. The **TEAM** was coming to an end as was the organisation.

There has been a concerted effort by some **TEAM MEMBERS** to keep the joy and spirit of the **TEAM** alive. Discoveries of long lost souvenirs, the vinyl bag with the logo, the orange overalls and spoons as well as Kevin Craik's mission to recover the **CYTA** patch.

Those orange overalls looked great on one of my family MEMBERs. **CYTA** spoons were only available for a limited time. Pictures of brochures, which still hold their colour, speculation on who was in photos, where and when they were taken.

These are symbols of another time. A time that some people do not want forgot. A time that cannot be relived, but which many former **TEAM MEMBERS** want to remember and have remembered, possibly treasured for many, while for a small number of people it is a time best forgotten.

None can ignore the fact that **CYTA** brought joy to almost 100% of the **TEAM MEMBERS** involved. However, we cannot ignore that the fact for some people they did not find **CYTA** to their liking.

Going places - CYTA

Former **TEAM MEMBERS** continued to use skills learned in CYTA and took on work as well as management of Christian camp sites. The sites included Naamaroo, Uniting church site at North Parramatta, Bonny Hills and Elanora Heights. Among the **TEAM MEMBERS** who continued to be involved in Christian Camping was *David* and *Ros Calder* at Naamaroo and *John Stone* at Bonny Hills.

George Cook spent the last five years of his working life working at the Uniting Church North Parramatta site. The *Jarret's* were managers of the Elanora Lodge for some years after serving at **CYTA LODGE**.

Daren Mann is the manager of the C.Y.C. campsite at Forest Edge Nerrim East Victoria. Daren's father Trevor managed **CYTA LODGE**. Christian camping lives on as does other forms of Christian service.

Cathy (who along with her husband Hans is mentioned in earlier and later chapters) talks about the Christian service in which the family has been involved.

> '*I (Cathy) worked for 16 years as Secretary to Canon Jim Holbeck, Leader of The Healing Ministry at St Andrew's Cathedral. We have 3 children. Benjamin, born 1979, was involved in the Christian ministry at Wollongong University and then went to Moore College. Timothy born 1982, now works for Youthworks training people for ministry and is on staff at Soul Revival Church Kirrawee, as their children's minister. Elizabeth born 1987 was recently music co-ordinator at St Luke's Miranda and now works for*

> Far East Broadcasting Company in administration. Our three children all attended Shire Christian School, where two of our four grandchildren now go. All four of our grandchildren who are aged 7-12, are now learning about Jesus's love for them. - **Praise the Lord!**"

James Gow grew up in the shadow of the **AUSTALIAN CHRISTIAN MUSCI seminar**. He is involved in full time Christian service. James is currently and has been for ten years the Manager of ***Logosdor*** Australia.

Logosdor founded by Simon Hood who has been the ongoing Managing Director Worldwide, states on its website that it is a world-wide missionary outreach to the children of over 190 countries. Logosdor material is produced in Hornsby, NSW, by a group of full-time, part-time and voluntary team of thirteen dedicated people. All material produced is provided free of charge and released from copyright. The material is translated into many languages by a large team of translators from all around the world.

Tea Pot Ministries (not a **CYTA** activity) was started by ***Robin Morris*** This ministry was more successful than Eagles Wings. It was a social and spiritual ministry for women that ministered to all women who wanted to be involved.

Robin Morris tells the story.

> "I (Robyn) head up the organisation and work with a committee of 8 other ladies. We are registered as a not for profit, organisation. A

fund has been established and this money allows us to bless a couple of women on most retreats who need to feel God's love and encouragement. We have given away on average at least $3000 a year to various ministries who are women and family- oriented.

Teapot Ministries is a ministry to women that I along with a couple of friends established in 2002/2003. The ministry offers events where women come together to share their love of craft in a Christian environment. God gave me the vision in 2002 and we were up and running and registered early 2003.

We hold at least three weekend long retreats a year. Each event has a theme, and we have a speaker who shares God's word. Jan Craik was our first speaker and has often blessed women in this way for us.

We have women from all over Australia attending our events. Retreats are one of our main activities. We have been going to Kiah Ridge at Tahmoor for over 18 years. July 2021 is our 19th year. We also do retreats on the Central Coast and Castlereagh Conference Centre at Castlereagh. As a result of the COVID epidemic in 2020 we established an online presence, running our retreats via ZOOM, email and Facebook. These were very popular, and allowed many women to be involved. We even had women connecting from their caravans.

Going places - CYTA

Many events including Quilt shows, Women's breakfasts, movie afternoons, and bus trips are offered each year. The group has made and donated quilts to various organisations. In 2020.2021 we donated over 130 quilts and 30 plus blankets to Bushfire victims as well as to flood victims from the recent floods. Quilts have been given to women's refuges, hospitals, and nursing homes. We also run charity workshop days and day retreats."

Our mission statement:

'Ministering to women through women's interests'

*Each week during the term we email devotions, and once a month we send out a thought of the month. Throughout each year we minister to over 150 women and email to nearly 200. We have small groups of women who meet on a regular basis to share fellowship and craft in different churches under the Teapot banner. Jan Craik has contributed to this after the death of Bronwyn McBurnie (Elizabeth Watson's sister) who attended **CYTA** weekends in the early years of the organisation."*

Robyn has ensured the group is and will be always open to all women. Each year an ever increasing number of women, who were never part of the **CYTA** TEAM and many women who have never heard of **CYTA** become involved in Teapot Ministries. Two thousand and twenty two was the twentieth anniversary of the Tea Pot Ministries group.

Chris Hill (Née Mascall) tells us:

> "I joined **TEAM** in 1982 after attending a January work weekend and stayed till 1988. While on the **TEAM** I met my husband, Jeff. Since 1985 I have worked in Christian Education and now Executive Manager for Education with Carinity (Queensland Baptists) where I look after their five schools, with more planned."

Karen and Kevin Hastie are now retired form paid work but are as they describe:

> "Bush Church Aid Nomads. We love supporting remote churches in Australia."

Karen and Kevin's son, Michael graduated from Moore College. He was an assistant minister at Roseville and Newtown/Erskineville Anglican Churches, for nine years. In January 2022 Michael moved with his family to take up the position of Senior Minister at Toongabbie Anglican, a church where he had been previously as an Associate Pastor.

Andrew Wardle before his retirement worked for **Bible Society in Ingleburn** for 10 years. He also worked for seven years for the **Wesley Mission (Sydney).** Andrew describes his time with CYTA.

> "I was involved with **CYTA** from 1972 till 1977. I first heard of **CYTA** when I was asked by my sister if I was willing to make up numbers on a Scripture Union staff snow trip in the winter of

Going places - CYTA

1969. I had recently been discharged from 2 Years of National Service in the Army. **CYT** *was using the Salvation Army facilities for accommodation adjacent to the old* **CYTA LODGE** *at the time.*

I became involved after the Cairns-Cooktown 1972 tour with **Graeme Leishman** *as the* **TOUR LEADER** *and* **Lois Riley** *as the* **HOSTESS***. The* **TOUR TEAM** *talked about potential volunteers for the team. Kevin Craik rang me at work (John Sands Printers) asking if I would join a group working at the Lodge over the October Long Weekend.*

At the **LODGE***, Merv and Daisy Clare put me through the third degree as to my suitability. They were like mum and dad at the LODGE to all the* **TEAM MEMBERS***. This is where I met my wife* **Paula (Née Watts)** *she disappeared for 2 years or so, on an overland tour. On her return we met up again and were married in 1977. We have 3 adult children and now have 5 grandchildren."*

A great story to finish this chapter

Shaun and Nerida Walker met when Shaun was assistant **TOUR LEADER** on a snow tour in 1985. Nerida joined Shaun on the **TEAM**, and they married in 1988. Shaun talks of their service for Christ, which occurred while dealing with personal adversity. Shaun speaks of the adversity that faced him and Nerida and how it has lead into ministry.

"In 1994 I was diagnosed as being Clinically Sterile and told we'd never have biological children of our own. However, through faith in Jesus we had four miracle children within four years.

Through her journey and heart to help others facing similar infertility, prenatal or childbirth complications, Nerida wrote two books, **"God's Plan for Pregnancy: From Conception to Childbirth and Beyond."** *and* **"It is finished - Transforming Your Life through The Finished Work Of The Cross.".** *She also founded New Life Ministries which along with the books have reached many people around the world.*

God also called us to move and plant a church on the Central Coast of NSW, which we have been doing since 2006. (Shaun also works in televisions filming and production)

I was never backwards in coming forward. I was the lead singer and guitarist in a band with other **TEAM MEMBERS***s that played a couple of times at the* **CYTA LODGE** *in Cooma. I was also a part of the worship* **TEAM** *in our weekly* **TEAM** *meetings.*

Nerida on the other hand was very shy and had a fear of public speaking and praying in front of others. The skills she learnt on **TEAM** *gave her the confidence to not only pray in front of people, but her Ministry opened doors for her to preach*

> in big churches and conferences in the UK, Malaysia, Singapore and India.
>
> **CYTA** was foundational in both of our lives in preparing our hearts to embark on a life of ministry where we both continue to share on the Goodness of God to anyone who will listen.

Kevin reflects on this story of adversity and the spark it gave for a life of ministry.

> "This story is about a couple who put their trust and faith in Jesus Christ. What a wonderful outcome. It all started, with a God given meeting, on a **CYTA** snow tour."

Nerida has a desire to reach others. She founded the ministry **New Life Ministries** and through her journey and with a heart to help others Nerida has written two books.

For Nerida's books:

> *God's Plan for Pregnancy: From Conception to childbirth and Beyond:* and *transforming Your Life through the finished work of the Cross*
>
> Check out: https://neridawalker.com

As the heading for this section suggested I think this was a great story of faith to finish this chapter.

Now to look at **Today and tomorrow** more stories of faith and service with the inclusion of the next generation, children of **CYTA TEAM MEMBERS.**

Going places - CYTA

11. Today and Tomorrow
The Next Generation
There are many more stories of today (the time after leaving CYTA) and of tomorrow (which is now). In this chapter we look at what has happened to the children of many of the **Team Members** and in some cases their grandchildren.

Peter and Heather Schabel had two children Jenny and Graeme. They were two of the **"Cooma kids"** who give us reflections on that time and talk about where they are today.

Jenny leads off.

> I'm now living in Goulburn, having moved to regional and rural parts of NSW after university.
>
> I've been following the Lord since I was a teenager, and appreciate all of the Christian fellowships I have experienced in my upbringing that have helped set a firm foundation. I've been involved in Scripture Union camps, studied at Sydney Missionary and Bible College, and have been a high school Christian SRE teacher for the last 6 years as well as coordinating a youth group at my local church. I worked with Bush Church Aid for a time while I was studying in Sydney too.
>
> Being part of the volunteer **TEAM** at the **AUSTALIAN CHRISTIAN MUSIC SEMINARS** was definitely a formative step in my journey of faith. Watching and learning in the Lodge kitchen

> developed a passion for camp catering, which I've put to use at SU ag camps (agricultural camps) and beach missions I loved being a driver for the Paul Colman Trio one seminar.
>
> As I've become involved in various ministries, it has been wonderful crossing paths with other **CYTA** kids. In particular, I've seen Clare Wimble, who has been involved in CRU (Crusaders) school ministries in Sydney for many years.
>
> I've seen Julie Layton, a school chaplain in Parkes. Julie is Jeanette Lane's daughter and was the corps leader of Parkes Salvation Army for a number of years. I have also been involved with Scripture Union activities under the leadership of Mike Hastie, son of Kevin and Karen Hastie, who met on a Fijian Tour and were **TEAM MEMBERS** for a number of years.
>
> It has been good to see that Mum and Dad have maintained connections with other **CYTA** couples, meeting for fellowship and a meal almost monthly for the last 40 plus years."

Graeme Schabel writes.

> "As a young kid I have many fond memories of **CYTA** friends. Our family would often catch up with other young **CYTA** families, and it was always a lot of fun. One evening I fondly remember watching the dads in their **CYTA** orange jump suits lighting fireworks and crackers near a huge bonfire to the oooh's and aaahs of

all. We kids had spent all day helping build that bonfire.

*Together our families spent many enjoyable weekends at Cooma C**YTA LODGE**. While the snow, tobogganing and later on skiing drew us there, we enjoyed even more being around friends. Memories of the fun evenings hanging around the warm fire, the cushion fights, films and especially the skit nights were great.*

We kids enjoyed the work weekends. There was plenty of fun had playing together. Saturday morning the parents were all divided into work parties. I remember one enthusiastic dad volunteering to sew and repair the cushions with the ladies. Us kids would often go out and rake the autumn leaves, and we would help with the food serving and wash up. One year I vividly remember helping demolish the internals of a small flat at the far end of Y block, doing various things like pulling the nails out of the wood. I especially remember one of the men who was a doctor (GP) really enjoying using the sledgehammer – I'm sure he didn't get to demolish flats too often!

*In our later teenage years, we kids had the opportunity to be part of the **LODGE TEAM** at the **AUSTRAIAN CHRISTIAN MUSIC SEMINARS**. We were busy serving, and we had a lot of fun too. It widened my world view**. TEAM** work and being with "big name" yet humble*

> Christian musicians was great, and I grew in appreciation to worship our Lord through music.
>
> I found the technology amazing. What you can do with lights, sound and recording interests me. It is through this interest that our Lord led me in July 2008 to become a full time missionary with Gospel Recordings, now known as Global Recordings Network."

I, Howard am happy to say that I found work in two organisations serving Christians, while still a **TEAM MEMBER** and after, I left the **CYTA TEAM**. Two years approximately was spent as Chief Financial Officer of the Wesley Mission (Sydney) and a further two years, which proved to be an exceptionally testing time, as Chief Operating Officer with Rhema (Music).

Both our sons have been involved in Christian service on a full time basis. Our older son David worked fulltime for some time with Jews for Jesus. Timothy our younger son worked for seven years, most of the time as a pastor, with Open Doors till COVID first struck. Open Doors, is an organisation that supports persecuted Christians throughout the world. Our daughter worked form sometime with a media company owned and operated by Christians. Our daughter, Chloe worked for some time with a media agency owned and operated by Christians

The daughter of **Barbara Wimble** is involved in Christian camping.

> "Clare, our daughter, has been a Crusader "CRU Camps" chaplain for 10 years. She, along with

> her brother Craig, served as **CYTA TEAM MEMBER**s on a number of music seminars."

Keith and Liz Jarrett have had children who have served others through teaching in a Christian based school. Their younger daughter:

> "Naomi married Mathew Burns, who she met at Morling Bible College. They trained to be overseas missionaries, while church planting in Hobart to gain experience." Naomi in time retrained to become a Speech Pathologist and is currently at the Gold Coast Hospital

Kevin reflects on the lives of the children of **Bruce** and **Heather Bolton**.

> **"Bruce and Heather** brought to the **LODGE** their three children: Alison, Murray and Nigel. Both Alison and Murray met their life's partner from the ranks of the short-term winter staff.
>
> **Alison** became Mrs **Woolly** after marrying, **Ian**. They both trained at Sydney Missionary and Bible College prior to serving as missionaries in Austria for nine years. Upon returning to Australia, Ian became the youth director before being invited to be the pastor of Heathcote-Engadine Baptist Church. Ian is now a part time chaplain at Hammondville Village
>
> **Murray** wooed and married Katrina Rayner and they now lives on the Central Coast. He is a successful builder of quality homes. He and his family are involved in Coast Community church.

Going places - CYTA

> ***Nigel*** *became a professional ski instructor and worked each winter at Smiggins/Perisher Valley. He would then head to the Austrian ski fields or USA's Vail ski fields. He and his wife Anne were in great demand on the ski fields due to their teaching skills*

Some of the children of past **TEAM MEMBERS** followed their parents into Christian Camping such as ***John Grinsell's*** son ***David***. David is a Camp Director of group summer programs for a Christian Camp in Texas. Camp Eagle caters for ten camps per summer season with 500 plus young people at each camp. David was inspired to get into Christian Camping by attending **CYTA** (family) reunion weekends at **CYTA LODGE** with his parents John and Judy.

This is what ***David Grinsell*** – a Cooma Kid says about his younger life and his life of service.

> *"My Name is David Grinsell. I am the son of the Infamous **CYTA** character John Grinsell. I am now 31 years old and living in Texas. For the last 7 years I have been involved in a Christian Camp called Camp Eagle Adventure camps, I am the director of our summer camp program that sees over 5.500 students a summer and lead a **TEAM** of 80 students.*
>
> *Around eight years ago, I fell into some jobs in Sydney that did not satisfy my need to serve the Lord in a capacity that was bigger than me, and I ended up taking a shot to work at a summer camp in the USA for 4 months. Four months*

turned into a Director's job, meeting the love of my life Brooke and a chance to influence over 40,000 for Christ over 8 incredible summers.

CYTA *played a huge role in my life over my early years, going to Cooma LODGE would be one of my favourite things I did every year. Mum would say that when I came home from the LODGE I would cry when I was 8. The reunion was one of the first times where I felt a sense of belonging, Christian community and being a part of something bigger than myself.*

There was just so much to do... I remember so much! I lay in bed awaiting the "good morning song", the pillow fights in the main hall, the pinecones out at the lookout, the abandoned buildings where we would jump on mattresses, Uncle Kev C handing out lollies from the stage. ***CYTA*** *really harnessed my passion to unite people together for a Gospel purpose. I used to call Cooma LODGE my second home, and I would feel at home as soon as we drove up that steep hill and saw familiar faces and that old wooden **CYTA LODGE** that held so many memories.*

*Still often today I think back to those memories and think about how God used **CYTA** to harness my passion for bringing people together and sharing the Gospel. He also used **CYTA** to harness my passion for adventure, relationships, and truth. **CYTA** changed my Mum and Dad's life (Judy & John) and in essence changed mine too.*

Going places - CYTA

> *At 31, I now take off on my next adventure which is starting my own business called the "Go Gateway". The business seeks to grow the impact and reach of small creative non-profits through fundraising, marketing & Event Management. A world changed through creatively acting out the tangible love of Jesus. We are about less talk and more action.*
>
> *Kev, I would call you a spiritual father to my Dad. You took care of him, believed in his abilities and gave him a sense of purpose! I am forever grateful for Kev, Jan & the **CYTA** crew for raising my parents to love adventure, community, and Jesus! I am also grateful for the many experiences of being involved with people who loved Jesus so much! Your impact and legacy lives on and is still impacting me on my walk with Jesus daily!*
>
> Love Dave Grinsell"

Darren Blood is the son of **Trevor and Lyn Blood** former **CYTA LODGE** mangers. **Darren** grew up at **CYTA LODGE**, managed by his parent's, worked at Mill Valley Ranch, where he met his wife **Sam** and was married at the camp. He was also part of CYC ministries and served as Ministry Manager for Baptist Camping Victoria. At the time of writing this book he is the manager at CYC Forest Lodge

Darren gives insight into his lie growing up as a Cooma Kid

Going places - CYTA

"I am happily married to my beautiful wife Sam, and we have two incredible boys, Jayden (18), and Noah (16) and we are all involved in camp ministry. (One of our boys is currently leading on a camp as I write this).

I have the incredible privilege of managing a great **TEAM** at CYC Forest Edge, as well as representing Christian camps at both a State and National level for CVA (Christian Venues Association).

I share this, as I genuinely believe that I am where I am today, as a result of my parents Trevor and Lyn Blood making the decision to take on the role of managers for **CYTA LODGE** in 1993. They took the step to journey into Christian camping and move our family from Sydney down to Cooma to follow what they believed was God's calling, and I'm so grateful they did.

What initially started as excitement to live on camp and have my own games room, turned into a life-long adventure of exploring God's call for my life.

One key person I met through **CYTA** was an amazing man named Kevin Pool, who had made a career out of camp ministry. He invited me to pursue what I now see as God's calling and led me down a path that has included ministry opportunities with Mill Valley Ranch, Christian

Going places - CYTA

Youth Camps (CYC), and Baptist Camping Victoria.

What started as a vision for **CYTA** *in the early days, to invest into the lives of young people through camp, is still happening today. It may look and feel a little different to back then, but this generation and the next, is just as passionate and keen to continue to build on the legacy.*

Through working with faith-filled young adults who would work for the winter season and include me in their daily lives, to being challenged and inspired through both through camping and the AUSTRALIAN CHRISTIAN MUSIC SEMINARS, I was encouraged to grow and developed into someone who loved God loved camping who embraced their gifting an talents to ultimately find that God had called me into a camping ministry

People's lives are still being impacted through the power and ministry of camp!! Mum and Dad Blood are parents in a season of Ministry as the Chaplains to the CVA Camps of Victoria."

Arthur and Bev Rickersy, two early **TEAM MEMBERS**, with their three boys looked forward every year to coming to the music seminar. All three boys were eager patrons of the Insomniacs Supper, the name of which as it implies went late into the night. *Arthur* shares his memories.

Going places - CYTA

*Glenn loved nothing more than to be part of the technical team, perched very high up near the ceiling operating the main spotlight. Darren earned his keep assisting on stage moving props, sound gear and other items around as directed by the stage manager(s), Jan, **Sallie-Ann Craik (Née Wilson)** and **Julie Everest (Née Prowse**), to mention a few.*

*Nathan graduated from the Children's program to help Dad in making sure the various school facilities were ready for morning electives and the afternoon workshops. Bev attended many seminars when at **ACMS**. However, for many years she let her "men have their time" at the seminar.*

Les and Ros Shakespeare had a variety of roles in the life of **CYTA**. Their son **Lyndon** is a **Bishop** in the **Episcopalian Church** in America. Daughter **Melinda** was in the Queensland police force for a number of years

Jeff Drayton, another one of the Director's Kids (son of Graham Drayton) had grown up at Cooma and was a great help to the Technical **TEAM** in setting up the required sound gear in each of the classrooms at the music seminar on a daily basis.

His love of music, led him into a time of managing a renovation of an historical theatre in Thirroul, NSW. He was also the music director of the Figtree Anglican Church. Jeff helped Jan Craik stage manage the World

Festival of Praise in Fiji, which was heavily promoted by Fiji Ministry of Tourism as a national event.

CYTA contributes to other ministries

The ministry lives on. **CYTA** was right for the time. It was unique in the Southern Hemisphere and nothing has come near to replace it. Times change and attitudes and interests move on. It has been a delight to hear of where our kids have ended up serving our *Lord* in successful professional and inn Christian ministry positions.

The final distribution of funds available at the time when **CYTA** ceased its ministry went to Christian activities in which, the children of **TEAM MEMBERS** were serving *God*. While the tours ceased in 1998, ACMS continued till 2002

People continued their service well beyond **TEAM** Membership and involvement in **AUSTALIAN CHRISTIAN MUSIC SEMINAR**. This chapter has included the service areas of former **TEAM MEMBERS** as well as some of the children of **TEAM MEMBERS**. It is important to note that service has continued in a variety of organisations beyond those mentioned in this chapter.

Occupations and groups in which they work include: Crusaders, Mercy Ships, As Pastors/Minsters in a variety of different denominations, Counsellors in Christian schools, teachers in leadership positions with some on school boards, and as Christian camp directors as well as the Samaritan's Purse including Operation Christmas Child, Logosdor as well **TEAM MEMBERS**

who took up full-time mission or acted as relief missionaries.

12. TEAM expansion - Melbourne and Brisbane
Melbourne
Melbourne over time provided more and more **TOUR MEMBERSs** and then its own **TEAM**. On the back of efforts by **Chris Otten (Née Peiper),** Melbourne established a smaller group than existed in Sydney but an equally enthusiastic group to match their northern counterparts. Chris came to Sydney for a year to be part of the main **TEAM** and to work in the office. The Melbourne **TEAM** rose to around 40 in number and existed for around four years.

Chris tells her story.

> "Some days in your life end up being extremely SIGNIFICANT and change the course of your life forever – I like to call these "DIVINE APPOINTMENTS" set up by God. It was around June 1975 that God set up for me one of these "Divine Appointments" – it just so happened I was attending my very 1st Gospel Music Concert at Festival Hall in Melbourne – a Gospel Group called André Crouch and The Disciples. I came to be there at the invitation of some great Christian friends I knew from Mill Valley Ranch – a wonderful Christian Camp I volunteered at. This camp was very special to me as it was where I became a Christian – forever changed and eternally grateful to that Ministry!
>
> But the significance of going to the concert that night was the discovery of the organisation that

*promoted this wonderful Christian Music Event as **Christian Youth Travel Association (CYTA)**. I had never heard of them before but as my eyes perused the Concert Program my eyes lit up and my "spirit" leapt as I read about **CYTA**. – I felt like I was hearing directly from God – **YOU CHRIS ARE GOING TO BE INVOLVED IN THIS MINISTRY! Who me**… **Yes You**! … But Lord I am not even 18 years old yet? You see the incredible thing was that only God and I knew that He had placed a "vision" in my heart – that there needed to be a **Christian Travel Organisation** for Young Adults… so they could travel together and explore His magnificent world whilst experiencing Faith and Community together. AND HERE WAS THE "ANSWER" TO MY VISION and PRAYER!! I was SO excited.*

*I just knew it was God's Divine Appointment for me! I loved the concert. BUT I could hardly wait for tomorrow to come so I could send a letter off to: Dear Sir at **CYTA**. … And express my desire to know more and to see how I could get involved … you see I lived in Melbourne and this organisation was based in Sydney. (This was before the days of mobile phones and computers you see… no Google Search back in those days!) – can you believe that?*

*The next day I excitedly wrote to "Dear Sir" at **CYTA**. and shared how I came to be at the concert the night before with some friends from Mill Valley Ranch – (Of course Dear Sir (who* *happened to be Kevin Craik) was good friends of Arthur and Bonnie Bartlett who ran the Mill Valley campsite – (so he could do a background check on whoever this young not quite 18 year old young woman was) – but I never came to know that part of the story until many months later..... I also told "Dear Sir" in my Introductory Letter to him that for the previous year of my life, I had the joy and privilege of travelling England and Europe for 7 months with my family in a Motorhome. As we travelled some 28 countries staying at all the major caravan parks, not only did it instil in me a DEEP LOVE of travelling BUT I also got to witness the life and adventures and "escapades" of young 16-30 year olds travelling on Coach/Camping Tours throughout Europe… and let's just say way too many escapades that compromised the quality and fun of young adults travelling, I thought.*

It's like God "seared" in my heart a VISION for a TRAVEL COMPANY that offered a "quality" alternative for 18-30 year olds who wanted good clean fun and adventure whilst travelling this beautiful world of ours!… You see I had become a Christian 2 years earlier and I had a clear VISION, that just "imagine" – a Christian Travel Organisation for that age group where you could experience the "joy" of travel, sharing the same Christian Values and exploring God's Creation together whilst enjoying Christian Community.

*Within 6 months of arriving back in Australia God had DIVINELY LED me to that organisation – the ANSWER to my prayers and vision that only God and I knew about! Back in 1975 with the technology available how on earth would I have ever found out that such an organisation existed! BUT God knew!! He knows the "desires of our heart" and He is SO FAITHFUL! Oh No! – **CYTA** only exists in Sydney! I live in Melbourne! Strangely it wasn't an obstacle to me – I just KNEW I was going to be involved somehow! But I had a lot to learn as a young Christian about "waiting on God" and "waiting on HIS timing" – which is always PERFECT!*

*I had done my part to be "pro-active and prayerful" and reach out to **CYTA**. But then there was the waiting, and waiting and waiting… in fact some 3 to 4 months later when I had another "DIVINE APPOINTMENT" that became another significant answer to prayer. Little did I know that by responding to a request for "volunteers" to help at the Inaugural Christian Camping International Australia Conference held at Mill Valley Ranch in 1975 I got to hear one of the Guest Speakers – who yes… you guessed it was Kevin Craik from **CYTA**. I could not believe my ears NOR contain my excitement that this must be the "Dear Sir" I had sent my letter to. With no hesitation I approached Kevin, introduced myself and told him about the letter I had sent some 3 months earlier. To my astonishment he acknowledged he had read my letter, said it was* in his Special File and that when he does reply...it will be worth the wait! – WOW – Thank you God for yet another "DIVINE APPOINTMENT"!

You see... as a young Christian I was learning and experiencing "first hand" profound lessons of "living by faith". I was learning to live one day at a time, trusting in Him to lead and guide me and to live obediently according to the guidance and prompting of the Holy Spirit. Amidst my disappointment over the past 3 months of not getting a reply to my Letter (why I didn't think to call the **CYTA** Office – I will never know!), I was also learning to respond to opportunities God was giving me to serve Him that were right in front of me. Because of the obedience it led me to meet "in person" Kevin Craik – The Director of **CYTA**.....How good is our God! Well with still a "testing time" of waiting on God some 4 weeks later THE LETTER arrived with the **CYTA** Logo on it... and I couldn't contain my excitement as I opened it –and true to his word Kevin, on behalf of **CYTA**, offered this "young" Chris some wonderful opportunities that would allow me to experience many dynamics in the life of **CYTA**. These were:

- Firstly, to fly me to Cooma (where on earth is that place?) to **their CYTA LODGE** to experience one of the "infamous" Work Weekends... this facility was the base for their Awesome Ski Tours.

Going places - CYTA

- *Secondly, I could choose any destination within Australia to experience one of the Coach/Camping Tours as an Assistant… over the Christmas Holiday Period. I chose Western Australia under the leadership of Ken McGill and his wife Diane as **HOSTESS**. They taught me a whole lot about **CYTA**.*
- *Thirdly, end up in Sydney for a week to experience the Administration Base, staying with a beautiful lady who worked in the **CYTA** office. It was **Elaine**:*

   *"Known and loved by many in the **TEAM**. This amazing friendship is still enjoyed today some 45 years later!"*

*Little did I know that the **DIRECTORS** of **CYTA**, had a desire to branch out to Victoria because there were many who came from there on the trips and here was God raising up an 18 year old young woman with a vision, a passion and desire to be part of this organisation… you see God had already written that VISION in my heart the year earlier – HOW GREAT IS OUR God! The answer was easy – I seized all 3 wonderful God-given opportunities – I had the most rich, challenging, exciting faith filled adventures of a lifetime over the next 6 years with **CYTA**.*

*Such was God's plan for **CYTA** to start in Melbourne that He also led a wonderful young man and his young family to visit **CYTA** LODGE in Cooma over that exact same Christmas Holiday Period that I was*

Going places - CYTA

away experiencing the Camping Tour! This man, **Graeme McSolvin**, a schoolteacher and a prominent leader in his church and youth group in Melbourne, felt God lay on his heart to bring a busload of Young Adults from Melbourne to the "infamous" Easter Camps at **CYTA LODGE** – a gathering of young adults to experience travel, fun and fellowship amongst a ministry of Christian Musicians and Chaplains.

So with Graeme's enthusiasm and connections along with the wonderful support from his wife and family that he and I set out to PRAY, PLAN and PROMOTE this first Bus Trip to many large churches in Melbourne and that Easter our first Inaugural **CYTA** Bus Tour to Cooma **CYTA LODGE** happened – it was AMAZING!

After that success we planned for the June Long Weekend and **CYTA** Victoria was really gathering momentum. It was meeting such a need for Christian Young Adults in the 16 – 30, age range. With Graeme's maturity, leadership skills and wealth of contacts within Melbourne churches and my "youthful" energy and passion we move ahead. God began to breathe HIS Blessing on the birthing of **CYTA** Victoria! Incredibly we began to build a strong foundation and presence of **CYTA** in Melbourne and promoting **CYTA** for its Coach Camping Tours within Australia and Overseas! We also began to promote our own Victorian Ski Tours and trips to Cooma **CYTA LODGE** too.

Going places - CYTA

As the momentum and profile was continuing to grow in Melbourne, the **CYTA DIRECTRORS** *offered me a "once in a lifetime" opportunity to shift to Sydney and live, breathe, work and learn ALL the many aspects of this marvellous Christian ministry. Well this adventurous 19 year old just knew this was right and embraced it – so many NEW challenges, NEW Friendships, NEW adventures, NEW learning and growth opportunities… but most importantly, learning to live a FAITH- FILLED life with VISION and PURPOSE! A highlight too was the weekly* **TEAM** *Training Nights for our 80+ strong Volunteer* **TEAM** *that came together for worship, teaching, training, and fellowship – this was such a wonderful time in my life and to this very day I am still blessed to have many special friendships as a result of this time.*

Early in 1978, not yet 21 years of age, the time had finally come for **CYTA** *Sydney to step out and officially start* **CYTA** *Victoria. I had completed a year-long training period and I became the first Full Time Secretary ably directed by honorary Director Graeme McSolvin, who helped energise, lead and inspire our* **TEAM** *whilst still passionately teaching in his day job. Our Head Office and* **TEAM** *Headquarters was at 1st Floor, 56 Burwood Rd, Hawthorn, where we too held our Weekly* **TEAM** *Training Nights with 35+ Volunteer* **TEAM** *Base with Young Adults, representing many different churches in Melbourne. We diligently promoted our local Victorian Ski Tours Program and extended Christian Youth Travel tours amongst many large churches in Melbourne, young adult gatherings, conferences and*

Christian Radio promotions and also helping sponsor alongside Head office in Sydney some marvellous Christian Music Concerts including Andraé Crouch and The Disciples, Evie, Ken Medema and the **AUSTALIAN CHRISTIAN MUSIC SEMINAR** – as a result many young people were reached with the Gospel and became Christians, many were strengthened and encouraged in their Christian Faith, many developed Leadership Skills as they served God through Melbourne **CYTA** and many, many of them met their spouses as a result of this unique and marvellous ministry. To this day so many of these couples are "raising" the next generation of Christian Young Adults who many are now serving in full time Christian ministry and passionately serving in their local church.

This four-year period of **CYTA** in Melbourne was a very rewarding and fruitful time for God's Kingdom… eternally impacting many lives. Such commitment, vision, sacrificial service, drives and passion was in the hearts of the original **CYTA DIRECTORS** and their spouses in Sydney – they too were Young Adults at that very time too. Without their obedience and conviction this incredible influential unique Ministry through the avenue of Coach/Camping Tours, Ski Tours, Gospel Concerts, Christian Music Seminars and much more was indeed RAISED UP FOR SUCH A TIME AS THEN!!

Only in Eternity will we fully see the "fruits" of this Ministry and the RICH HARVEST of so many people for Jesus! I personally am ETERNALLY GRATEFUL TO GOD… that He so DIVINELY LED me to be a part of this amazing Ministry! It has impacted me to *this very day in every area of my life and most importantly my FAITH IN GOD!*

Little Chrissie, (the Mexican from down South), as I was affectionately known… is now 64…and I have been married to a wonderful Christian guy for 35 years. We have 4 adult children and 4 precious grandchildren – how BLESSED am I… we have throughout our marriage been committed to church life… served our Lord passionately… BUT I will NEVER forget those AMAZING blessed six years of serving my Lord and Saviour through the powerful ministry of Christian Youth Travel Association…

*Thank you, Kevin and your Leadership **TEAM**, for giving me the opportunity to be part of **CYTA** – I was SO blessed and honoured to be part of the **CYTA** Family… eternally thankful! As a familiar chorus goes, This IS MY Story...This is My Song… to Follow My Saviour All My Days Long...*

My Life Verse (as provided by Chris)…"

> "**Ephesians 3:20**… Now to Him who is able to do immeasurably more than all we ask or imagine, according to HIS power that is at work within us...to Him be glory in the Church and in Christ Jesus throughout all generations, for ever and ever, Amen.'

Kevin Craik adds that he believes

> 'He Never Changes', "a song sung by Evie Tornqist and Chrissie's testimony. It is a

> demonstration of Christ's love for her and her commitment to HIS ministry."

Ultimately **CYTA** Melbourne after Chris's time decided they would run their own tours independent from **CYTA** and the cost of supporting the Melbourne **TEAM** became prohibitive. Bookings in other Australian cities had grown quickly. Over time there were greater numbers of bookings for tour places, in each of Adelaide and Brisbane than Melbourne.

Brisbane

Vic and Colleen Barrington who were long term Team Members formed a small Brisbane **CYTA TEAM,** with an office in their home. They had a lot to do with the music of **CYTA** when it travelled to Brisbane.

Colleen Barrington remembers.

> "Christian Youth Tours was mainly for young people, but we had from time to time a church group complete with older people. Well, that was fun. We would pick them up on Friday night and arrive at our destination around midnight to put up the tents. We planned to always have a nice, neat camp on every tour but on one tour with a church group, we found once the sun had come up the tents were all over the place, which was the cause of much laughter.
>
> Another challenge with a church group was rain. The group came back drenched after taking a long walk together. Vic and I moved the kitchen into the communal tent and when the coachload

> *of mature-aged campers arrived back at camp, they crammed into the tent with us cooking their dinner so they could get warm.*
>
> *We started with **CYTA** in Sydney and then moved to Brisbane in 1976 where we set up the Queensland **CYTA** office in our home. Vic and I spent many wonderful years with **CYTA**. We have made lifelong friends and were privileged to serve in so many ways. We praise God for the lives we saw changed and the amazing experiences we had with **CYTA**."*

There is more about the great work of the Queensland **TEAM** and Colleen and Vic's enthusiasm for *Christian* music in later chapters as well as the citing of the significant work of Vic and Colleen particularly in the early days of CYTA.

The **CYTA TEAM** in the early to mid-seventies for at least a short time was not just a one city based group. It was an "east coast phenomenon."

13. Death, Faith, the TEAM

A separate chapter has been given to the death of three **TEAM MEMBERS**. The two situations differ markedly. One was young and the other two not so old.

Of course over time other people have died who contributed to the mission field of **CYTA**. The Honour Roll of those people that have died who were **TEAM MEMBERS,** and/or who contributed to the ministry that was **CYTA** are too numerous to list. If there was a list it would also run the risk of omitting someone. But we thank *God* for every one of them for their service to **CYTA** and ultimately to *God*.

Death in youth - Anne Macdonald

Life for a young adult is almost always new, with often many new experiences every othe day. Almost always each **CYTA TEAM MEMBER** was without the encumbrance of mortgages, laughed at how poorly there second hand cars ran and enjoyed life. New friends were made. Time was spent seeing how you fitted in with other **TEAM** people, finding your niche in the **TEAM**.

There were presentations on a "life ever after" as promised through the sacrifice of Christ but few if any of the **TEAM MEMBERS** during their time on the **TEAM** thought about the end of a physical life. When it came to one young **TEAM MEMBER** it was possibly one of the most jarring events in the history of **CYTA**, certainly to that point in the organisation's history.

Kevin Craik first met *Anne MacDonald* at a travel expo at the old Sydney Show Ground (now the Entertainment

Quarter) in 1976. I remember us cooking sausages in the large show ground halls. It was a highly dangerous activity, (no doubt not allowed today), but great fun.

Anne went on tour, joined the **TEAM** and was a **HOSTESS** on several tours including a 1979 tour with *Max Watson* to Central Australia.

Glennis Craig (Née Richardson) while on a Fiji tour remembers the sadness she felt when she heard of Anne's passing. *Max* Watson recalls how he felt hearing the news from Kevin of Anne's death:

> *"It was the worst day of my life, when Kevin rang me to tell me about Anne's death."*

Tragedy had struck the **TEAM**. A **TEAM MEMBER** had been *killed* in a car accident. *Anne MacDonald* was travelling in a car with a male friend along the Pacific Highway just south of Swansea. A car on the other side of the road crossed to the wrong side of the road and crashed into the car in which Anne was travelling forcing it into the guardrail on the roadside. A fire broke out.

Anne was killed in the crash. Her friend survived and has been left with permanent scarring.

TEAM MEMBERS were shaken by the death of the young, dynamic, committed and active **TEAM MEMBER**. Her funeral, as with most, was a sombre affair, with many female **TEAM MEMBERS** crying, along with a few male **TEAM MEMBER**S. The funeral was a new experience for almost every **TEAM MEMBER**. It was the funeral of someone at or close to their own age.

Though the mood was sombre, Anne's mother, clearly a strong Christian woman hugged every crying young woman at the funeral. She was assured that Anne was now in God's *Kingdom* with *Jesus*.

Anne McDonald Fund

A fund was set up in Anne's honour called the Anne McDonald Bible College Scholarship Memorial Fund, which raised $31,375. The breakup of the distribution of funds is included, as one of the addenda found at the end of this book. The following is the text of the letter from Kevin Craik establishing the memorial fund.

> "*17 September 1980*
>
> "*Dear friend,*
>
> *Many past and present CYTA **TEAM** remember Anne McDonald as a real friend, and a **CYTA TEAM MEMBER** who was always willing to go the second mile.*
>
> *Her death late last year (1979) not only shocked and saddened us all; it also brought back memories of many happy times we all shared with Anne when she was with us in the **TEAM**, on tour, and serving at **CYTA LODGE** in her most joyful and helpful manner.*
>
> *Anne went Overland with **CYTA** in 1978 and during her time in Europe she was able to spend some 13 weeks studying at L'Abri in Switzerland to further her understanding of her commitment to Jesus Christ and the Christian way of life.*

Going places - CYTA

> *It was evident from the numerous letters Anne wrote to her friends while overseas that she was a very caring person, one who was not only concerned about her friends but also concerned about their spiritual well-being.*
>
> *As a continuation of this concern for her friends and her love and dedication to her Lord who she sought to serve daily, it is fitting that some on-going remembrance of Anne be established.*
>
> *To this end it is proposed to establish a fund of $3000 from gifts of those who knew Anne as a friend and as a fellow **CYTA TEAM MEMBER**. This amount would be invested and the interest each year would be used to help a young person meet part of a term's fee at a Bible College or other place of Christian study.*
>
> *It is proposed that the first grant would be late in 1981 and that the fund would continue for a period of 5 years. At the end of this time the amount held would be distributed in to several young people in training or study.*
>
> *While we may never see the fruits of Anne's witness, you can be assured that by your contributing, others will come to know and have a real faith in Jesus Christ which was so characterised in Anne's life."*

Mr Richard Horsnell, a member of Holy Trinity Panania Anglican (Anne's church), was invited to be the chair of a little committee with two **CYTA TEAM MEMBERS**, who met yearly to consider the applicants. Richard

Going places - CYTA

chaired the fund for the entire project. We say, "Well done, Richard!"

The **CYTA** office administered the fund. All donations received by **CYTA** for any reason other than the Anne McDonald Fund, unless earmarked for a specific purpose, were placed in this fund. Over the period of 1982-2001, grants of varying amounts were made to 31 students studying at 10 different Christian colleges. When it was decided to close the fund, after nearly 20 years, the balance in the fund at that time $16.600 was allocated equally to Morling College and Holy Trinity Panania Anglican Church Jubilee Fellowship Fund. The overall total that was raised was $31.375 honouring a wonderful young woman whose influence won't be known this side of heaven

Kevin sums up the objective of the fund

> *"The fund honoured a wonderful young woman whose influence won't be known this side of heaven"*

Holy Trinity Anglican Church which is now known as Panania Anglican Church, established an Honour Book to remember Anne McDonald

Brian West, an early **CYTA TEAM MEMBER** (and still a proud **TEAM MEMBER** after 45 years), who met his ***wife Roslyn*** on a USA Tour spoke in recent times at an evening service at the Panania Anglican Church (Anne's old church). Brian is a Trustee of the church's Jubilee fund to which **CYTA** contributed $8300, saying it was a privilege to report that it was still giving support to students of Moore College – Anne's memory and ministry continues and will well into the future.

Paul Webb - A death of a Christian man

Paul Webb came to Australia with his family as "*ten pound poms.*" Part of the post second world war program to add skills to the Australian work force (such as with the snowy scheme mentioned in chapter one) and help populate the nation.

Paul's parents managed Camp Saunders and a number of other church homes in Newcastle, which existed to house teenagers and younger children in need. At some stage the family moved to Sydney around Liverpool where Paul attended high school. He became a qualified electrician and also held credentials in Air Conditioning and Refrigeration.

Paul always had a touch of the theatrical about him. He was involved in the Anglican Harvest Theatre company. He was active in his church.

Being a Team Member for twelve years he gave exemplary service to **CYTA** both n his work at the **LODGE** and as a **TOUR LEADER**. He led many tours including the Overland Tour, Europe tours, New Zealand, and the Barrier Reef and off course all those snow tours.

It was always clear even from the first days of their forty six year friendship having met through their involvement in **CYTA** that **Paul** and **Linda** (***Née Sykes***) would be together at some stage. Diligent **TEAM MEMBERS**, but

Going places - CYTA

they were never too far apart for a long time on work weekends.

Together they were marred for thirty six years, and have five children four of whom are two sets of twins. I, (Howard) was delighted to be in Paul and Linda's wedding party as I was delighted that Paul was in our wedding party.

Linda adds the following very personal thoughts on Paul.

> "Paul was a loving, kind, caring husband, father and a good friend to so many people. He always saw the good in everyone and always had a great sense of humour.
>
> Paul died from melanomas that had grown in his body and travelled to his brain. He wanted to live and had four brain surgeries. Due to the research the Melanoma institute did on Paul and other sufferers of the disease, progress is being made towards the management of melanoma."

Paul was able to see his and Linda's first Grandchild born before he died. He lived life long enough to see his children grown but still died young in respect to current expected length of life. Again we never know when *God* will call us home.

Death and a life well lived - Kim Forsyth

Kim Forsyth, a former **TEAM MEMBER** that some of you as readers will have known died in recent years. She was just 65 when she died. She was not an old person by today's expectations. Kim died after living a life of faith including some years with **CYTA**

At her memorial service one of her children spoke of his mother as being someone he always saw in Christian service, wherever she worshipped. A family tribute was handed out at the memorial service, much of which was composed of words written by *Kim* on an earlier occasion where Kim had spoken of her faith and of some of the trials she experienced in her life:

> *"Life is not all plain sailing. Life at school was not all plain sailing. Life at school was difficult at times and so was my family situation. My dad left home when I was 19 years of age and my world fell apart.*
>
> *Luke (one of her children) became sick when he was just thirteen years old. He was diagnosed with cancer and had intensive treatment for fourteen months but sadly lost the battle one summer's day.*
>
> *I questioned God and asked where He was in these situations. Why me? Why my family? I don't know the answers to those questions, but I do know He was with me through these troubling times, comforting, helping and guiding me through. I have heavily relied on Him as well as others in my family and my church family."*

What is not mentioned in the service publication was that Kim's husband Ross passed away around five years before her. Kim was hospitalised for 16 months

Going places - CYTA

from the end of 2019, during which time she was diagnosed with Guillain-Barré syndrome"

> **As side note** Kim, had a verse she added to her statement she made about her life, which is quoted from the service program at the thanksgiving service for her life. I think it says a lot about how she lived and thought about her life.
>
> **2 Timothy 2:12**(New Intentional Version)
>
> *"If we suffer, we shall also reign with him"*

We started this chapter with Anne MacDonald. Anne's death was a death in youth. Anne was someone who touched people's lives and was gone too soon. Paul was a helper and a friend to many. Kim lived a life of faith and service.

What might we say about or think about our life lived, when *God* calls us home?

> **CYTA** was but a bus stop in **HIS** service along the way

Going places - CYTA

14. TEAM, Work and Training weekends
Work Weekends

Work weekends were spent completing endless tasks. It could be painting or cleaning, grounds work or one of the numerous jobs around the **CYTA LODGE**. Some of the **TEAM** were skilled trades' people such as electricians who installed and fixed lights. Some people like me, with little skill at anything, just lent a hand wherever it was needed.

The day always started well as **Robyn Hunt** recalls the start of each day.

> Good memories of being on work weekends and being woken up every morning by that song, good morning good morning good morning it's time to rise and shine. Good morning good morning good morning I hope you're feeling fine. You got to get up you sleepy heads

In the early days of the **CYTA LODGE**, one of the heavy jobs as we mentioned in an earlier chapter was removing non-working water heaters from ceilings of cabins. The heaters were heavy, covered in dust and dirty. The job required two people in the roof to move each heater to the manhole and two people beneath to take the heater down. Kevin was often in the ceiling directing the removal. It was a job with the possibility of injury occurring. Every **TEAM MEMBERS** regardless of gender could take their turn in the roof. I can assure you it was not pleasant.

When you were working in the roof, there was always the possibility of a foot going through the ceiling. People did go through the ceiling. One **TEAM MEMBER**, *Paul Webb*, went through a ceiling twice.

Andrew Drylie remembers one such incident

> *"Paul came crashing through a ceiling when removing a water heater, fortunately without injury"*

A side note: Things were safe and worked after maintenance work was carried out. Sometimes sets of adjacent room lights after being fixed behaved in strange ways. One such instance was when adjacent lights were fixed the pull down cord switches seemed to be reversed. The light on the left was switched on by the hanging cord switch of the light on the right and the reverse!!

But there was time for fun. *Andrew Drylie* remembers the nonsense that went on whenever the **TEAM** was the **LODGE**,

> *"One night as I was about to get into bed I found the bed had been filled with tree leaves that I and others had raked up during that afternoon. The next morning I was on kitchen duty. I was asked if I had **slept like a leaf**."*

In an earlier chapter it was mentioned that Kevin Pool would stroll around the LODGE precincts on work weekends, with a group of female **TEAM MEMBERS**, linking arms together which then linked onto Kevin Pool's arms.

Going places - CYTA

Christine Pegram remembers these times fondly:

> "We would take AMOOC on a lead into Cooma. Stares came from passers-by who saw a sheep on a lead, with one male and several females in company."

Elva Harris also remembers a walk with AMOOC

> "One work weekend some of us decided to go to the Cooma shops for a milkshake, taking with us AMOOC on a lead. A group of people trying to figure out what breed of dog he/she was finally had to ask us. Trying to keep a straight you **Kevin Pool** replied:"
>
> 'It's a sheep dog!!"

AMOOC (Cooma spelt backwards) was an orphaned female lamb that Kevin Pool had found. AMOOC grew into a sheep, a large sheep. A sheep is an unusual pet, but one that received enormous affection from **MEMBERS** of the **CYTA TEAM**, as well as from Kevin Pool. Unfortunately AMOOC died after being injured in a dog attack.

Geof Hyde recalls,

> "The year CYTA LODGE was being fitted on its perimeter with half logs I helped on many work weekends often collecting the logs on the trip down to CYTA LODGE. Over the years when in bible-college and later when not on tour I also helped out at the LODGE. It was on one of the work weekends I met Rossanne my wife of 40 years."

> **A side note:** The fitting of the LODGE to which Geof refers was the decision to cover the fibro inside walls with pine half logs. The fibro was painted black so no gaps could be seen after the logs were in place. Kevin and Geof were unsure before painting whether the black paint would cover the gaps and look acceptable. It worked fine. The half logs were nailed to the fibro. Geof spent a whole week doing the inside front wall.

Sue Hayes remembers that:

> "I was on the **TEAM** and volunteered to work at the **LODGE** almost weekly. I went to Cooma Baptist Church more than my home church."

On another January long work weekend there was the building of one of two planned cabins. The pre-cut cabins had been purchased by **CYTA** from a supplier who had, had a customer- a camp site - go into receivership. **CYTA** bought the two buildings. One became the games room, which was erected over several work weekends.

The second cabin became the manager's accommodation, which was expanded from the 60 feet pre-cut frontage to 80 feet. This building was constructed over some weeks by **Les Shakespeare** who also logged the side walls of the main **LODGE**. Les brought his family to live at the **LODGE** while construction of the new accommodation building occurred.

Max Watson recalls his time at the LODGE on work weekends

> "The **LODGE** held so many great memories. As an electrician, I spent a lot of time under floors and in roof cavities, which was not always very pleasant as there was "wool' insulation in the ceilings. It was horrible stuff that worked its way into everything you were wearing."

A side note: Max is right. The wool insulation stuck with you till you showered. Clothes may have come out of the home washing machine clean but the insulation often continued to stick to them and needed to be picked off clothes by hand.

Poor **Max** got possibly the worst job.

> "Once I was involved in cleaning the grease pit".

Lucky you Max, though Max was not the only person to be given "challenging" work to do.

Marion Veerhuis (Née Chant) was given a job that was testing.

> "I remember on work weekends that **Robyn** and I were the shortest people on **TEAM** but had the tallest job, cleaning out the drain pipes."

Vertically Challenged?

Gai Henderson remembers that things did not always go to plan and improvisation was sometimes needed.

> "On a work weekend, I arrived with some other people quite late in the evening. The person in the main building gave us our room allocations but when two of us got to our room the door was

> *locked and no one could find the key. The other people in the room were all asleep.*
>
> *It was very late by now and most people had to be up very early so we didn't want to bang on the door and disturb them so I used my name badge to undo the window latch and we crawled in, quietly found beds, didn't unpack, went to bed in our clothes and woke up in the morning to find we'd been sent to the wrong room! Ours was nearby, open and empty!"*

A gathering of TEAM MEMBERS for a weekend time was a time for important announcements. **Max Watson** recalls:

> *"When the centre at Homebush was purchased, Kevin gave me the honour of announcing it to the **TEAM** on a **TEAM** weekend at The **LODGE**"*

People who attended the work weekends were to be **TEAM MEMBERS**. One **TEAM MEMBER** while packing coaches for snow tour departures on a Friday night met a young woman who had recently arrived from a country town. The woman was looking for a particular **TOUR LEADER**, who as it turned it was not on tour that weekend.

The **TEAM MEMBER** explained to the young woman that the same tour staff MEMBERs were not on every weekend. He assured her that all **CYTA TEAM MEMBERS** were of a high standard and she would have a great time away.

As she was new to Sydney the **TEAM MEMBER** also said there was a **TEAM** work weekend in the near future. If she came she would meet a lot of young people. The **TEAM MEMBER** invited her to come to the work weekend without reference to the office.

The young woman went on and enjoyed the snow weekend. She did come to the work weekend. Kevin sees a person at the work weekend he did not know, walks up to her and says: "*Hello I'm Kevin.*"

She introduced herself and they got chatting and laughing. The new person had a natural laugh. Kevin never asked how she got on the weekend and before the weekend was out the new arrival had asked Kevin if there was any work in the **CYTA** office.

The young woman gained work in the office and became a **TEAM MEMBER** and an integral part of **CYTA** for many years. Kevin does not know to this day who invited this person on the work weekend.

Work weekends accomplished much in relation to the development and maintenance of **CYTA LODGE**. It was a time of friendships developing as well as a time of serving *God* in the ministry of **CYTA**.

Family reunion work weekends

CYTA always had a legacy element. The friends of **CYTA**, (covered in an earlier chapter), kept former **TEAM MEMBERS** involved with the **TEAM**. Some of the work weekends were accorded the name of "Family Reunion Weekends". Again former **TEAM MEMBERS** could meet up at Cooma, reacquaint themselves with old friends as well as continuing to contribute to the maintenance of **CYTA LODGE.**

For *John Grinsell* and his wife *Judy,* who were both **TEAM MEMBERS** it was truly a family affair with their children in tow. *John,* and *Judy's* son continues in Christian service which stems from his attendance at the family work weekends. John recalls one of reunion weekend.

> "My family used to attend the Family Reunion weekends. These weekends were a great time of friendship and fellowship and even some work around the **CYTA LODGE**.
>
> The men usually were given the chore of painting to do. So as a joke Mark Bradbury, Paul Cleasby and I decided we would rather join the knitting group and selected the group as part of our workload over the weekend. When we arrived at the group we were presented with large knitting needles."

Graham Schabel, son of Peter and Heather, as a teenager came regularly with his dad on work weekends

Training Weekends

TEAM training weekends were often held in an outdoor area out of Sydney. One such location used was *Wombeyan Caves.*

Marilyn Lee reflects on the weekend.

> "It was so cold the tent pegs bent when hammered in because the ground was so hard. I

Going places - CYTA

> shared a tent with Glennis Craig and we both slept fully clothed (including shoes) in our sleeping bags covered in blankets. We also wore hats and gloves.
>
> **Geof Hyde** (who was an employee of **CYTA** at the time), *slept in the bin of the coach (usually a no no) and claimed he was warm all night."*

Another to remember the cold was **Elva Harris.**

> "There were the **TEAM** weekends away at Wombeyan Caves where we all froze but came back a year later for another freeze! Some of us discovered a hot water heater in the middle of the night, right near the toilet block, after we had struggled to walk there with every bit of clothing on that we had brought!"

The training weekends covered many of the outdoor activities that could not be covered in the Thursday night training sessions. Overcoming the fear of an exploding pressure cooker, setting up camp next to a coach and then packing it in the most efficient way into a coach were highlights of the training. Sometimes the packed coach looked perfect. Other times it looked like your shopping bag after the milk, which is dripping with condensation, was packed in the bottom of the bag upside down. Such a shopping bag would be considered a mess as was some of the coach packing.

Going places - CYTA

> **A side note:** Fun was always on the cards. Playing soccer with two people tied together as if in a three-legged race, each from opposing teams competing for the ball. Male **TEAM MEMBERS** helping female **TEAM MEMBERS** across a creek when out walking, though some of the males left the females stranded in the middle of a creek.

The training weekends were fun times. They also doubled as **TEAM** building activities.

Robyn Hunt remembers it being cold at the caves

> *"I remember a training weekend at Wombeyan Caves. When we woke up one morning on an October Long Weekend it was sleeting. James Mann, I remember slept outside in his sleeping bag which could withstand the cold."*

Though, **James Mann** disagrees with **Robyn** that it was sleet.

> *"That wasn't sleet Robyn, it was snow and I was as warm as toast."*

Whereas, **Max Watson** suggested somewhat unkindly that the ability James had to withstand a snow storm resulted from a neurological problem:

> *"I remember it was a very cold time, but you were young and possibly didn't have your nerve endings properly connected"*.

Wombeyan Caves provided space for activities and as it was in a campground there was always practice at erecting tents. Timing of this practice was excellent for

Going places - CYTA

the summer tour schedule. However, not all training weekends and **TEAM** weekends were held at the caves.

Teen Ranch was the location for a 1980 April **TEAM** weekend. Everyone was warm in their cabins, though the horses kept at the ranch proved slow for some people and too fast for other **TEAM MEMBERS**

Bawley Point was the location for a training weekend over the Easter long weekend 1981. The town of Bawley Point on the New South Wales South Coast has less than 700 residents today. **CYTA** led an invasion which added more than twenty-five per cent to the population for one weekend of training. Though Bawley Point is a tourist destination, it would not have been surprising if some of the locals had "taken to the hills". On this weekend there was almost 100% attendance by **TEAM MEMBERS**, over 80 people plus **DIRECTORS**, chaplain etc.

It was this weekend that some of the **TEAM MEMBERS** including *Paul Cleasby* were baptised in the surf by the then **CYTA chaplain Geoff** Rowcroft. It was appropriately an Easter training weekend where several **TEAM MEMBERS** decided to continue to commit or recommit their lives to *God* through a baptism of immersion.

> **A side note:** Any time is a great time for nonsense. On this weekend, **Rod** and **Ros Hills** found a child's portable toilet outside their tent after the first night and a box of apples the next night. The perpetrator remains at large.

Going places - CYTA

Apparently, this was also the weekend *Liz Calder* and *Keith Jarret* announced themselves as a couple when they chose to drive to the camp site together. Later of course they were **Mr Keith and Mrs Elisabeth Jarret**. It was the talk of Bawley Point. Trivia and gossip just like love makes the world go round.

The Basin in Ku-ring-gai Chase National Park was the location of another **TEAM** training weekend. The Basin is accessed by boat from the Palm Beach wharf by ferry. This location offers lovely surroundings and views to the Central Coast of NSW.

It is large, grassy area that overlooks the Pittwater, which is a port area, for small sailing craft out of the way of the ocean. **CYTA MEMBERS** used the ferry transfer service from the wharf to get to the location for another **TEAM** training weekend. This **TEAM** campsite is one with multi-million dollar water views. I have often eaten lunch sitting in the green space at Palm Beach wharf and enjoyed the view across to the Basin

Not just the practical aspects of camping were emphasised on **TEAM** training weekends. **CYTA** tours, was a mission field unlike other mission fields.

All **TEAM MEMBERS** were encouraged to stand firm for *Jesus Christ* while on tour.

15. The people of CYTA LODGE

Everyone needs to eat. Have you a bed allocated? Is there someone to issue linen? Who can't find their room?

Paid staff was needed as the ministry grew. Volunteers gave a lot of time to **CYTA** but could not be there all the time. Paid staff provided continuity for customers.

It is not possible nor are we attempting to name all the people who gave dedicated paid and voluntary service in the full-time administration staff, short-term winter staff and the friends of **CYTA**, not forgetting the reliable local casual staff. However, the efforts of all paid and voluntary staff that worked for **CYTA** are not only appreciated but were essential to ensure that the organisation ran smoothly. Many thanks to those named below and to those that have not been named

The first employees at the **CYTA LODGE** were ***Mervyn and Daisy Clare***. They were the all-rounders of all-rounders. Hired as the property managers, they operated the property, organising and completing much of the maintenance required to keep the property operating. When tours were in, they took up management of the kitchen with Daisy involved in organising and cooking the meals.

Originally from Newcastle from a Methodist/Uniting Church background, they responded to an advertisement in the religious press for staff to work at **CYTA LODGE**. In the interview for the position, they expressed a desire to be a strong witness for Christ and to provide help to young people. The first employment contract for the Clare's was for six months during the snow season with the understanding they would need to find another source of income for the other six months of the year. The couple had accommodation for the whole year but were only offered six months of paid work. Merv and Daisy lived in then A Block, Unit 2.

Merv and Daisy were employed for six years. Nothing more was provided in writing other than the initial agreement. Their salary was paid for a whole year, each and every year. They never had to look for other work.

During their tenure they always maintained a high standard of work. The two balanced each other beautifully with Merv being a rules man, a disciplinarian, whereas, Daisy was all fun and a bit of mischief. Merv built and maintained strong relationships with key people in the community and with trade's people whereas, Daisy was involved in ensuring **CYTA LODGE** was a place where **TEAM** and **TOUR MEMBERS** felt at home and were relaxed.

Daisy's sense of fun was complimented by a desire to try new things. Daisy also went on tour as a **TOUR LEADER**. After stopping in Coffs Harbour, on an overnight stop on the way to the tour's final destination, she was seen with a large group of women, in a Mini-Moke speeding down the main street.

Joining Merv and Daisy during their time at the **CYTA LODGE** was *Kevin Pool*. Kevin lived in Bankstown and spent much of his time with the North Bankstown Soccer group. He was a sometime attendee of the Highway Methodist (later Uniting) church, before joining **CYTA**.

Going places - CYTA

Kevin was an employee in the clerical staff in Sydney Rail before his employment with **CYTA**. As a result of going on a **CYTA** tour that came from the Highway Uniting Church Bankstown which was led by *John Craik,* Kevin Pool made a personal decision to follow Christ.

Following the tour Kevin Pool felt called to offer his services to **CYTA**. His offer to work for **CYTA** included a statement that he did not need to be paid. While in discussion with Kevin Craik in regard to future employment a test of his camping skills came about as a result of **CYTA** being asked to assist with travel and meals for *Kairos '73*

> *A side note:* CYTA had limited involvement Kairos 73. CYTA supplied food and transport. The 1973 meeting followed as similar program to that of 1988.

This event was prompted by Christians, who were concerned with the then fractured nature of the world. The group decided they should meet in Canberra and pray holding hands in a circle around the old Parliament House.

CYTA was involved in another Kairos event at the opening of what was then the new Parliament House. Again people joined hands around parliament house and prayed for the parliament of the day.

Kevin Pool acquitted himself admirably at Kairos '73. Kevin was always a big man but he got to running speed as he charged from one task to another. "Poolie" (as he became known) was part of his first CYTA event and acquitted himself well.

In his time at **CYTA LODGE**, Kevin worked in the kitchen as well as around the lodge with small repairs, laundry collection etc.

Kevin Poole (and his large personality) soon attracted a fan club. Groups of female **TEAM MEMBERS** could be seen on work weekends walking arm in arm with Poolie. These were called, "Poolie's Girls". It was a common occurrence for a group of girls to attach themselves to Poolie and walk about the **CYTA LODGE** property.

Kevin never married but did enjoy the company of one of the female **TEAM MEMBERS**. We are not going to reveal here who it was, but suffice to say Kevin Pool would invite the **TEAM MEMBER** out with the promise of an activity which involved spiritual or personal development. The person remarked once on her outings with Poolie, "but we just went out"

Is this the cutest way to ask a girl out on a date?

During his time at the **LODGE**, Kevin Pool felt the need to be baptised as an adult. Previously attending a church which only offered confirmation did not ring true with Kevin. The baptism was conducted at the Numeralla River, which is in between Cooma and Bredbo.

At the river baptism a rock was thrown into the water causing a ripple effect on the water. Starting as a small hole where the rock hit the water, the impact caused a ripple outwards across the river. For some people the ripple of the pebble was symbolic of Kevin's life. A short comment, a conversation of no great length could have a ripple effect for someone's life.

Kevin Pool spent 9 years as the assistant manager at the LODGE. Kevin Pool was so well respected by his peers and was made a life member of the Christian Venues Association. He served in the ministry of *Christian* camping for over 41 years.

He died at 61 from cancer. At least three hundred people came to the funeral service in Melbourne. His family said how wonderful it was that Kevin had so many friends and people who loved him. The coffin in a hearse leaving the funeral received a standing ovation. A thanksgiving service of Kevin's life was also held in Sydney.

Merv *was 56* when he took up the position at the **LODGE**. Daisy was of a similar age. They stayed six years at the **LODGE**. The ever increasing workload was beginning to take its toll on Merv. The numbers of people staying at the **LODGE** started at 40, went to a 100 fairly quickly and then to over 300. A decision was made that Merv and Daisy would move to Sydney, and search for a smaller venture, a new job, a two or three hour drive north of Sydney, which would fit better with their stage of life. While on their search for work beyond Sydney they stayed in the flat above the Homebush premises. No job came about.

Eventually by mutual agreement they finished working for **CYTA** and returned to their Newcastle home that

Going places - CYTA

they still owned. Merv went on to write a book of poetry that **CYTA** helped to promote.

With the departure of Merv and Daisy a new a family took over the management of operations at **CYTA LODGE**. The Bolton's arrived, after a period of management by Les and Ros Shakespear.

Les Shakespear: offers the following input on his time as **CYTA LODGE** manager with his wife **Ros.**

> "Having been associated with the **CYTA DIRECTORS** and **TEAM** for a number of years and being involved in leading **TEAM**s of young people on Tours around Australia and NZ, it was a real honour and privilege when Ros and I were invited to move to Cooma and manage **CYTA LODGE** in 1976.
>
> We were taking over from Merv and Daisy Clare who were managing the LODGE from the time of establishment. They had served faithfully and were 'hard shoes to fill'. We teamed up with Kevin Pool and **Alan** and **Pam Mc Hardy** to carry on the work which God had established and, which was such a blessing to countless young people who visited during the snow season and older folks who met with church camps out of season. Many public or private school groups were accommodated on weeknights during the snow.
>
> The Saturday night during the season ministry was outstanding with visiting music groups and

speakers and was a great opportunity for presentation of the Gospel. It was a highlight when overseas artists participated. Even during school visits, grace was always said before meals and the **CYTA LODGE** staff members were available to witness to students and teachers alike.

Our two children were young when we moved. Melinda was 7 and Lyndon 4 and they have commented that their time at the **LODGE** was a lifetime experience. They loved mixing with the groups that came and the freedom which the beautiful property afforded. It was a marvellous experience for us as a family."

Kevin Craik remembers the great work of **Les and Ros Shakespear**

"Les was my assistant director for many Baptists camps from the early sixties. He took a tour to Expo. Japan. Both he and Ros were **COMPANY MEMBERS** in the formation of **CYTA**. He took a number of camping tours and formed a partnership with Alex Leishman creating Sunliner Coaches.

After Merv and Daisy, were to finish up, the **CYTA DIRECTORS** invited Les and Ros to take up the management of **CYTA LODGE** as fulltime employees. In true Les style he supercharged the development of the Lodge.

In September 1978 they resigned to take up the management of The Malborough Motel (next

> *door to the LODGE). Kevin Pool was Acting Manager of **CYTA LODGE** till Bruce Bolton and his family joined us in January 1979."*

Bruce and **Heather Bolton** were the new managers of **CYTA LODGE**. Bruce had been in real estate sales in the Parramatta (NSW) region for some time. Bruce was the top salesperson for the agency for which he worked. The business also held the largest rent roll in the Parramatta area. Looking for a new challenge in his life he, along with his family, was selected to manage the **LODGE**. His salary dropped considerably but his enthusiasm to serve *God* rose exponentially.

The Boltons arrived at the **LODGE** in February 1979 and finished up in January 1993. In the fourteen years they were at the **LODGE**, they subscribed strongly to the ethos and Christian witness of **CYTA**. Bruce required a disciplined group of paid staff and **TEAM MEMBERS** to be working with him. If a **TEAM MEMBER** was late for duty Bruce would straightforwardly admonish the **TEAM MEMBER** and require them to be on time for duty during the rest of their stay.

For staff at the **LODGE** (and **TEAM MEMBERS** who volunteered for a week a service) a *Bible* study was held each Thursday. Devotions were held daily.

When dinner was served the Boltons and their children sat at the table with other staff and **TEAM MEMBERS**. If there was unacceptable behaviour, Heather would remind those present that this was a family dinner and a poor example should not be set for the children present.

Going places - CYTA

> **A side note:** Along with permanent staff and the labour provided by **TEAM MEMBERS** at the Lodge there were other temporary staff members. Short term winter staff could be hired locally but some of the winter staff came from as far away as France and Switzerland. These staff and volunteer **TEAM MEMBERS** working at **CYTA LODGE** were taken to the snow once a week for skiing.

Kevin Craik credits the time the Boltons were in the Lodge as being one where Bruce and Heather had a great influence on the **TEAM**.

> *"They had the knack of getting on with everyone. Heather was a great support for Bruce and had a wonderful 'motherly' influence on all who served at Cooma".*

Bruce Bolton continued to build and maintain the trust with local suppliers that Merv Care established. Such was the trust that Bruce was afforded by local suppliers that he was given a key to the Cooma Butcher shop for any after-hours emergencies.

Bruce and Heather Bolton also challenged non-Christians by asking them directly to think about giving their lives to Christ.

Bruce Bolton recalls his time as **LODGE** Manager.

> *"Our appointment as managers to the **LODGE** we believe, was God's calling on our lives and He took us on a journey that we would never have imagined and one in which we have never stopped thanking Him for.*

Going places - CYTA

In January 1979, Kevin Pool was the only other permanent employee and the system in place was that local folk would be employed as casuals, plus volunteers, would be called on to help when we had guests in. When we finished in 1993, our winter staff consisted of husband and wife as assistant managers, full-time cook, along with four girls and four guys hired during the snow season. During this time, we also developed a scheme "A Holiday with a Difference". This was aimed at young people who would take annual leave and come and share the load with us. This meant we had other young people join us each week, not to mention **TEAM MEMBERS***, who often stayed on for the next week.*

By 1982 we realised that with everyone living on site, we were much more than just employees of Christian Youth Travel. We were "family", "A Christian community" sharing together every day and night, all the ups and downs of life 24/7. The first thing we would ask when interviewing new winter staff was to "tell us your faith story". The range was from babes in Christ to those who were filling in time to go to Bible College. We realised we had a great responsibility to nurture these young people spiritually – we were their church, their youth group. And so began a ministry within a ministry.

At the conclusion of lunch each weekday, working from a Bible Study book (having done

> their homework the night before!), we would discuss the study and pray with each other. This was so embraced that it then led on to each Thursday afternoon, which would normally be their free time before guests returned for the evening meal, when we gathered at either of the managers' homes for a mini church service, where worship, testimony, prayer and God's Word was explored. These times were life-changing for us all and testimony after testimony still today, speak of the blessings these young folk received from just spending 4 months of their lives at **CYTA LODGE**".

Kevin Craik remembers with fondness the work of the **Bruce** and **Heather Bolton.**

> "Under the leadership of our wonderful **LODGE** managers, many significant renovations were carried out by full-time and short-term winter staff. Murray Bolton, son of Bruce and Heather, served part of his building apprenticeship with a local builder, Graham Trevor, in the construction of the extensions to the kitchen and dining room. From this initial training, Murray has gone on to achieve great success building top-of-the-range homes.
>
> **Mel Kroenert** also contributed much to the renovations at **CYTA LODGE** and also the **Homebush CYTA CENTRE**. After Bruce and Heather moved on **from** managing **CYTA LODGE**, both the Bolton and Kroenert families formed a partnership to purchase, improve and

Going places - CYTA

> operate Carinya Lodge in Jindabyne, using their skills honed at **CYTA LODGE**.

Upon the departure of the Bruce and his family a new couple took over the management of the **LODGE**, *Trevor* and *Lyn Blood.*

Trevor and *Lyn Blood* became the fourth managers of the **LODGE**. It was a big jump for *Trevor* from delivering new cars to clients. *Lyn* initially felt daunted by the size of the **LODGE** kitchen.

Kevin reflects on how they faced the new challenge of managing the **LODGE.**

> "They went about the task of managing **LODGE with humble servant heart.** They coped brilliantly weigh the support of the fulltime staff and the winter staff hires along with **TEAM MEMBERS."**

Trevor and Lyn were shocked by the sale of **CYTA LODGE** to PHCS as they saw their work at the **LODGE** as *God's* long-term plan for them. They had become well acquainted with the **TEAM** and the operation of the **LODGE** when new bosses arrived, PHCS arrived. They continued at 'Pacific Lodge' for some time and then took up employment and residence in Cooma. Subsequently Lyn and Trevor moved to Victoria and are still involved in Christian camping as chaplains to the staff at Christian camping sites throughout Victoria.

A side note: The sale of the LODGE was not planned. PHCS approached CYTA to purchase the property. Hence Trevor and Lyn were surprised at the sale. They had not been consulted on a plan to sell the site as none existed.

A word of thanks from **Kevin for all the staff** who worked at the **LODGE:**

*"Over 27 years many other people were employed as full-time staff at **CYTA LODGE**. It is not possible to list all those wonderful people. I fear that if I begin listing them some wonderful contributors will be missed. You know who you were, and we give our sincere thanks to each and every one of you"*

Whilst this book is dedicated to those who made the **CYTA TEAM** so successful, and gave so much of their time, in the operation of **CYTA LODGE**, under the guidance of dedicated managers we were also blessed by the continuous support of local Cooma businesses and tradies. We mentioned a few but there were many others, like Bob the butcher, Mama the fruiterer, Steve the boiler man, Ian the plumber, Graham the builder, Keith and family the locksmiths, Cec the ski hire outfitter (for the school kids' snow tour excursions), Col the weekend ski hire expert at Snowline in Smiggin Holes and Tony the Rotary leader, and many others.

For many years, managers Bruce and Heather Bolton helped Rotarian Tony Slater coordinate the annual RYLA (Rotary Youth Leadership Awards) camp. This was a wonderful opportunity for the use of **CYTA LODGE** for the wider community.

At Bruce and Heather's farewell, they were presented with the "Pride of Workmanship Award", a rare and well-deserved Rotary honour.

Going places - CYTA

16. Office Administration Team

The first office for **CYTA** was the dining room table at the house of Kevin Craik's parents. The phone number on the travel brochures was the home phone number. Time came where paid staff was needed. This was replaced by the Craik's family home then in Strathfield.

Through the 1960's many people volunteered to do '101 things' needed to make CYT tours operate successfully. However growth made it clear that paid staff available all day was necessary.

Without the Office staff, the tours wouldn't have operated. Someone was needed to do all the backroom work necessary for accommodation, airline tickets, coach hire and on, and on, and on.

The first paid staff member was **Heather Anderson** working in the first office. The first "Office" was in Homebush. It was an $8 per week "cubby hole".

Heather recalls those early days:

> "The beginning of my link with **CYTA** is the late 1960s, and after 2 tours to the Gold Coast, and Central Australia, I was "hooked" on these amazing holiday tours. The fare was $100 for the 16-day Gold Coast tour. Bookings were made to a PO Box in Marrickville. It should be noted that in the late 1960s and into the 1970s, young people did not own motor cars (like they do today) and hence **CYTA** tours were popular with young people old enough to travel."

Going places - CYTA

In 1970 I applied for, and successfully became the first fulltime employee of **CYTA**, *working as a secretary. My weekly wage was $50 gross. The office was in Kevin and Jan Craik's home in Beresford Road, Strathfield. Over the next 3 years the office was relocated to a small shop in Knight Street Homebush and then to larger premises in Everton Road Strathfield followed by premises in Symond Arcade Strathfield.*

Offices in the early 1970s all had typewriters and land-line telephones. It was the pre-computer and IT age. **CYTA** *stationery was yellow with brown logo and address details. We even had brown pens to sign letters! Remember carbon paper? Yes, we used lots of it.* **CYTA** *even had brown typewriter ribbons. Anything and everything that needed office work was my responsibility. Extra duties included assisting in buying catering-size food items for camping trips at a wholesale outlet. The souvenirs for our snow weekends were also bought at a warehouse and sold during the return trip to Sydney, each Sunday, travelling from Cooma to Canberra.*

Winter snow trips were busy times and before each trip left Sydney, the number on each coach were phoned to The Paragon Café in Goulburn. The staff would have raisin toast and hot drinks ready for us. It was always a good way to start the snow tours.

Later on, we changed to a little French restaurant—The Celebrity – operated by Palasa and Peter Salvi. They allowed **CYTA TEAM** to take over the whole restaurant for Friday night one-inch-thick raisin toast and hot chocolate. Then, on the Sunday night, do the same thing for dinner. Sometimes there were six coaches which were served in 90 minutes. Sadly, they sold up and we had to make alternative arrangements.

The staff of **CYTA** grew when Merv and Daisy Clare were appointed as Managers of **CYTA LODGE** in Cooma. They were well-suited for the role. Under their guidance the **LODGE** thrived. A million memories are mine of Merv and Daisy's dedication and hard work at Cooma.

My secretarial position enabled me to have contact with prospective tour **MEMBERS** booking on all types of tours and weekends away. Fifty years on, I keep in touch with friends made this way. Some now live overseas, interstate and in NSW.

CYTA also did charter trips for schools. I particularly remember a Point Clare Primary School trip to Lightning Ridge and The Back Of Bourke and a Newcastle Girls High School trip to the Barrier Reef. I went on both, as the cook. **CYTA** sent me by Flying Boat to Lord Howe Island with a small **CYTA** holiday group.. I've returned several times as this has become one of my favourite NSW holiday destinations.

As the office work expanded, I was assisted by **Olive Edmonstone**, wife of the then Baptist

> *Minister at Strathfield/Homebush church. In 1973 I left the employ of **CYTA** on a salary of $65 per week and remained a **TEAM MEMBER** till 1977. **Priscilla Gordon** replaced me in the office.*
>
> *I never had another job like **CYTA**. I learnt so much, including life skills which have sustained me in my life journey, both in Australia and extended periods of living and working overseas, including 2 years in Pakistan. Whenever I'm in Goulburn, I still enjoy the food at The Paragon Café!"*

Heather has given us two highlights that appear as addendums to this book. They are:

1. **Heather Andersen's A-Z List of "I've Been Everywhere With CYTA"** and
2. **The A-Z of what CYTA means from Heather Anderson, Kev's first Personal Assistant**.

Check them out now, if you need a break from reading or when you finish this book.

Upon the move to the Everton Road office staff numbers grew as the number of **CYT** tours and other activities of the organisation grew.

Priscilla Gordon later married. She married **Harold Isberg** and became **Priscilla Isberg** became Kevin's personal assistant. Priscilla was a valuable addition to the staff. She was Kevin's second personal assistant. Priscilla was able to carry out Kevin's directions as required especially when he was not around. She made a valuable contribution to very busy '70s. **CYTA** grew at its most rapid rate during that decade. Priscilla was able to fully support Kevin though Kevin was work, not in the office during the day except for a rushed lunchtime visit, when possible.

> **A side note:** The ministry was growing but Kevin had a fulltime job while being Managing Director of CYTA till well into the 1970's. Instructions to Priscilla were given in a rushed lunch hour briefing. No mobile phones or SMS in those days

Priscilla was taken home to be with *God* in 2015.

Megan Norberry (Née ***Edwards)*** Kevin Craik's last personal assistant remembers the fun of **CYTA** that went right to the end of the life of the ministry.

> *"One of my favourite stories was when I went to the last **CYTA LODGE** weekend. I went to bed and was trying hard to be quite as other people were asleep. **Director Cornflake** (aka **Paul Cleasby**) made that impossible, as a practical joke someone had filled my sleeping bag full of cornflakes."*

Diane Wilson (Née Saunders) worked for some time in the office. She came straight from completing an Office/Business course at Bedford College (a Baptist owned and operated accredited business college). It was 1995. At seventeen Diane was excited at starting her first full time job at **CYTA** as a receptionist. For a new starter there were a lot of new people to meet, including ***Alison Bronger (Née Firth),*** who became one of her best friends. Alison worked for Kevin as his personal assistant for four years.

Kevin remembers **Diane** well. The following is the combined comments of **Kevin** and **Diane.**

> *The training Diane undertook and learning on the job while employed by* **CYTA** *proved to be invaluable. She has become a best-selling author, published by Harper Collins and Random House. Diane gives group talks on issues of the body and their connection with the, Soul, the Spirit, heathy living, body image, perception of peroneal value and personal identity.*
>
> *Dianne's entrepreneurial approach to her life and her message of freedom in Christ has created a platform that reaches a diversity of audiences.*

She now lives in Newport, Orange County, California with her husband Johnathan. She returned to Australia for her wedding and then moved to the United States, after Johnathan and she accepted a call from God to start a church in the United States, which occurred after being key leaders in their Sydney church for 21 years.

Diane is the mother of four gorgeous children, which includes twin boys and two girls. At the time of writing, Bentley and Beaucara are 29, Bella is 25, and London is 15. Bentley who is a United States Air Force fighter pilot, based in Virginia married Morgan. Beaucara who is real estate developer is married to Kylee and they live in Texas. Bella lives in Las Angeles and is

> completing a master's program in psychology. London is in Grade 11 and is on the Varsity (school house in Australia) volleyball team.
>
> In 2015 Diane become a citizen of the United States and enjoys every day loving and serving, God, her family and her community. She is a passionate church builder who loves God, people and life.

Geof Hyde, worked in the **CYTA** office for some years, delivered devotionals at **TEAM** nights, chased up **TOUR LEADERs** who were still gathering and packing gear close to their tour deadline and was an **ASSOCIATE**, (non – voting) **DIRECTOR** on the **CYTA** Board.

The relationship between Kevin and **Geof** began on a street corner during a rest stop on a Barrier Reef tour. Geof who was studying at Bible College approached Kevin:

> "If you ever need a chaplain, I will make time for you."

Geof proved to be particularly adept at facilitating small group studies and discussions. He also owned a minibus, which was used by **CYTA** for weekend trips, mainly for **TEAM MEMBERS**.

Raelene Schoonbeck worked in the Strathfield and Homebush offices

> "I started working at **CYTA** on 11th November 1974 in our Strathfield Office! I was a young nearly 19 year old!! I remember the day I was offered the position. I felt so honoured and very

excited and nervous for my new job! I started out as the receptionist the front desk girl. I welcomed so many people by phone or in person and was always told, "Remember… the receptionist is the most important person... the first point of call… introduction to **CYTA**"!!

No pressure… ha … but I loved it. I went on to also be the Tours coordinator for some of the Australian tours and helped with the snow tours. What a time that was! Helping to bring young people from all over the country together to join our tours, heading off on adventures to many beautiful parts of Australia, not to mention all the amazing overseas tours that **CYTA** had operating as well.

Our Cooma **LODGE** and Snow tours!! Weren't they the best?!! I have so many memories I will hold in my heart forever. I could never ski but I had fun trying. I remember helping prepare lunch in the snow. Hotdogs and soup… I loved it all. Also back at the **LODGE**, helping in the kitchen and whatever else needed to be done. It was so great being part of the crew there.

My husband John and I still love going to the snow. We now go in our caravan and stay in Jindabyne. But no, we still can't ski!! Ha!

I also loved the concerts we organised and they were a highlight of my time in the Homebush office. Overseas Gospel artists such as Andraé Crouch and The Disciples, Evie Tornqist, Ken Medema, Sandi Patti, Barry McGuire and *others!! So amazing!! Working in the office I always felt that we were a **TEAM**… working and serving God together in this wonderful ministry.*

Kevin was a tough boss. Ha! (I have told him that, so he knows and I say that with much affection!) He ran a tight ship but it needed to be run like that. That is why it was so successful. Kev taught me very good skills. I learnt great 'life' and 'business' skills, which I have carried on in my life and also in the running of our own business on the Central Coast. I'm so grateful for that time and for what I learnt.

*I worked with some lovely friends over the years and one was my now "sister-in-law" **Denise**. I met her when she started in the office, and we became very good friends. I introduced her to my brother in-law and they were married a year after us.*

*I was so blessed to work with such a great **TEAM**. I was with **CYTA** for six and a half years, from 1974-1981. I left to have our first son, Nathan. What an honour and privilege it was for me to work and serve God in this incredible ministry. I will never forget this time! Love and Blessings* appreciated by Kevin and the other MEMBERs of the **CYTA** Board as well as by many **CYTA TEAM MEMBERS**

Raelene and her husband John have a leading real estate agency on the Central Coast of NSW. It is a family business, managed by Raelene's husband John

Going places - CYTA

with Joshua and Luke, two of her three boys. As well as sales, they specialise in strata management of over 450 strata plans, in addition to a very large rent role.

A last word from **Elaine Aurel Smith** (Née **Thrupp**) who came into the organisation as Andraé Crouch and the Dsiciplines were about to do their first tour to manage ticketing and stayed for a while.

> "My time with **CYTA** was undoubtedly, one of the most significant and pivotal experiences of my life to date and was such a catalyst in how I moved forward to where I am now. In moments of reflection, I always give thanks to God from the bottom of my heart, for the awesome impact **CYTA** had in my life, and the amazing opportunity I was afforded to grow in confidence, as I was taught new skills that stretched both my mind and my spirit – always unto a purpose in God!!
>
> The outstanding quality of **CYTA** for me has ALWAYS been the "body life" concept – all part of one **TEAM**, many different gifting's, and always headed in the same direction with the same common purpose unto God. I relished being a part of that. It was incredibly life-giving.
>
> I knew my part and I **BELONGED**! This has always been my hope for how I imagined the Church, but sadly, I struggle to remember another time in my life, where such a significant and outstanding corporate quality has been supported and allowed to exist in the way I experienced it way back then."

Going places - CYTA

These are just a few of the **CYTA TEAM**. Many staff passed through the doors of the various **CYTA** offices. ***Bev Caruthers*** and ***Liz Calder***, before she married were among **TEAM MEMBERS** who worked in the office for periods of time. Some **TEAM MEMBERS** took on temporary office roles. Such people were employed to help make special events happen.

You may have noticed that ***Robyn Morris*** is missing. Fear not ***Robyn's*** involvements directly and indirectly for more than 45 years receives special mention in a future Chapter.

You know the drill. Check the detailed contents in the appendices to this book. I know, you did not need to be told that.

A final note to this chapter - Please be assured that even though your name may not be mentioned, **the efforts of all office staff members that worked for CYTA was valued and appreciated.**

Going places - CYTA

17. The Chaplains behind the TEAM

The significance of Chaplains

As the **TEAM** grew, **CYTA** appointed a series of *Chaplains*. Some worked part time, while others were fulltime employees. Kevin and Jan in particular and other board **MEMBER**s in general, believed that given the amount of voluntary work given by the **TEAM** to **CYTA**, that support and counselling should be available to **TEAM MEMBERS**.

Jan herself has provided a wealth of support and time to female **TEAM MEMBERS**. The chaplains not only provided spiritual input but also provided an additional resource to support **TEAM MEMBERS** in their lives.

The first Chaplain - Geoff Rowcroft

Geoff Rowcroft was commissioned as **CYTA**'s first and only, fulltime Chaplain, and he and his wife Elaine were welcomed to the **CYTA** family. He was welcomed to his new job in February just at the time the TEAM and CYTA as a whole were commencing a new year.

Geoff brought a whole new approach to the Ministry of **TEAM** MEMBERs, Staff and the Directors and their spouses. A more comprehensive selection process was introduced to select **TEAM MEMBERS**, and a new streamlined and more cohesive **TEAM** emerged as a result.

Elaine, Geoff's wife who had at one time worked in the **CYTA** office met Geoff when he was in Bible College.

She became a key participant in a monthly prayer meeting and luncheon for the Directors' spouses and some **CYTA** Prayer Partners, and was always available with a listening ear to all those involved in the Ministry. Elaine had previously been on staff in the **CYTA** Office with responsibility for the administration for the first *Andraé* Crouch East Coast Tour including the Sydney Opera House.

After three years of sterling service, Geoff and Elaine resigned from the ministry of **CYTA**, as they once again felt called to take up a full-time Church Ministry. Under their leadership and ministry, every area of **CYTA** went from strength to strength

John Crowther – Number 2

The Chaplains to **CYTA DIRECTORS** and **TEAM** included *John Crowther* was a minister in the Church of Christ.

John Crowther reports his thoughts of his of his time with **CYTA** with his *wife* **Marianne.**

> Marianne and I were called into the life of **CYTA** after spending a year in PNG in 1984. We were both passionate about Christ, camping and Christian leadership.
>
> At our first **TEAM** meeting, Thursday night at Homebush, in 1985, we sensed a heart and enthusiasm for the ministry as Young Adults re-connected after the Christmas break.

We were welcomed in at the training retreat held at the Basin where I was unceremoniously baptised into the role by being thrown off the wharf on Saturday afternoon!

There were so many opportunities to support, equip and train young leaders to live intentionally with Christ in every aspect of their inner and public lives. Over the 5 years at **CYTA** *we played a small part in the life of* **CYTA TEAM MEMBERS***, Thursday nights,* **TEAM MEMBERS** *Missionaries, marriages and vocations that have been Christ centric.*

An example of faith in practice was in 1985 when the **CYTA DIRECTORS** *met one Sunday afternoon for prayer and discernment. It was a month before the first* **Beyond the Black Stump** *Christian Music Festival and numbers were not looking great. The DIRECTORS decided to underwrite the event against the odds of a huge loss.*

I remember **John Smith's** *passionate preaching and invitation to follow Jesus wholeheartedly, which led to hundreds of young adults excitedly responding and going forward for prayer. Whole youth groups encountered a move of the Holy Spirit at that time.*

Many Christian leaders, (some 250,) state that **Beyond the Black Stump** *was a key turning moment in their life. Little did I know in 1985 the long weekend in October would continue to be a* *key event in our family's life? Our daughter Tamara who was 6 weeks old on the first event attended every Black Stump for over 25 years.*

***CYTA**'s ethos of pioneering new ways to creating a safe community, where opportunities to have natural conversations about Jesus occurred. The Cooma weekends, Easter Adventures at the Lodge and on the road, Kiah Ridge, Silverwater events, **TEAM** training days and retreats which all showed expressions of creative ways to do healthy community. It was a privilege to be invited into the dreaming and the actioning of these opportunities.*

*The **CYTA TEAM** became a treasured space for over 5 years as we were challenged to grow as disciples of Jesus and to serve in practical ways. While at times we reached the end of our rope, (Cooma **LODGE** on Friday night at times felt like a journey to the centre of the earth with our two pre-schoolers). But with encouragement from Kevin and Bruce there was a growing resilience and an invitation to grow deeper in our relationship with God.*

*The season at **CYTA** provided countless opportunities for Marianne and me to learn and mature. We are deeply thankful for the privilege of being supported by the Directors, **TEAM** and the staff.*

Going places - CYTA

Garrett (Garry) Coleman
Could he be called the Rev Head?
Rev. Dr. Garrett (Garry) Coleman OAM remembers his time as chaplain to **CYTA**.

"My time of serving with **CYTA** began with being chaplain on a Coach trip to the snow in the early 70's. Following further tours, I was asked by Kev and Jan to become Chaplain to the **CYTA TEAM**, meeting weekly at Homebush for training and orientation of **TEAM MEMBERS**, leading tours to the snow, into the Australia countryside and overseas tours.

I had the distinct privilege of being guest speaker at the **AUSTALIAN CHRISTIAN Music SEMINAR** at **CYTA LODGE** on two occasions. During those years the special music guests included Ken Medema, Barry McGuire, and Jimmy and Carol Owens. With my wife and three daughters, we became regular attenders at Cooma for our summer breaks. I was also a MEMBER of the ACMS organising committee for a few years. (The story of ACMS is found in the chapter dealing with the Australian Christian Music Foundation).

During the years of my involvement with **CYTA** I was often a guest preacher at YFC (Youth for Christ) and BYF (Baptist Youth Fellowship) rallies. Other roles were National Director of Ambassadors for Christ Aust., then Pastor of Parramatta Baptist Church, later at Islington

Going places - CYTA

Baptist Church, Newcastle, and led and taught "Walk Thru the Bible seminars".

During one year, c 1983/84, it so happened that three regulars at the Cooma seminar each experienced ministry "Burn Out". *They found the seminars that year very beneficial for fellowship.*

They were **Bob Goodfellow**, **John Smith** and me. *Years later, I would drive Hopkinson Coaches to Cooma during the snow season.as well as Cooma, I was guest Speaker at the first and second Adelaide Christian Music Seminar, which was organised by a good friend, Fred Grice.*

*These amazing seminars, based on similar seminars in Estes Park in the USA, were a defining period as the Australian Christian community moved from Youth Rallies in major cities and travelling evangelistic **TEAM**s across the country, featuring a preacher with musician supports, to a Christian Concert format.*

This was the rise of many Christian musicians with almost no learning context to develop their platform skills. **AUSTALIAN CHRISTIAN MUSIC SEMINAR /CYTA** *was the first serious structure to teach platform presentations, involving drama, dance, stage settings, and band refining, and showcased the spectrum from Christian Rock to Operatic singers on the same platform for nightly concerts. It was a great privilege to be a part of this transition process in our country. Kev and Jan Craik and the serving committee were* unique producers of these formats of touring and giving seminar. With very good memories Garry Coleman Rev. Dr. OAM "

Garry Coleman was a pastor with the Baptist Church of NSW and ACT. He worked as a Chaplain in the days of the Homebush Centre, He and his wife Betty attended family weekends away. He spoke (preached) on these occasions. Later in life he was awarded an **OAM** for his services to motor sport. Garry and his wife were the special guests at a number of **CYTA** TEAM family events. Garry was a chaplain to the **TEAM** for 12 months.

This section has a tag The Rev Head? Garry Coleman also had an interest in Super-Cars. In an interview with *Eternity* magazine at his retirement from his involvement in Super Car racing *Garry* said:

> "I get to pray for sixty seconds on international television at the major sporting event of the year (Bathurst 1000). There is no other sporting event in Australia that does that."

A side note: For the initiated Super-Cars are those that race at Bathurst and around Australia each year. Note the street cars they used to race at Bathurst in its early days. These cars look like street cars but they hyped up true race cars.

Steve Kearns the last chaplain

Steve Kearns was a part time staff member at **CYTA LODGE** for some time, and became a later became a chaplain to **CYTA**. His wife Karen came up with the idea

Going places - CYTA

of deportment classes for the CYTA TEAM mentioned in an earlier chapter. While he was a chaplain for **CYTA**, he also pastoring a church, the Church of Christ at Burwood (NSW).

Steve Kearns *reflects on his various forms of involvement with* **CYTA.**

> "Question: How would God redeem a crushed and widowed 22 year old runaway and give him a foundation to recover and gain the resources to minister in HIS GRACE.
>
> Walking towards Sydney in 1984 from two weeks at the bistro in Jindabyne, he thinks
>
>> 'I remember staying at the LODGE while in primary school. I wonder if I can bunk there for a few weeks till the snow comes back and the season reboots.'
>
> Upon arrival at **CYTA LODGE**, Bruce and Heather ask
>
>> 'Are you a Christian? We have been praying for another person to complete our team for CYTA LODGE. Yes' he says without thinking too hard.
>
> The Boltons interview him (me) and we all retire to bed for the night, having been given a bed for the night.
>
> Damon, a room-mate, asks,

> ' Are you the new **LODGE** team member?'

I reply,

> 'I don't know but can I borrow your BIBLE'

I read, **Isaiah 42:3-4** (as quoted in notes from Steve Kearns)

> 3 A bruised reed he will not break, and a smouldering wick he will not snuff out. In faithfulness he will bring forth justice;
>
> 4   he will not falter or be discouraged till he establishes justice on earth. In his teaching the islands will put their hope.'

Two snow seasons later, with a gentle and unassuming father heart **Bruce** tells me in a letter I still have:

> 'I am not your father but if I was, I would say to you, that boy who has experienced some graphic abuse, the death of his young bride and his own crushing injuries, has been enabled by God to take on guiding, solo, five back to back New Zealand tours and has completed five years of full time Bible study sponsored in part by the Anne McDonald Memorial scholarship fund.
>
> The once wanderer begins a ten year pastoral calling to the Church of Christ,

> Burwood (NSW). He also takes up a role as a part time chaplain with **CYTA**. He with Karen Johnson establishes with **CYTA** the, 'First Impressions Deportment School.
>
> The nub of this story is that **CYTA**, driven by Kevin and Jan's faith, trust, wisdom and strategic ministry, along with the love, grace and wisdom of the Heather and Bruce were instruments for a lifelong Pastoral ministry. It turns out that **I AM** that man, redeemed and equipped to minister to a church and to **CYTA** its **DIRECTORS** and its **TEAM.**
>
> Now, as I write, I am in my seventh year of pastoral ministry at Kurrajong Village Baptist Church. The CYTA ministry I believe continues to shape the many men and women to serve thorough accepting God and receiving the saving GRACE that comes through the sacrifice of JESUS CHRIST."

Philippians 1:6-7 as quoted **by Steve Kearns**

> 6 being confident of this, that he who began a good work in you will carry it on to completion until the day of Christ Jesus.
>
> 7 It is right for me to feel this way about all of you, since I have you in my heart and, whether I am in chains or defending

Going places - CYTA

> *and confirming the gospel, all of you share in God's grace with me.*

> **A side note:** Though after I was involved in CYTA do you think that it was extraordinary foresight for Kevin and Jan had to introduce chaplains' to minster to Board of **DIRECTORS** and to the **CYTA TEAM**? I certainly do.

Were there some temporary chaplains?
Fun and food - Word of Life

Dick Andes and *David Hillis* were two guys sent to Australia from their mission base in Schroon Lake, New York State to start the ministry here. Part of their brief was to obtain a site suitable for a youth camp and Bible College. Not long after they arrived in Australia, they were invited to be chaplains on the **CYTA** Easter tour to Lightning Ridge.

Robert Leishman was one of the coach drivers. This was a side "hack", as his day job was as a real estate salesman. In discussions with Dick and Dave with members of the **CYTA** Board, they indicated they were looking for a property to base their Word of Life Ministry. In true salesman style, Robert indicated that he had just listed such a property! Two days after the tour returned, the trio inspected a property near Wiseman's Ferry, which is an historic town 75 Kilometres west of Sydney, and as they say, the rest is history!

> **A side note:** One of our End of Year Christmas functions was held at the Word of Life Ministry Camp. A wonderful BBQ spit roasting two big pigs and the fun of a huge water slide ending in a mud hole. As with every

Going places - CYTA

end of year event, there was a lot of fun and plenty of food.

Going places - CYTA

18. A safe place to date
Here comes the bride

As with any organisation where women and men meet, relationships may develop. **KEVIN** and **JAN**'s marriage in 1966, while they were involved in the establishment of **CYTA** (which of course preceded the establishment of the **TEAM**) might be said to have been the most significant marriage for **CYTA**. Their union underpinned what was to happen with the organisation.

So let us look at some happy outcomes.

Rod Derly was slow off the mark but finished in a whirlwind. He met *Janice* in 1983, but their first date was September1, 1984, engaged on the same month on the 24th and married in February 1985.

One of the earliest **TEAM MEMBERS**, *Greg Roby* was leading a Tasmanian tour. At one stage the tour group split into two groups. Greg and his group walked and camped out for six days of the tour starting at the Cradle Mountain walk. There was a girl named **Anné** in his group. They took a liking to each other. As they say the rest of the story is history, for Greg and Anné as they became **Mr and Mrs Roby**.

Stuart Charles met the love of his life, **Debbie** on one of the weekend snow tours. He was the **TOUR LEADER** and **Debbie** one of the **TOUR MEMBER**s took his eye. Yes, you could say their eyes met. I know this because I was there as his assistant **TOUR LEADER**. Not that long after they married and moved to Canberra where Stuart took up a new job.

Going places - CYTA

Elizabeth Watson (Née Kelly) met **Greg Watson** while they were both on **TEAM**. They married in 1975.

During one work weekend training trip in 1976 **Steve Castle** recalls meeting his future wife **Jenni (Née Plumb)**, another **MEMBER** of the **CYTA** TEAM.

> "We were married in September 1977, bought a house in Kings Langley, and had many wonderful years together, travelling the world together courtesy of the discount airfares through my job with Qantas and produced two wonderful children, Kathrine and Lindsay. Married life meant I could no longer devote spare time to **CYTA** so I left the organisation, although we did attend a few reunion weekends and day reunions in subsequent years. Unfortunately our marriage ended in 1993."

Brain West proclaims that:
> "I was blessed to be a passenger on several longer **CYTA** tours to, Central Australia 1977, Europe 1978 (Anne MacDonald was also on that tour) as well as USA/Canada 1979. Not only did I meet my wife, **Roslyn Heslop**, for the first time on the USA/Canada but we were engaged after 4 weeks before the tour had ended (possibly unique in **CYTA**'s history). Ros was from Newcastle and had been on **CYTA** tours to New Zealand and Central Australia plus a ski weekend and mystery tour before we met."

Wow what a love story.

Going places - CYTA

Brian goes on:

> "**Ros West**, (Brian's wife) joined the **CYTA TEAM** after we were married, several months later. The last weekend of our honeymoon was spent at a **TEAM weekend at Teen Ranch**. We still keep in touch with some **TEAM MEMBER**s from our era. Later we became friends with several **TEAM MEMBERS** from the tours we had been on and during my time on the *CYTA TEAM* including **Lester Terry, Rod Derley, Chris Pople** and **Geof Hyde**."

I thank *God* that he persuaded me to go to America in '79 instead of doing the Milford Track with **CYTA** as I had originally planned."

Rossanne Hyde (Née McDowell) met **Geof Hyde** while in the **CYTA TEAM** 1981.

> "I left Australia and Geof followed me to Sri Lanka where we got engaged then I did the overland tour and married Geof 6 weeks after arriving back in Canada".

Another WOW – he chased the girl to Sri Lanka

Marilyn Lee meet her husband **Garry** at **CYTA** and

> "We've been happily married now for 42 years in 2023. My bridesmaids were **CYTA** girls. Wonderful memories, wonderful friends and a time in my life I will always cherish."

Coralie McAlpine-White met **Phil White** on the January work weekend 1973, engaged in June the same year and married in 1974.

Going places - CYTA

CYTA was into music ministry. Groups of **TEAM MEMBERS** went on the road with performers to country towns in NSW. On one tour to Wagga, six vehicles, cars and a utility, set off on a Friday night. People were carrying passengers who did not drive. In one vehicle, a one ton utility was *Ron*, who took a passenger down to Wagga Wagga. His passenger requested a change of vehicle on the way back.

A girl named *Robyn* said she was happy to ride in the utility. By now it is a familiar story. Ron and Robyn would later become **Mr Ron and Mrs Robyn Scanes**. Even a short weekend music tour cemented a lasting, loving relationship.

Robyn Spencer (a lot of girls six in fact, were named Robyn/Robin) enjoyed her five years in **CYTA** from 1983 to 1988. A bonus was that she met electrician *Donald* during her time with **CYTA** and they married in 1986 and became **Mr Donald and Mrs Robyn Horne** and subsequently stayed on the team till 1988.

Malcolm Power (Tour Leader) and *Shayne Standen (Hostess)* *(Née Henderson)* took a tour together, where *Malcolm* met *Joan.* Malcolm made a "provisional" date with Joan.

> *"If things don't work out with x would you come to a $21st^{st}$ with me?"*

It was Shayne's 21st. Malcolm and Joan went together to the 21st and off course they became **Mr Malcolm** and **Mrs Joan Power** who have three adult children and seven grandchildren.

Going places - CYTA

A post script to the story is that **Shayne** and her husband *Geoff* (they have four children and ten grandchildren) moved to and lived in the same suburb as **Malcolm** and **Joan** for many years. They all remain good friends today.

So much could happen on any tour that could positively affect many lives forever.

Max Watson recalls that he met his wife, **Chris Everett** in **CYTA**.

> "Chris and I were in the same small group at **TEAM** meetings and events in 1979. We started dating in October; a few ups and downs and we married in December 1980. We have 4 adult children and 6 grandchildren".

Chris and Max have been married for more than forty years, a lasting marriage. **Chris Watson** has recorded on the **CYTA** Facebook page on their fortieth anniversary how pleased she was:

> "That Max had chosen her."

I bet **Max** is pleased **Chris** chose him. He is recorded as saying:

> "I never imagined any girl would put up with me."

Going places - CYTA

Andrew Wardle.

> "Kevin Craik rang me at work asking if I would join a group working at the **LODGE** over the October Long Weekend. This is where I met my wife **Paula (Née Watts)**. She disappeared for 2 years or so, on an Overland tour. On her return we met up again and were married in 1977. We have 3 children and now have 5 grandchildren".

Elisabeth Calder met **Keith Jarrett** while on **TEAM** in 1982.

> "We got together at a **TEAM** training weekend at Bawley Point and we were married in April 1983, 12 months later."

Shaun Walker encountered **Nerida Storey** on a CYTA snow tour in 1985. *Shaun tells us of how it all unfolded.*

> "After meeting Nerida on a snow tour in 1985 when I was an Assistant **TOUR LEADER,** Nerida joined the **TEAM**. Our relationship blossomed and became official at the inaugural 1985 Black Stump music festival. We served the next three years on **TEAM** together leading tours and as Assistant Leaders, until we were married in November 1988 and moved to the Northern Beaches of Sydney."

Rick Gribble and **Beverly Long**

> "At the **CYTA** Training Weekend at Mount Seaview inland from Port Macquarie, I noticed Beverley Long from her Bible Study contribution. Subsequently at a pre-snow season work

> weekend at **CYTA** Cooma LODGE, I assisted Beverley, a registered nurse, who had gone to medically care for a young lady suffering a fitting episode on the homeward coach trip. Afterwards we chatted for the rest of the journey back to Sydney as Beverley watched over her patient. Beverley had already planned to go to Swiss L'Abri and I encouraged her in her plans. Upon her return to from L'Abri we talked about what we had experienced. There was much in common.
>
> We married in August 1979 supported and surrounded by family and friends many of whom were from the **CYTA TEAM MEMBERS**."

Robin Morris (Née Rodway)

"**Garry** and I met on a Warrumbungle tour in June '74 and married Jan '76."

A side note: Kevin would like it recorded that Robin Morris has been a staunch ally of CYTA for over forty years. Her story has been captured in the chapters dealing with: **The other tours of CYTA** as well as **Yesterday and Today,**

Kevin Hastie

> "I met **Karen** on a NZ trip in December 1974, it was not love at first sight, but the Lord brought us together on a mystery tour in October 1975."

Kevin and Karen until recently have spent most of their later years working with Bush Church Aid.

Going places - CYTA

Peter Wills took the first American tour. He met his wife **Rhonda** on the tour. Not to be out done the **HOSTESS Kay Mckerlie** met her future husband **Ross Frizelle,** (both of whom were on the team for some years), on the America tour.

Barbara Wimble (Née **Moore)** met Warren through **CYTA.**

> "I met Warren soon after joining CYTA and we were married the next year. The ideals of CYTA were a great influence on our life together and in our children's participation through activities at the **LODGE.** "

Cathy met **Hans** and travelled to London just to say hello to him.

> 'I met Hans at the Cooma **LODGE** on a ski weekend in 1974. I joined Hans in London after his arrival off his Overland Tour on which he was **TOUR LEADER** in 1975. Later that year, we travelled in Europe and America together for a few months, then came home and we married in June 1976."

Well done Cathy, all the way to London for a date.

Cathy and her family have been, and are still involved in Christian service, which is discussed in the chapter – **Yesterday and Today.**

Lesly Bennet was on **TEAM** in 1983 when she met her husband, **Mark.** They married in 1984.

Going places - CYTA

Even one of the original **CYTA DIRECTORS**, *Graham Thorburn* found love on a **CYTA** tour. As recorded in an earlier chapter, Graeme met his wife *Jenny* on the 1968 Gold Coast Tour.

Did you know that Kevin also walked a **TEAM MEMBER** bride down the aisle on one occasion?

There are many other people who were on **TEAM**, met and married including *Yvonne* and *Gordon Bubb* who met on an October long weekend tour dated the first time on October 18, 1974, and married one year later to the day.

James Mann and *Judi Garrard* met on **TEAM** and married in 1986.

"*Ashleigh White (Née Bennett)* writes of love and marriage through time.

> "My brother Nathan and sister Hayley are the KIDS generation of parents who met and fell in love at **CYTA**. Our family holidays were at the **CYTA LODGE** at Easter with the other kids of **CYTA**."

Paul and Linda Webb met while on the **TEAM**. Best friends for a long time till they connected romantically and married

This could go on forever. There were, no doubt more couples who wedded. Apologies from me if you met and married your life partner while involved in **CYTA** and you name(s) are not listed. The whole book could have been about the **TEAM MEMBER's** romances and marriages. But we must move on.

Going places - CYTA

CYTA at one time introduced a **pre-marriage course** given the number of young couples involved in the **TEAM**. **Kevin** reports on this innovation.

> *"Given the number of young couples who were part of the **CYTA TEAM** a pre-marriage course was introduced. The course was conducted by Rev Ian and Gerlinde Spencer of then Family Life Movement of Australia (NSW branch). Attendance at the course was voluntary. The course included a live in weekend at **CYTA LODGE**. Even fifty years on, many **TEAM MEMBERS** who chose to take part in the program remember the importance of the time they spent with the Spencers."*

Jan Craik, who was a trained registered nurse educator at Royal Prance Alfred Hospital, also gave guidance to the **TEAM** on relationships between **TEAM MEMBERS** while on tour

Kevin acted as a *"relationship guidance expert."* He would keep his eye on the dating habits of **TEAM MEMBERS**, particularly dating **TEAM MEMBERS** Where he thought a couple had been dating for a while and he thought the male was "playing games", upsetting, leading on the female member of the couple, Kevin would first check with the female in the couple as to whether they were ok and if she was not ok with what was going on, he would pull the male aside for a chat, which began along the lines of, "What are you doing? What are your intentions?"

> *A side note:* Any volunteers who wish to nominate as someone who received a chat? I would like to state categorically I did not have one of these chats with Kevin. While talking to Kevin about this book I found he did not know as much as he thought about the dating habits of **TEAM MEMBERS**. However he says "he did know many of them."

Kevin's actions were out of the love that Kevin and Jan had for the **TEAM MEMBERS**. They cared for each **TEAM MEMBER**, their welfare, their happiness and their future even after they left the **TEAM**.

What a legacy.

Disappointment and hurt

There are some people who have not realised their hearts desire. You may have been interested in someone or wanted to form a closer relationship which did not occur. Of course not all relationships between **TEAM MEMBERS** and of **TEAM MEMBERS** and **TOUR MEMBERS** finished poorly. CYTA was generally a safe and happy place to date. Many lasting marriages occurred between **TEAM MEMBERS** and between **TEAM MEMBERS** and **TOUR MEMBERS**.

However, some marriages between **TEAM MEMBERS** and between **TEAM MEMBERS** and **TOUR MEMBERS** did not last. Some long-term marriages collapsed after many years. Some couples that were to marry broke up before they got to the altar.

In undertaking research for this book some former **TEAM MEMBERS**, were reluctant to be involved. A request for general information about the organisation awakened negative thoughts long buried.

Also, being part of the **CYTA TEAM** did not make people immune from the day-to-day pressures of life. In some **TEAM MEMBERS'** lives there was/is sickness as well as disappointment not with **CYTA** but with how their life was turning out. Broken relationships, mental illness and the unsatisfied human need for fulfilment lead to unwelcome consequences for some **TEAM MEMBERS**. Inappropriate things happened.

A separate group of **TEAM MEMBERS** believed there relationship with **CYTA** never reached the point to which they might have aspired. They were never or rarely appointed to the role of **HOSTESS** or **TOUR LEADER**. In life many people tend to feel disappointment and possibly resentment when they believe they are overlooked.

Dating with *God* the ultimate relationship

It may sound clichéd, but it is true. It is *God* with whom we should be seeking to date. I leave this topic with the following scripture passage

The organisation **Mission without Borders** uses the verse **Isaiah 46:4,** to illustrate their mission to the poor and down trodden in Europe regardless of the belief or otherwise of people helped in the Christian life. Though addressed to Israel the passage may provide some comfort for people in each of, or both of, the groups of people cited. I quote from Mission without Borders.

> *"Even to your old age and grey hairs I am HE, I am HE who will sustain you. I have made you*

and I will carry you; I will sustain you and I will rescue you"

Kevin offers the following apology on behalf of all the Directors

*"During the time **CYTA TEAM** supported the ministry of **CYTA**, many hundreds of people chose to be part of the Christ-centred not-for-profit Christian youth organisation. We were all part of a big family and no family is ever perfect. Some **TEAM MEMBERS** and staff were hurt during their time within **CYTA** and perhaps still carry that hurt. Whilst the past cannot be undone, I, Kevin, on behalf of all the Directors of **CYTA**, say a **SINCERE SORRY**. I and Jan feel it unwise to elaborate on details and express their understanding to all for not publishing further details."*

As side note: I would note the disappointments and failures written about in this chapter were not the fault of CYTA. CYTA always acted for the good of the TEAM and for those people that toured and/or those people who worked for CYTA. Personal disappointment could be characterised as the devil working to disrupt the *Kingdom of God* on earth.

CYTA was created for and **always** had as its first key priority *Christian* service.

Going places - CYTA

19. The Outstanding Speakers

There was noise of another type but it was not music. Speakers presenting clear and simple Bible Based talks, rather than sermons or homilies, spoke at each snow weekend as well as special events such as, **TEAM** training and work weekends and at **ACMS**. This chapter should be read as an adjunct to the key note speakers and presenters' whose contribution to the ministry was restricted to being a guest presenter with **ACMS**. (Check the detailed contents list at the end of this book for the chapter information.)

Some of the Key-note Speakers included:

Rev Dr Brian Willersdorf - Brian's relationship with the **CYTA DIRECTORS** dates back to the mid-1960s. Brian and his wife Christine were special guests at the 1990 and 1991 **AUSTALIAN CHRISTIAN MUSIC SEMINAR.** Brian is a man who had a close encounter with God through cancer and wants to make God known to as many people as possible. Their son David is a well-known Christian singer, guitar player and composer. Their daughter Karen set up *Samaritan's Purse Australia* and was instrumental in establishing Australia's first Christian TV channel.

During the period of 1960-1970, Brian became well known as a powerful speaker into the lives of young people. His early training came from, Youth for Christ, (YFC) and he completed his theological training at Morling College in New South Wales. He became a much sought-after speaker across Australia and around the world. Brian pastored several churches, including four years in Texas, and spent one year in the UK, training with Selwyn Hughes, author of "Every Day with Jesus".

Brian's qualifications have led him to a ministry in advising senior management, both in the commercial world and the church. He has had a great deal of experience in counselling church leadership and discerning with them the future direction of the Church.

Brian was always prepared and usually spoke without notes and without equivocation when presenting the gospel on a Saturday night at **CYTA LODGE**. Brian spoke in many locations in Australia as well as making speaking trips to the United States. Brian's contribution to the music mission of **CYTA** is also recorded in other places in this book.

Jim Gibson – On his LinkedIn page, Jim Gibson, describes himself as a theologian of the gospel and evangelist at large that saw him become a key-note speaker for **CYTA**. He is, at the time of writing, the Senior Pastor of the Salisbury Baptist Church in Brisbane.

John Dickson – A degree in theology and a PHD, John Dickson at the time of writing presents a course on the "*Historical Jesus*" at the University of Sydney. This is probably the John Dickson that many Christians would know of today, which is how he was known when a speaker for **CYTA**. But before this and his extensive writing in Christian literature, starting with his first book, "*The Best Kept Secret of Christian Mission*" to his latest book being, "Is *Jesus* History?" (2019), John Dickson was the lead singer of the Christian rock band ***"In the Silence"*** through the late 1980s and early 90s. The band would play up to six shows a week. They played in pubs and clubs and on occasion in high schools. In song introductions and between songs members of the band talked about their faith.

Whether as the lead singer in a now ancient band, a church pastor, a speaker for **CYTA** or in a large auditorium, John Dickson has always been a powerful advocate for the gospel.

John Smith – God's Squad, formally called God's Squad Christian Motorcycle Club is a Christian motorcycle club established in the late 1960s in Sydney. It was in the 1960's till John Smith's death under the leadership of the **Rev. *Dr. Kevin John Smith*** the club who over time expanded the club and grew the club into a diversified group of bikers.

John Smith - ***God Squad*** (no other titles or credentials were needed to be advertised wherever John Smith spoke) as he was billed wherever he spoke, ministered to other biker groups. He was a popular speaker who spoke in straight-forward terms about *Jesus Christ*. Wherever he spoke which included **CYTA**, and many churches, the normal congregation numbers would swell with leather clad usually young men as well as some young women, to hear the man in "leather" talk about the *Kingdom* of *God*. He continued teaching/preaching till his death from Cancer in 2019.

Going places - CYTA

Not just the tours or the music but the message of a noteworthy speaker penetrating lives.

> **A side note:** Though this chapter is restricted to becoming informed of the powerful speakers that served CYTA, I am taking a moment of indulgence to record some thoughts by those who listened when **John Smith** spoke at **ACMS.**
>
> **Glen Powell** recalls hearing John Smith preaching at **ACMS** and making a decision for Christ *"Hearing John Smith preach for a week in 1983 (at the music seminar) is when I made a decision to follow Jesus myself, rather than just as one person of a Christian family."*
>
> **Geoff Stevenson** also remembers John Smith speaking.
>
> *"I was there, I think, 1984 - a great and inspiring week. John Smith dropped by and spoke. It was an excellent week and I was grateful for the teaching."*
>
> There are more reflections on **John Smith** speaking at **Beyond the Black Stump**, earlier in the chapter.

What a powerful man of God

Barry McMurtrie – has a relaxed and down to earth style in reaching the hearts and minds of thousands with the gospel message. This is the style which was often best suited for the holiday atmosphere of

Going places - CYTA

Sean and Anne Sanborn – An International Spouse for Christmas!

Sean remembers a past holiday.

> "As missionaries, our family couldn't be picky about when we celebrated our holidays. We were scattered around the world for Christmas of 1995. Mom and Dad – Ellen and Art Sanborn – were leading a mission school in Singapore. My brother, David, was performing in a musical in Florida. My sister, Calah, was studying medicine in the Caribbean and I, Sean, had just started a computer programming job in California.
>
> My parents were invited to be the guest speakers at the January 1996 Christian music/worship conference at Cooma (**ACMS**), in the Land Down Under, Australia. Of course, I had always wanted to visit Australia, so I decided to meet up with my parents so we could celebrate a January Christmas. My brother and sister were also able to make the trek and we enjoyed a beautiful Christmas at the house of the leaders of the Cooma camp, Kevin and Jan Craik. As soon as David and I arrived at Cooma, we became the centre of attention from some of the lovely ladies.
>
> In America, we were just ordinary guys without an accent, but in Australia, we had an "accent" and soon we were beset by these beautiful girls,

seeking our attention. This was the pinnacle of bachelorhood!

There was one girl who seemed to ignore me and I wanted to learn her name. After a group meeting, I watched this darkhaired beauty float over to my mom. I seized my chance. I ran over and, using our secret language, Thai, asked my mom to introduce us. I learned her name was Anne, and soon I was backing away, mesmerised as she focused on my mom's advice about music. I stared at her until I tripped over a fold-back speaker on the stage.

Anne and I were married in September 1996, having known each other for 8 months, and I began working at computer companies in Silicon Valley in California. Two years later, as we returned from work one day, separately but simultaneously, God instructed us that now we should take the time to prepare to become fulltime missionaries.

We quit our jobs and drove to Florida for further mission training. We then spent a few months in Switzerland assisting the founder of the **YWAM** (Youth with a Mission), Loren Cunningham. We then for 12 years helped to plant churches in Chiang Mai, Thailand. In 2012, we returned to Florida to assist the YWAM mission training base.

> *We now have two children Samantha and Timothy. Sean has written The Missionary Kid Chronicles Series - The Naga Trilogy, (**https://mkchronicles.com/**), a great read for children."*

Anne an Australian, born and raised in Australia, moved to America after marrying Sean. She gave her life to Christ at the age of 10, and committed her life to missions at 15.

Anne gives her side of the story.

> *"I had always longed to join the rest of my church worship **TEAM** on their yearly trek to the Cooma/worship conference. Each year, obstacles had prevented me, but I really felt it was important that I attend and did so in January 1996. I started a new job in downtown Sydney and was sure that once again, I would be kept away.*
>
> *After a month of work, my boss approached me and asked me if I'd like to take some time off for Christmas. I was astounded and grateful, and I quickly made plans to go to Cooma. Ironically, none of the rest of the worship team could attend that year. When I prayed, I felt God prompting me that this would be a significant, life-changing conference and I was excited to see what God had in store for me.*

At the conference I met an American guy who was constantly surrounded by other girls. He attempted to flirt with me. When we met, he rudely stared at the pimple on my nose. While getting my picture taken, he was saying, "smile", which made my picture come out weird. He kept trying. Dream on guy!

I needed to find out what God had for me at this conference. I had dreams of becoming a missionary to Asia and I wasn't going to be slowed down. One day, in the dining room we sat together and soon the rest of the world dissolved away. We had a lot in common and had the same sense of humour. When we came back to earth, our food was yet uneaten, and most people had left the building. I was concerned that this meeting might take me away from the special gift God had for me.

Each day we kept talking and I was surprised to learn that he also wanted to be a missionary to Asia and had even grown up in Thailand. He was a preacher's kid! "

After several days, he bluntly asked me if he was what I was looking for in a man. I went and read my journal and as it turned out, yes, this intense guy from America was exactly the kind of husband I was looking for. By the time we left Cooma, I suspected that this was the man I might marry. By the time he left Australia a week *later, it ripped my heart in two because I knew then that I would marry this man.*

A month later I bought my wedding dress with my best friend. The month after that I flew to America so Sean could propose to me. In August, he came to Australia, where we had an amazing engagement party at Kevin and Jan Craik's home. The following week, I flew to America to marry the man who would take me around the world as a missionary. Yes, God indeed had a special present for me that Christmas".

Sean and **Anne** are a **TEAM** with complimentary missionary skills, state on their website that they believe:

> "*Everything they have experienced in their lives has been in preparation for serving our Lord Jesus as Missionaries*".

Going places - CYTA

20. Kevin Recognises

True and reliable, I think this was everyone I met connected with **CYTA** and I suspect the many hundreds I have not met. Every MEMBER of the hundreds and hundreds of **TEAM MEMBERS** that came and went in **CYTA**, the paid staff, chaplains, **BOARD MEMBERS**, paid staff etc. played a valuable role in making the organisation work, grow and be sustained. I never met anyone who was not true and generally reliable and for the time they spent with **CYTA**, committed to the work of the organisation.

However, this is a chapter where Kevin wanted to recognise those who worked closely with him in CYTA over many decades.

A list of people who had their life affected positively by their involvement in **CYTA** and contributed strongly to **CYTA** could be almost endless. Though some people are mentioned in detail below, any publication runs the risk of leaving some out.

The story of **CYTA** would not be complete without mentioning the following people who amongst a fabulous **TEAM** put in a great effort over the years that Kevin remembers:

From the CYTA TEAM

Geof Hyde, Wendy Dierikx, Mel Kronert, Geoff Robinson, David Joyce, Mel Kroenert, Chris Otton, Kevin Pool, Bob Dierikx, Jill Heyworth, Paul Webb, Mel Kronert

Going places - CYTA

Non-**TEAM MEMBERS** that greatly assisted Kevin Craik to make CYTA work and grow in the Lord are listed immediately below.

- *Merv and Daisy Clare* – 1970-1975 First **CYTA LODGE MANAGERS,** who set the high standards we all still follow.
- *Alex and Graham Leishman* – Established Sunliner Coaches coach company primarily for the ministry of **CYTA**.
- *Ros and Les Shakespeare* – 1976-1978 Second **CYTA LODGE MANAGERS.**
- **Rev Brian Willersdorf** – Brian's recommendation to bring Andraé Crouch to Australia led to CYTA's continuing music ministry.

> **A side note:** Brian's story is included in the chapter on the speakers who provided exceptional service to CYTA.

- **Bruce and Heather Bolton** – 1979-1993 Third CYTA LODGE MANAGERS.
- **Trevor and Lynn Blood** – 1993-1997 Fourth CYTA LODGE MANAGERS.
- **Graham Hopkinson** – Purchased three double decker coaches especially for CYTA use.
- **Ronald Drayton, Steven Doran, Lyndon Rumsay, Geoff Rice and Aurora Wilton** – Our very supportive office managers
- **Coach Captains of note: Cliff (Cliffy) Waburton**-whose story appears later in this chapter), **Fredy Smith, Fred Jackson and Jeff**

Going places - CYTA

      Cowper (who doubled as a **CYTA** Chaplain whose story is in the chapter on the **CYTA** chaplains).
- **George Higglet** of **Higglet Coaches** who not only supplied coach services to CYTA but also bailed the organisation out of a corner on some occasions
- **Tony Royal** from Forest Coach lines that gave CYTA Cliff Warburton.

Though the people listed above are not mentioned in detail in this chapter, they gave much support to Kevin. Most of their names and some of their stories appear in other chapters of this book. There are many more that could have been recognised

If you as a former **TEAM MEMBER** feel that your life was as affected as those to be described and you contributed to the mission of CYTA as the people listed below have done, I am sorry you have not been included. God will know of your service to CYTA, which was to God, even if others don't know how you served. Please share your story with others.

In an organisation such as **CYTA** where up to a thousand people were involved from a short time or for a long time, not everyone's story is known to me. **CYTA** days were great days for so many people. I hope they were great days for many of you reading this story.

Kevin Craik describes **Ros Hills** as:

      "One of the most capable people I have met."

Going places - CYTA

Ros began developing her skills in understanding and managing people as a tour **HOSTESS** with the Christian Youth Travel Association from 1978 – 1988. She then went on to be Executive Producer of *Stand Tall*. Stand Tall states on its website it is an organisation committed to arming young people with resilience, the strength and the ability to stand up to bullying, the power of perspective, plus the ability to make good decisions.

Ros is particularly passionate in seeing volunteers within organisation used effectively and purposefully to the fullest of their capabilities. She is now an independent organisational and event manager committed to executing events and organisational strategies with companies particularly in the field of community services and in the non-profit sector. She has been working with, and to the good of, other people for more than forty years. Ros inspired, and was inspired by, her time with **CYTA** which helped to set a pattern of positive interaction and concern for others.

Kevin also remembers times other than working on **CYTA** business with *Ros* and her husband *Rod*, who became a Director of the organisation. One such instance that *Kevin* relates is:

> "One of the **many** highlights of Jan's and my involvement with **TEAM MEMBERS** has been the special time with **Rod and Ros Hills, Paul and Carol Cleasby, Mark and Beth Bradley, and Heather and Bob Pearce.**
>
> To top off one of those special times was a very scrumptious fish platter meal on the harbour on a

> *luxury cruiser which they had hired for the night that was positioned for a 9pm firework show.*
>
> *This is the night I put my knee well out of joint. Back on the wharf I could not walk and had to be supported by two of the boys. Ros, in her usual manner, rose to the occasion and believe it or not found a wheelchair nearby, which was used to get me to the car. The group later that night used my office chair to wheel me into the house."*

Marilyn Hinton started her work life as a primary/infants school teacher. Her desire was to assist the development of the young chidden in her care. In her time with **CYTA** she was an active **TEAM MEMBER** and an encourager of others within the **TEAM**.

She at a particular point in time re-evaluated her life and decided to deepen her relationship with *Jesus Christ* by attending Bible College. Marilyn became a pastor in an outer suburban area of Melbourne. She has pastored a congregation of up to 500.

Over many years, Marilyn developed a deep love for silence and found it to be a space of inner healing, refreshment and renewal, providing space for deepening our inner journey. She has facilitated a number of soul nurture days and retreat days, over the years at the **Wellspring Centre** in Victoria as well as being part of retreat **group** on other retreats.

Going places - CYTA

She has also enjoyed introducing silent retreats in her church community. She is especially interested in people ensuring they have a deepening in a loving, life-giving relationship with *God*. Marilyn's life of service was influenced by her time contributing to the work of **CYTA** and her relationship with other **TEAM MEMBERS** as well as her relationship with Kevin and Jan Craik.

Father Jim McKeon is currently the parish priest at Epping/Carlingford Parish. His path to his current vocation was influenced through his life intersecting with **CYTA**. Not on a tour but through attending the **AUSTALIAN CHRISTIAN MUSIC SEMINAR** and working on staff at the **LODGE.**

His interest in **CYTA** extended to becoming friends with Kevin Pool. Jim McKeon decided to take a "gap year" during his seminary training. He decided to take on a season of work as winter staff staying at the **CYTA LODGE** where he met up with "Poolie". A combination of factors influenced Father Jim McKeon in his Christian journey, not least of all his friendship with Kevin Pool.

Jim McKeon held many different roles in the Catholic Diocese of Broken Bay. A blogger and social commentator, he spoke at variance to church policy when discussing sexual harm by Members of all churches towards people. Father Jim McKeon said in a Sunday morning sermon:

> "Denying that such crimes are impossible is a form of fundamentalism which does us no good, and harm to others."

He further highlighted the pain of victims, those close to victims and parishioners affected by the unveiling of sexually based crimes against people:

> "Scandalised, betrayed and disillusioned by what has happened in the church".

When carrying out a first communion service for a group of young children, Father Jim showed them the cup he was holding and asked,

> "What is in this cup?"

> "Holy Water" was the response from the obedient seven-year olds.

> "This is just water from a tap I used to fill the cup before the service. What makes this water special is that I prayed to the Lord over it."

Father Jim McKeon has been asked by Kevin to speak at his funeral. **Kevin** particularly:

> "I *want through Jim McKeon to illustrate that **CYTA** was inclusive and did not discriminate against any one denomination as well as to show that there is believing alive Christians in the Catholic Church."*

Father Jim also attended and became a Board member of Beyond the Black Stump. Black Stump had been where he had first considered a commitment to Christ. He decided to establish a stall where visitors to the Black Stump festival could experience the life lived by

Going places - CYTA

the poor through living in Humpies. He presented the gospel of Christ Crucified and Risen. Our saving is through grace flowing from Christ's sacrifice.

David Ohlmus was the **TOUR LEADER** on the tour where Paul Cleasby made his commitment. David was an enthusiastic and committed **CYTA TEAM MEMBER**, who led each tour with a calm and commanding manner but was deeply committed to presenting the gospel.

David married and moved to Canberra but never lost his enthusiasm for **CYTA**. When Priscilla Isberg left **CYTA**, David took a year off from his public sector job and worked in the role of Kevin's personal assistant. However his work extended to being an assistant to Kevin to someone who helped shape the future of **CYTA**.

Carole Reece was mentioned several times in the early chapters of this book. She was a tower of strength in the early establishment of **CYTA**, especially in her skilful ways of preparing camping tour menus along with Jan, Colleen and Jenny (which is mentioned in the chapter dealing with the original Directors).

Carole also assisted greatly in getting **CYTA LODGE** up and ready for our first booking, in nine weeks after obtaining access to what was then known as West Camp. Carole appears regularly in the story of **CYTA**.

Paul Cleasby, (aka Director Cornflakes) was an Associate Director of **CYTA** for five years. An elder in his church, Paul came to a real knowledge of Christ on a New Zealand tour. **David Ohlmus** was the **TOUR**

Going places - CYTA

LEADER. *Kevin recalls* what Paul told him about his experience on the New Zealand tour.

> *"I saw the **TOUR LEADER** up front. I believed I was a Christian. However, he had something I did not have and I wanted, though at first I was unsure of what it was."*

Paul joined the **TEAM**, led several tours and then served **CYTA** as a **DIRECTOR**. He was nick named "Director Corn flakes". He played practical jokes of people, particularly putting cornflakes into beds at the **LODGE** and into the desks of office staff.

Paul early in his time at **CYTA** used to ask Kevin Craik every week if help was needed at the **LODGE**. A very enthusiastic young man you would think. The real reason for his enthusiasm was that he had met a young lady in Cooma. Like all good love stories, they married, have four children and lived happily ever after.

But let's hear the *Paul Cleasby* story from Paul.

> *"In December 1979 I went on a **CYTA** tour to New Zealand. My brother and sister had been on **CYTA** tours to NZ and said they were good. Just sleep in and you can miss the religious bit. I didn't need churchy stuff, it's just for weak people who need a crutch and can't cope. But God had a plan.*
>
> *'Coincidentally' the late David Ohlmus, a long-time family friend, was the **TOUR LEADER**. The people on the tour were different, kind, warm, friendly, caring, but also normal, fun loving and*

adventurous. Not only did they break my mould of what a Christian was they made it attractive. On 11th January 1980 on a wet night in a **CYTA** tent in Queenstown with 3-4 other **TOUR MEMBERs**, I gave my life to Christ.

"After returning to Sydney, David invited me to a **TEAM** night to share my story. What an experience that was. It didn't take long before I joined and looked forward to **TEAM** nights at The **CYTA Centre- Homebush** every Thursday night. Eventually I was rostered to lead **TEAM** Nights, which led to Work Weekends, Snow Tours, WA and Nepal."

In 1984 I booked a one-way ticket and went on the Europe Tour. Kev connected me with Ian Mayo the CEO of Oak Hall, a UK-based Christian Travel Company. For Oak Hall I lead tours to French Riviera, Africa, Scandinavia and snow tours to Black Forrest in Germany. After leading the 1985 Europe Tour I returned home.

Going back to The Centre this time was different. The winter staff had just finished a season under Bruce and Heather Bolton at Cooma **LODG**E, turned up at the same time. In particular **Carol Stuut** with her tight pants and cute bottom. It didn't take long and we were going out, 9 months later engaged and 9 months after that we married on the 16th of January 1988.

> *Carol and I were privileged to continue to serve through **CYTA** for several more years, including Uncle Kev's Pancake nights, Uncle Kev's Bush dance (in Sydney Town Hall and on Sydney Ferry's), True Colours at Silverwater and also myself as a **BOARD MEMBER**.*
>
> *I am so thankful for how God used **CYTA** to minister and shape me. I have been privileged to continue to use those leadership skills in work and church life, leading small groups, heading up Young Families, on Mission Committee and as an Elder for 15 years.*
>
> *Carol and I have seen our four kids accept Christ and seek to serve Him through their Church and professional lives. More recently over the last 6 years **Carol** has become the full time Children and Families Pastor at our Church, Thornleigh Baptist, where we have worshipped for the past 30 years. Thank You God for **CYTA** NZ tours and for all you continue to do in our lives. - **Carol and Paul Cleasby.***

Robyn Harris may be well-known to many **TEAM MEMBERS** for her tireless service. Many **TEAM MEMBERS** did not see or know about what Robyn did behind the scenes and the hours she spent working such as, running a coffee machine and making many hundreds of aprons over the years for the music seminar time as well as making the hot chocolate before snow coaches left Homebush.

Going places - CYTA

Robyn spent many winter seasons in her caravan at the **LODGE** in Cooma and the rest of the year working in the Sydney office, her speciality being looking after concert ticket sales. Many days, Aunty Rob was the kids' taxi pick-up after school and dropping them off either at home or keeping them occupied in the office.

Cliff Warburton was a regular **CYTA** coach driver from the Forest Coach company on the Northern Beaches of Sydney. Cliff was a favourite with both **TEAM MEMBERS** and **TOUR MEMBERS**. He was always happy when on tour and entertained all with a dry sense of humour. He often entertained coachloads of young people happy to sing along with his rendition of:

"There's a hole in the bottom of the sea."

Over a period of 23 years, he developed many strong connections and friendships with those who were on **TEAM** in that period of time in our history. He was a lovable larrikin in the true Aussie sense, but he was also a person who shared in the load of camping tours which were his favourite tours. His first tour with us was Chatswood Primary School in 1965 and drove continually till 1987.

The memories of *Cliff Warburton - Coach Captain – Forest Coach Lines* (until end 1987) and always was and is considered a **CYTA TEAM MEMBER.**

> *"My recollection of one of my first* **CYTA** *trips was of a ski weekend at Smiggin Hole departing Friday night with all night travel to Jindabyne for breakfast then a day in the snow at Smiggin*

*Holes. Then back to Cooma for overnight in motel (prior to **CYTA LODGE** days) and then off to Canberra on Sunday to look at the sites and go round in circles and a fancy lunch at Hotel Kurrajong. Then we returned to Sydney arriving around 11pm. It was a long weekend but full of great fun and fellowship.*

*I remember a Central Australia tour in the brand-new Denning coach. It rained and rained. As the dirt roads were impassable – we bogged, we ran out of fuel and had to wait at Curtin-Springs roadhouse for a fuel tanker which was also bogged. It was a great adventure. During this time the **CYTA TEAM** never faltered – keeping up the morale people on a coach with typical high spirits and grace.*

*Then there were the great Mystery Weekends. Nobody, not even the coach captain, knew of the destination. The 1968 Gold Coast holiday tour was a highlight, where I met **Jenny**, my wife of 50 years. It was two weeks of all sorts of activities – sight-seeing, horse-riding, water skiing, restaurants – enjoying all the Gold Coast and a side trip to Noosa had to offer.*

*The acquisition of the **LODGE** at Cooma and its transformation was another highlight during my time working with **CYTA** – lots of fun working bee **TEAM** weekends, snowy trips and conferences. It also became a great venue for school excursions to the snow. I have many happy memories of those times.*

Going places - CYTA

> *I could write a book on the adventures over a period of 21 years of association with **CYTA**. I often think back that there were so many young **TOUR LEADER**S not even born yet when I was working with **CYTA**."*

Robin Morris has been involved with **CYTA** in one form or another for more than forty years. She started work in the **CYTA** office as the first employee of **Travelways Australia** in 1975, taking her first tour to New Zealand just weeks after her employment. Robyn met her husband *Gary* on while tour.

She and Gary were **CYTA TEAM MEMERS** and continued their involvement with **CYTA** by joining the friends of **CYTA** after active **TEAM** involvement was no longer possible.

Robyn also founded **Teapot Ministries** (not a **CYTA** activity) which was and is designed to reach women of all ages and background, this ministry reaches more than 200 people each year. With its twentieth anniversary in 2022 the ministry is strong and lives on.

> **A side note:** Information on Teapot Ministries can be found in the chapter, "**Yesterday and Today**." and you can also read more about the Robyn's work work for Travelways in the chapter dealing with "**The Other Tours**" (which covers the activities of Travelways)

Robin recalls key moments in her ongoing relationship with **CYTA**

> *"My first experience of **CYTA** was a work weekend January 1974. I do not remember how I*

*came to go or who I went with, but that weekend set the course for the journey I was to travel in my life. On the return trip from Cooma I sat next to John Craik. As we travelled, we talked. He encouraged me to apply for the position in the **CYTA** Office for the first Travelways Tour Coordinator. This I did and was employed that year.*

*My overall role in the organisation was to handle Australian **CYTA** tours, Weekend Snow Tours, Long Weekend Tours, and Travelways which then was the individual travel component of **CYTA**. I credit **CYTA** and in particular Kevin for honing my secretarial skills which helped in my many PA administration positions I filled throughout my adult working life. Other skills acquired during my **CYTA** experience included Event Management, Leadership skills, and Public Speaking. I have used these skills working in several Christian Ministries over the past 45years.*

*Within the first couple of months of joining the **CYTA TEAM**, Kevin had me go and speak to a church group about **CYTA** and from then on, I have represented other Christian Ministries in this way. As a Christian through **CYTA** I grew in my faith, knowledge of the Scriptures, relational skills and care for others.*

*In the early family years along with **Gary** my husband (yes who I met on a tour to the Warrumbungles) we took part in the many family* weekends at the **LODGE** sharing our **CYTA** experience with our Children. Their trips to the **LODGE** still hold a special place in their memories.

Following my experience of working for **CYTA** I worked in many Christian Organisations, including **ANZEA** Bookhouse and **Scripture Union** where I was involved in the Christian Book Industry. This included setting up programs for distribution of books and Daily Bible Notes as well as designing and constructing stalls for the Christian Booksellers Conferences for Scripture Union over several years.

On our life journey Gary and I faced many challenging experiences. We were sponsored on an Emmaus weekend that both refreshed and renewed our faith. This led to my involvement in the Emmaus movement and Kairos Prison ministries.

Later employed by Kairos to establish the Kairos Office and serve on Kairos TEAMs ministering to those in prison, I became the face of Kairos. In their early years I used the office skills I had gained through my **CYTA** experiences to establish office procedures, as well as my event management skills to create and manage the early Kairos' conferences. The joy of being a Lay Director and leading a **TEAM** of 30 plus for both Emmaus and Kairos Outside weekends helped me to understand the need women have, to feel loved and cared for.

> In 2002 I put together a weekend Retreat for everyday Women at Kiah Ridge and as I was handing out a piece of Agape which was the shape of a Teapot saying: "When the kettle is up to its neck in hot water it still sings so in:
>
> > 1 Thessalonians 5:16, "Rejoice in the Lord always".
>
> I felt a nudge from God to establish a ministry called Teapot Ministries. I waited 6 months and prayed about it, asking God to rise up two other people who had a similar vision which He did. Early 2003 Teapot Ministries it was registered as a not-for-profit organisation.
>
> I thank God for that first **CYTA** work weekend back in 1974 and for the impact it had on my life. The **Christian Youth Travel** Association had an enormous influence on my life and I have been able to honour God and serve Him using the gifts He gave me which were honed through my time with **CYTA**.

Robin concludes:

> Praise God for the vision He gave **Kev** and **Jan** and for their willingness to listen and serve Him. How many others have gone on in ministry using their God-given gifts because they attended and served through **CYTA**? I am sure mine is just one of many stories of young Christians trained though **CYTA** and the way God used us to reach others.

Going places - CYTA

James Gow. James's mother **Jan**, served as assistant to Kevin for the **AUSTALIAN CHRISTIAN MUSIC SEMINARS**. James was a small boy when he began attending the seminars. He helped set up rooms, cleaned up, collected bottles etc. The music seminar became a large part of his life. James also helped in the **CYTA LODGE** who when at Cooma became a dab hand at arranging the bread display in the main hall of **CYTA LODGE**.

James grew into **CYTA** and the Christian life. Starting his association with **CYTA**, as a young boy he became a follower of *Jesus Christ* and stayed with **CYTA** in one form or another throughout the growing years of his faith.

James recalls the training he had with **CYTA** that has held him, and his wife, in good stead even in recent years.

> "My **CYTA** training came in handy last week (during 2021). I was asked to cook for our church youth camp of 100 people. My wife, **Min**, wasn't so sure that we should say yes, but we did!
>
> I surprised myself, recalling how most things worked at **CYTA**. It was the "little things" we did, such as counting the plates before the meal. Everyone was fed on time. We didn't run out of food and there wasn't much left over either. The energy and effort of those years ago is still paying off."

John Geering was one of the early **TEAM MEMBERS**. He was always ready with a smile, a jibe for Kevin and almost always dressed in white overalls which showed the signs of many hours of activity.

He was affectionately known as "Gearbox" - on and off tour. John gave many hundreds of voluntary hours as a qualified electrician in rewiring the Cooma **LODGE**. He was a dynamo! He was also thorough in his preparation and maintenance of camping tour equipment. **CYTA** owes a huge debt to John for his work in the early days of the organisation.

John and his wife had two daughters. He passed away in 2019

Arthur & Bev Rickersey unlike most other **TEAM MEMBERS**, had been married a year before their first **CYT** Tour. Arthur was a volunteer with Baptist Youth Ministries. He and *Bev* were planning to travel in January 1971, to a Baptist Pan Australian Youth Conference (PAYC) in Launceston, Tasmania. With much trepidation, given they did not know anything about **CYTA** they booked travel to the Conference and on a Camping Tour that followed (to be led by **Graham** and **Sue Drayton**). The rest, as they say, is history.

Together, **Arthur** and **Bev** led tours to The Great Barrier Reef, Central Australia and New Zealand. Arthur also led tours to New Zealand and Fiji. As a **TOUR LEADER** in New Zealand with (*Selma Pik Née Hokin)* and *John Stone*, Arthur was in the coach that "rolled off" the road into trees at Punakaiki, near Greymouth, a short time after devotion on "God's care and protection. The road, before and after this section of road, dropped straight to the rocky coast below!

Going places - CYTA

Following the second ACMS in 1979 **Kevin Craik** visited the Rickersey family, now including their 3 young sons, Glenn, Darren and Nathan. They were signed up to work at the next **AUSTRLIAN CHRISTIAN MUSIC SEMIINAR** at Cooma. This was to become an annual family adventure for more than 20 years. Their 3 sons continuing to attend the seminar until it finished in 2002.

Arthur was a Founding Director for the Black Stump festival, (which has its own separate chapter). This also became an annual highlight for the Rickersey family. Arthur was a Company member (refer to chapter one for more information) and went on to serve on the **CYTA** Board and as a Director/ Company Secretary.

A final comment from *Arthur Rickersey*,

> "We express our thanks to God for our family involvement in such a strategic opportunity for ministry and service."

Les and Ros Shakespeare

The story of Les Shakespeare starts back in the sixties. Les was the youth leader of Green Point Baptist Church. He had been an Assistant Director to Kevin (as the Director) on many BYF camps.

Les was a very well-liked and appreciated leader of a large group of enthusiastic young people of Green Point Baptist Church. Les regularly brought down coachloads of his young people to the monthly BYF rallies held in Scots Church Sydney using Richter Bros Coaches (a NSW central Cost company in Umina).

Going places - CYTA

There is much written about **Les** and his wife **Ros** in various areas of this book, including the erection of a copse of pine trees to damp dawn sound coming from **CYTA LODGE**. There was also a period where **Les and Ros** were **CYTA LODGE MANAGERS**. The connection of Les with Richter/Sunliner coaches proved to be a significant connection in the life of **CYTA**. That story is told in the **TEAM** chapter. There are stories about Les in many different areas of the book.

Kevin concludes the chapter with his reflection on the work of *David Inder* for **CYTA.**

> "David Inder went on a weekend snow tour with his youth group from St Andrews Uniting Senior Fellowship of South Turramurra church in around 1970 or 1971.
>
> He joined the **TEAM** in 1975 and he is still involved in 2023, even after many years! He is still a "go to" person who is always willing and able to assist despite his recent medical issues.
>
> David, along with his friend the late **Graeme Hoose**, also a **TEAM MEMBER** travelled to Cooma for 9 weekends in a row in order to install an exhaust fan in the already built Dining Room chimney. They adopted an extractor fan to fit and then got it working 100%. It sure did make a difference!
>
> David was a "gopher" for me for countless music seminars, the official photographer at many and made sure the local processor of his photos processed them in a timely manner. You never

had to chase David up to make sure my request was completed as it needed to be.

David maintained the **TEAM** database. This was a never-ending task. He catalogued hundreds of the early **CYTA** 35mm Kodak slides. (Who remembers them in the digital age?

Thank you David for many years of service!"

Going places - CYTA

Part Four - The Tours

Going places - CYTA

21. The Other Tours of CYTA

Travelways Australia the not often mentioned fully commercial arm of **CYTA** operated there first tour under the name *Christian Trailways.* Travelways Australia operated as a public commercial travel agency from its first day of operation.

> **A side note:** A search of registered names found the registration of the name Christian Trail Ways had lapsed, so **CYTA** snapped it up but only used it the once. The name Christian Trail Ways was only ever used for the 1969 tour to Melbourne for a Billy Graham crusade. It was the tour that birthed Travelways.

Travelways Australia supported **CYTA** tours with airline tickets, accommodation etc. The business became a registered travel agent, when registration was required by law.

Prior to 1974 travel agents were unregulated. Due to a large number of travel organisations collapsing and people with bookings losing their money, the NSW government legislated that if you sold travel which included an overnight stay, you needed to have a licence as well as maintain a bank trust account and not make use of a client's money till after you provide the service.

When legislation was introduced for the licencing of travel agents, **CYTA** trading as **CYT** and **Travelways Australia** received the first travel agency licence. Travel agency license 1 (No. 01) and as a second license which was Travel Agency 2 (No. 02). The second licence confirmed there was someone with qualifications to operate the business. Once registered Travelways had to, and did, hire an IATA accredited travel agent this being a key requirement for travel agency licensing. **CYTA** always operated a trust account which became a legal requirement upon the passing of the agency licensing legislation.

> *A* **side note:** I did not know until she told me, that Bev Caruthers qualified herself as a travel agent and spent time working in the office for **CYTA**.

> *A side note:* The late **Steve Doran**, the then office manager, took up a position in IATA (the International Air Transport Association) and later the management of the Travel Compensation Fund (TCF) and licensing of all travel agents in NSW, which has since been disbanded. Followers of **CYTA** Facebook will know that **Steve Doran passed away** in 2023.

When the registration was through, **Kevin Craik** held up the registration certificate, (which showed that **CYTA** and its travel arms had the number one license), along with the folder containing the documentation at a **TEAM** night proudly declaring:

> "The licencing people have complimented **CYTA** on the extensive and fully documented paperwork that was submitted. They hoped further applications would be as good"

It was thought Travelways could tap a local market as a separate walk-in off the street agency when it was set up in the Homebush shopping centre. Though

Going places - CYTA

Travelways traded profitably, two attempts to offer it as a walk in off the street travel agency were not successful for **CYTA**.

The secret for Travelways success proved to be largely found in "going to school". There was no age limit on Travelways tours. Being established as a commercial tour operation, Travelways principal area of custom over time became school groups.

The first High School Excursion was in 1962, with Bass Hill High going to Canberra and back in one day. In the following years sometimes more than one hundred schools in well over 100 coaches annually were carried by Travelways, mainly to Canberra and the Snowy.

The fame of **CYTA** Camping Tours, whether they were operated through **CYT** or through **Travelways**, spread over time.

There were tours undertaken for a number of primary schools within NSW and a tour to Perth for Newcastle Girls High School. *Jef Hyde* along with *Richard Brown* had the pleasure of taking the group of over 40 girls and teachers across the Nullarbor.

In 1970 *Peter* and *Margaret Crofts,* along with *John* and *Lorraine Cronshaw* led two coaches from Oberon High School to Central Australia.

Peter, a primary teacher at Excelsior Public School in Castle Hill, hosted three annual tours of up to three coaches on a week-long tour to Rennie in Southern NSW and the Murray River. Highlights of the tour included staying in the Rennie Oval Grandstand, spending time on and enjoying a local farm owned by a family who's three children Peter had taught as a 1st year out teacher, years earlier at Rennie Primary School. A trip on a Paddle Wheeler on the Murray River caused great excitement.

> *A side note:* Peter the primary school teacher at Excelsior Public School went home to heaven in 1990.

Tours were also hosted by volunteer **CYTA TEAM MEMBERS** and staff from **CYTA LODGE**. Cliffy Warburton was always one of the Coach Captains used on these tours.

In addition to the **CYTA** office, **Travelways Australia** had its own office in Homebush in rooms in Rochester Street. These offices were vacated when **CYTA** bought the **CYTA Centre Homebush** at The Crescent in Homebush, which could accommodate all its activities.

Travelways Australia had been sharing toilet facilities with the co-inhabitant Westpac, also the building's owner. Two strange bedfellows sharing bathroom facilities together

After the sale of the **CYTA Centre, Homebush**, Travelways Australia Returned to Rochester Street in an adjacent building to where it was first housed which offered expanded space.

The Travelways Australia operation was to appeal to a different market to **CYTA**. Though the key market niche of this operation were school tours, older groups made up a key secondary market. The business held its first

Going places - CYTA

adult overseas tour by taking an adult group to New Zealand.

Robin Morris (**Née Rodway**) was the first staff member of Travelways and had only just started in the **CYTA** Office in 1974 when she was named **TOUR LEADER** for the trip to New Zealand. Accommodation on these tours was a mixture of hotels and motels. Time has shown the leadership and customer care shown by Robyn who having only been employed in the organisation for a few weeks when she took the tour, was exceptional.

John Geering – otherwise known as "Gearbox" – an early **TEAM MEMBER** was passenger on the 1969 Billy Graham Melbourne Crusade. A few weeks later he went on the October Long Weekend tour to Lightening Ridge and got so excited about the work of the **CYTA TEAM**, he joined the TEAM immediately on his return from the tour. In his three years of service from, 1970 to 1973 John gave greatly of his time. He worked for **CYTA** relentlessly during that time in his occupation as an electrician a much needed talent in the early days of **CYTA**.

John married Norma (Née Nasia). They had two daughters. John passed away in 2019

> **A side note:** In John I saw a dynamo, in his electrical work and in his meticulous preparation and maintenance of camping tour equipment. More of John's story appears in the chapter detailing loyal and faithful **TEAM MEMBERS** to Kevin

Going places - CYTA

By the middle 1990s, Travelways Australia, Schools Excursions were renamed Student Learning Experiences and Travelways Australia was one of the leading operators out of Sydney. Year six, and some Year seven students could receive government subsidised travel to Canberra. This was a lead market for Travelways.

Other tours were mounted, under the Travelways Australia and/or **CYTA** banner. Four coaches travelled to Brisbane to enjoy two days (never enough) to The Great Exposition which when it appeared in Australia was named **EXPO 88**. It featured 41 countries from around the world. Last time I looked one country had left its pavilion fully erected on site on the Northern side of the river that runs through Brisbane.

In 1974 **CYTA** organised for 80 young Australians led by **Graham** and **Sue Drayton** to travel to the eighth Baptist World Youth Conference in Portland, Oregon, after which the group travelled in two coaches touring Western USA. This was **CYTA**'s first "camping tour" in the USA. No tents but the use of church halls and other facilities.

Christian Camping International Australia (CCI) Australia, now known as Christian Venues Association began in 1975. **CYTA LODGE** hosted the first National CCI Australia Conference in 1976. A year later, Australian delegates travelled to the Banff Canadian Rockies and joined with hundreds of others who were involved in Christian camping from around the world. Upon arrival in Seattle Airport, a great friend of **TEAM**, *Evie Tornqist,* was there to greet them.

Going places - CYTA

In 1978 **CYTA** had the responsibility of the Australian contingent to the ninth Baptist World Youth Conferences conference in Manila, in the Philippines.

In 1983 Carlingford Baptist Youth Choir were invited to take part in the 2nd Asian Baptist Youth Conference in Hong Kong. Prior to the conference the choir visited a number of Christian Churches in Manila, Philippines. This was a **CYTA** tour.

In 1993, 32 coaches took over 1200 high school students on a one day trip, to the initial Science Exhibition in Canberra. An optional breakfast (which doubled as a rest stop) was available for students who wished to have it at McDonalds Sutton Forest. Travelways staff made forward arrangements which included checking with the manager of the McDonalds whether the store could handle such a number. It is reported the McDonalds manager had up to fifty staff on that day to handle the crowd.

For the groups travelling on this occasion, more than 250 individual venue appointments throughout Canberra went without a hitch.

To help promote Travelways availability to schools, the first school folder/catalogue, which included brochures supplied by all of the leading attractions and accommodation houses used by Travelways and other operators, was sent to almost every school in NSW.

In the chapter recording the work of some of the staff of **CYTA**, it was noted that **Daisy Care**, the co-manager at the **CYTA LODGE** was appointed a **TOUR LEADER**, of

Going places - CYTA

a mature adult Travelways tour. The tour she led was to the Carnivals of Flowers of Toowoomba.

Toowoomba is one of the Queensland towns that hold annual garden contests involving domestic and commercial gardens in the town. It was on this tour that Daisy was seen driving around Coffs Harbour, in an open mini-moke during a stop-over on the way to Toowoomba.

Travelways decided to invest in the then obsession for the musical theatre piece the Phantom of the Opera. The Phantom was showing in Melbourne a long time before it came to Sydney. Travelways booked a block of 400 tickets and advertised a tour. They did not sell out. This was not a successful venture. However **CYTA**/Travelways always believed in the saying, nothing ventured, nothing gained.

Prior to **CYTA** finishing up Travelways Australia was sold to a Western Sydney Bus business, **Hopkinsons**. Travel ways/Christian Trail Ways was an area of operation not often involving the **TEAM** but an integral part of **CYTA**.

> **A side note:** Hopkinsons is mentioned in some detail in the chapter dealing with **Buildings and other things**.

22. The tours - the good, unusual and the ugly

The purpose of the tours

Not every tour went smoothly. Some tours seemed to go off without a hitch whereas other tours had problems along the way. Regardless of the smoothness or otherwise of a tour, the Good News of *Jesus Christ, HIS* sacrifice and redemption and the gift of being involved in an enduring relationship with *God* (saved through grace) was always proclaimed and explained on tour. Unchurched people as well as existing believers heard the gospel proclaimed on every tour with **TOUR MEMBERS** coming to Christ on tour as well as after the tour.

This chapter deals with tours that did not go to the snow. The snow tours have their own chapter right after this chapter. The first non-snow tour for **CYT** (the ongoing operating tour name which was owned by **CYTA**) was led by *Graham Drayton* to Tasmania in 1965. This was a motel tour.

Soft bunch weren't they!

The unusual from the tours

Graham Drayton also led the second extended tour which was to Central Australia in 1966/67. *Jan* and *Kevin* led their first tour together to Central Australia in 1968 at which time the nexus of the **CYTA TEAM** had been established. *Peter Croft* led a tour to the Barrier Reef in 1969.

Going places - CYTA

The **Nepal** trip, which departed on Boxing Day, was generally a three week tour, and included hiking and sleeping out on the trail. The tour visited well known places such as Kathmandu and less well-known places such as Anna Purna.

Those young people who had the opportunity to travel with **CYTA** to participate in a Himalayan Trek, or on an Overland to London adventure, found some extra luggage they were able to take and distribute in Kathmandu, Nepal.

A visit to the Shining Light Hospital Pothra Nepal

Anna Purna in Nepal was the location of the *Shining Light Hospital*, a hospital operated by Christian staff, expat missionary medical staff and some locals. Each time the **CYTA** tour arrived there was a supply of wind up cassette machines included in the luggage of people on the tour.

Once it was clear how many people would be on the tour, an order (along with payment) was placed with *Gospel Recordings* for the cassette machines and one cassette, on which had been recorded a selection of Christian music, Bible verses and stories. The number of machines and tapes ordered was matched to the total number of people on each tour.

Each person on a tour, including **TEAM MEMBERS** leading the tour would have one of the cassette players in their luggage. Before leaving Australia, the **TOUR MEMBERS** were given a pack of "goodies" The goodies were bags of personal care items that could not be sourced locally such as toothpaste, shampoo, and non-perishable treats such as Vegemite and Tim Tams. These items were gladly received.

Kevin reflects on the Nepal trips.

> *"Never once was there a problem with customs in bringing the cassette players and tapes into a predominantly Hindu nation. Who knows where and how these tape recordings were used of and for our Lord. Gospel Recordings Ministry became Global Recordings Network and continues its work in many other countries today. They now have "solar-operated" mp3 players."*

A side note: The above information is shared with you for your information. However, though these events happened more than forty years' ago it could be that the packs taken to the Hospital are still considered as a sensitive issue by the appropriate authorities. I would suggest that you might be circumspect in sharing this information with other people.

Besides the Shining Light Hospital, The Nepal trip offered unparalleled viewing experiences. One of these was the world famous **Chitwan National Park** where the group stayed at Tiger Tops Lodge deep in the National Park. There Royal Bengal Tigers, leopards, deer, rhinoceros, and a host of other wild animals grazed and lived together. One of the most remarkable activities was the elephant ride into tiger country.

> **A side note:** Though Elephant rides are considered unacceptable in today's world in Western Countries. It is part of the work life and culture of other countries in previous times and still continues in some locations today.

Now to the Pacific

The *South Pacific Safari* (known colloquially as SPS) featured a tour through *Samoa* where the **TOUR MEMBERS** and **TOUR LEADERSHIP** slept in a school. In Tonga sleeping quarters were in a hall of a Uniting Church building and Fiji, where the people on tour slept in the villages.

One SPS tour with **Mark Standen** and **Bev Carruthers** being the tour staff was disrupted on one occasion by the King of Tonga. Though seats were booked and paid for on a flight from Samoa to Tonga the arrival of the **King of Tonga and his entourage** demanded and secured the plane for their trip home. They were to load first followed by the **CYTA** group. Fortunately there were enough seats to accommodate the entire group though they were facing a Fiji cyclone.

How dare the King of Tonga disrupt a CYTA tour?

Kevin remembers the (SPS) tour of 1984/5

> *"**Mark Standen and Bev Caruthers** led the Christmas Fijian Tour 1983. The tour was caught up in a cyclone, Cyclone Eric. **TOUR MEMBERS** were holed up in a concrete bunker, i.e. a cyclone-proof motel rooms.*

The group for the trip home was split in two. The tour flight home was delayed. They had to wait till the King of Tonga and his entourage boarded one of the planes.

Mark went to Sydney with Sydney based **TOUR MEMBERS** and **Bev** went to Melbourne with the Melbourne based group. Bev then had to hot foot it back to work as she was at that time a qualified travel agent working for **CYTA**.

Mystery Tours

Mystery tours were just as the name implies. They could be for a weekend, a single day or for an extended time. No two tours were ever the same. Some involved camping, others went somewhere of interest and came back. These were popular tours. They booked out within days of being announced.

One such tour was a mystery train tour. **CYTA** booked a 35 (sorry not the well-known 38) class train, with six carriages. The unknown destination was the Otford Conference Centre. Upon arrival a barbeque would be available. Special 9 inch (approx. 23 cm) wide buns had been bought for the occasion. They were piled with steak and salad.

Close to 300 people were booked on this tour. Once the train had left the main line and entered the National Park, there was an increasing crowd of people along the line as the train got closer to its destination.

The passengers saw these crowds of people waving to them so they waved back. Clearly **CYTA** had recruited an army of volunteers to greet them. Well at least many of the passengers thought so. However, that wasn't the truth.

The crowds of people along the track waving were steam train enthusiasts who were waving at the train and of course, by default, the passengers. Not a specially recruited group to greet the mystery tour travellers.

The day was fabulous, a great success and by the time everything was cleaned up and the train returned to Sydney it was almost midnight.

I wonder how many passengers really thought the crowd was just for them or is this just one of those urban myth**s.**

Going places - CYTA

23. The TEAM is on Tour
This is the **TEAM**'s time. Here we go with reflections of tour staff on the smoothness or otherwise of some of the many tours conducted by **CYTA**.

A tour to New Zealand
I *recall a trip to New Zealand that could be best forgotten but still the Holy Spirit worked in the lives of people.*

> "For me the best part of the trip to New Zealand was the flight over and the flight back. When the group arrived, some of the luggage was lost including paperwork necessary to the tour. A promise was made and kept that the lost luggage would be there in the next day or so.
>
> The luggage was a small problem compared to the state of the "school" bus waiting outside the airport.
>
> "Is this the bus to take us to the coach?" A question asked by a somewhat young and possibly at the time out of his depth **TOUR LEADER**.
>
> "No" said the driver. "This is the coach to take us around the island. We use it regularly for tours".
>
> The lost luggage slipped from my thinking as I mounted the steps of the bus. Yes, this was a school bus. Looking down the cabin most people but not all were smiling as the bus moved off.

Fortunately, someone complained early in the tour through their parents back to **CYTA** about the lack of fresh fruit on the tour. You might say surely a complaint is not a fortunate event. Kevin called me.

As this is many years ago, the shops in the areas of New Zealand in which we were travelling were closed for four days around New-Year. At the time of this tour there was a half day Saturday trade and no Sunday trade. Around new-year the half day on Saturday did not happen. The explanation in regard to the fruit completed, I went on to say

"**Kevin,** about this coach..."

We started our New Zealand tour in the South Island, which allowed the **TOUR MEMBERS** to see the beautiful Milford Sound. We had a new ferry. It was a clear day. There was just the odd fluffy cloud on the horizon. I can assure you the Sound is as beautiful today as it was then.

However, a new ferry means new technology. Our captain miscalculated the return to the wharf crashing into an overhanging pole, covering those sitting underneath with splintering wood and breaking glass.

We were back on the school bus which was about to be replaced. The replacement had not come soon enough. We went nowhere. The bus did not start. The bus had broken down. A coach courtesy of Kevin was on its way but would not reach us till the ice had run out on the meat and an esky full of dinner to be cooked had "gone off".

"Enough" you say. Ok but tour difficulties were not over.

Crossing the straight to the North Island went largely without incident with only one of our **TOUR MEMBERS** suffering from sea sickness.

Making our way north we reached the "town" of Hamilton. More like a village then, it only has 176,500 inhabitants today. It was raining. Tired after helping the **TOUR MEMBERs** set up tents and establish camp, I and two of the male **TOUR MEMBER**s who had been helping put up the tents in heavy rain decided to sleep in the camp laundry. It was after 10PM (2200). Sleep came quickly but not for long as we laundry squatters were awakened by two police officers.

"Are you in charge?" said one of the officers, directing his question to the group camping in the laundry.

"Yes", I replied exhausted,

"Three **MEMBERS** of your tour have been run over. You need to come to the hospital now".

One person had suffered a badly broken leg. Two others had been hit by the car. One was grazed and ill from shock but not badly injured. She was kept in over-night. Another TOUR

MEMBER kept in overnight limped into camp the next morning at breakfast time.

Kevin was rung long after midnight Sydney time.

The tour group was advised of the accident, the next morning. There was an unscheduled trip to the hospital for the whole tour group. The driver wanted to continue with the tour immediately. The injured weren't coming so he wanted to get on the road. The driver lost the argument but moved the coach to the next street. Only three people were allowed in to see the injured.

With one of the injured back on tour, coming through the ward door we were greeted by another of the three injured **TOUR MEMBERS** who had convinced the hospital staff she was well, had not thrown up and was feeling fine. "I am re-joining the tour" she said. Promises were made to keep a watch on her and go straight to a hospital if she had any problems.

Right everyone on the coach. Wait, where was the **HOSTESS** and two of our **TOUR MEMBERS**? The driver was fuming, with the further delay. No sign of the three. We left, me wondering what had happened and what to say when I rang Australia.

We found all three hitchhiking around 70 km up the road. The **HOSTESS** had believed the threat I had made to leave anyone behind, the next time someone was late. The coach had been *moved to a side street by the driver while parked at the hospital and she thought we had gone.*

Oh, the injured **TOUR MEMBER** *kept in overnight, a young woman who said she was well enough to travel almost vomited shortly after the coach began to move. Was this a slight twisting of the truth for the hospital staff? My language was a little more focussed than that when I talked to her.*

No. She admitted that everything she told the hospital nurses was untrue. The young woman did make it home to Australia in one piece.

Parents flew in from Australia. But that is enough of this story. There is more but let's move on. Happily, the badly injured **TOUR MEMBER** *(a Christian) made a full recovery.*

The flight home was great.

However, with all that was said and that which was not, still people came to Christ as a result of the tour and are still solid Christians today."

New Zealand yet again more good than bad

Ross Killick remembers his introduction to touring, which occurred in New Zealand.

"I believe that Les Shakespeare a church leader at my church Green Point Baptist convinced Kevin Craik to allow me to go on NZ trip as "leader in training" in summer of 1970-71 with possibility of leading NZ trip the following summer. So the following summer (1971-1972) that's what happened. It was an amazing experience. There were about 25 girls and 10 boys, one dodgy old slow bus, a local driver who liked a beer, and a wonderful **HOSTESS Lois McCaffrey** who kept me in check.

We were caught in a cyclone and had a very rough crossing on the Cook Strait Interislander ferry. As we were not able to camp due to the cyclone, we arranged to sleep over in Nelson Baptist Church Hall. We cooked inside which was a mistake as the pressure cooker popped spraying food onto ceiling. When we got to Queenstown we set up camp only to be surrounded by 30 bikies wanting to cause trouble. We survived and continued to endlessly play Peter, Paul and Mary cassettes while travelling in the coach."

Margaret Quinn (Née Hollier) remembers that:

(On another tour to New Zealand), *"the Maxi Brakes failed while we were coming down a winding road and about to cross a bridge at Hass Pass. Of the choices available to stop the runaway coach, the driver chose to cross the bridge. There was a car with two girls in it heading toward us. The coach collided with the car but no one was seriously hurt. That accident with the car saved us from more serious injuries."*

Barrier Reef - the good and the unexpected
I remember a trip to the Barrier Reef with **Joan Power** as the **HOSTESS**, where two girls caused a furore back in Sydney and two young enthusiastic Christian men put me on the spot:

> "A Barrier Reef trip went well except for one incident. One night rain was about so the **HOSTESS** and a few of the **TOUR MEMBERS** decided to sleep in a recently constructed yet unused toilet block. Among the small group were two young girls, about sixteen years old. They had been offered help to put up their tent but declined. Two of the male **TOUR MEMBERs** offered to sleep outside to provide an obstruction should anyone try to enter. Having checked several times during the night it was clear to me that these two gallant men had been good to their word. I should note that one of the men was **Paul Webb**."

A side note: **Paul Webb** was a man of substance, a man of *God*. Paul was not short on words but his presence, rather than words, was a great support to me. He was a great support to many other people. Paul was a gentleman who would always be available if someone needed a hand. You will find out more about Paul in the chapter dealing with **Death coming to the TEAM**

> "The next day of the Barrier Reef tours comes a call from Kevin. The two young girls had told their parents they slept in a toilet with two men. Of course they had forgotten to mention that one of the **TOUR LEADER**S, our **HOSTESS Joan**,

was with them and that they had been offered help more than once with their tent. The two men had slept outside and the toilet block as distinct from a single toilet was unused. Why did they omit these details? "

"To …….. our parents" (words somewhat censured)

> **A side note:** I wonder if these once young girls now in their sixties have encountered a similar experience if they have had children.

"On the same tour two young men from Newcastle had befriended a woman from another tour. They had explained something of the Christian life. Approaching me they rapidly convinced me to preach the gospel in the hearing of this woman after dinner that night.

Camp was set so that the **CYTA** group were adjacent to the group the woman was travelling with. I preached on John 3:16 breaking the verse down into component parts. No one knows what if any impact the sermon had on the woman, but the gospel was preached, and the rest is with the Holy Spirit to complete."

Barrier Reef - the bad but all good in the end
Glennis Craig (Née Richardson) recalls another Barrier Reef tour that was a wash out.

"The Barrier Reef Tour was literally a wash-out. The first night at Tallebudgera ended up with us all floating on our air beds as it rained all night.

> The nearby creek broke its banks right into our tents. Under way again and we almost make it into Mackay. The Queensland police closed the flooding roads behind us.
>
> We spent the week in the local church hall having concerts, card nights. A story of our plight and pictures ended up on the front of the local paper. Just to "keep spirits up" **Glen Calnan** swung a billy that emptied on his arm and ended up burnt. One overcast day we made it out to Green Island. Myself, and a few other **TOUR MEMBERS** only remember feeling green all the way there and back! On another day we were out swimming when one of the girls fell through a pontoon and got badly hurt and spent 2 days in hospital.
>
> We came up with a motto:
>
>> 'Barrier Reef or Bust' - we did make it eventually!"

Glennis did work at the **LODGE** on many occasions and was part of the tour staff on a snow tour and one an unusual tour.

> "**Mel Kroenert, Linda Webb, Geof Hyde** and myself, (**Glennis**) took a group of Kiwi Youth Leaders to Port Macquarie for a week."

Glennis adds her graphic memories of a Barrier Reef tour.

> "One particular creek looked passable according to the driver, so he drove through it. Although the coach made it through OK, the luggage

compartment was flooded and many of the suitcases were saturated. I was lucky, as my pack was on top, it survived without getting wet. Everyone except me spent the next day in an outback Queensland town, Emerald, using the local laundromat to dry their clothes and sleeping bags.

The next leg of the trip was to Rockhampton, due to the floods we had to drive along dirt roads into Rockhampton that were covered with about 30 cm of water. The area we were in is well known for the black soil plains and we got bogged. A local farmer was luckily nearby and was able to pull us out with his tractor, but we all had to get out of the coach to make it lighter. Consequently we were all wet and muddy by the end of the day!

Most of the camping grounds we were scheduled to use had been flooded out, so we ended up staying in an old school building in Rockhampton, sleeping in the open veranda.

One of the girls on the trip was a tourist from Ireland where they don't have any creepy crawlies. Early one morning a huntsman spider dropped down from the roof directly onto her and she was in an absolute state of shock for hours.

In spite of the dramas in getting to the Barrier Reef, the rest of the trip was uneventful and very enjoyable."

Going places - CYTA

Yet another trip to the Barrier Reef this time with **Max Watson.**

> "The 1974/5 Barrier Reef trip was led by **Bob and Wendy Dierikx** and I was the Assistant **TOUR LEADER**. This was my first extended trip on **TEAM**. **Les Shakespeare** (a popular coach driver from the Central Coast) was our Coach Captain. It was a full coach.
>
> It was a very wet time. Cyclone rain hit the camping ground and we were playing soccer during the rain. A little old lady came out of her van and said":
>
> 'You's must be Christians, no one else would be silly enough to play soccer in this rain.'

To Perth and back with an unusual request

Christine Pegram was the HOSTESS on a WA tour at the end of 1972 with *John Stone* as TOUR LEADER. Christine recalls:

> "Kevin asked us to bring back one of the unused telegraph poles from the Nullarbor. When we found an unused poll everyone got into helping get it out of the ground. It took a lot of twisting and pulling and whenever a vehicle went past we stopped and looked like we were just having an innocent break in the middle of nowhere. Finally it was removed and put on the floor of the coach. We had to stop for quarantine inspection at the SA border so there was a move out of the coach to try and stop the inspectors boarding it and

seeing the pole! We finally, got it back to Sydney, but I've never heard what happened to it. Maybe Kev has it in storage?"

> **A side note:** Kevin has now revealed why he wanted the pole. It was to be used and was used as a **flag pole**

"On the same trip, again crossing the Nullarbor, our wonderful driver, the late **Paul McCaffery** (also known as **Rusty Wrong-way**), chased a Pioneer coach which was leaking water at the back. Paul finally caught up with it and the driver met Paul at the back of the coach. Paul put his hand under the leak and said to the Pioneer driver."

"You're losing water, mate" to which the Pioneer driver replied:

"Oh, that's just the john overflowing!!"

The look on Paul's face was hilarious and that was at a time before anyone had heard of hand sanitiser."

The good and the unusual
Max Watson recalls

"The 1975/6 WA trip was led by Ken and Dianne McGill, and I was the assistant; this was an epic trip and the last **CYTA** WA trip that travelled over the Nullarbor on the dirt road".

This trip had its share of characters, including a guy who insisted we call him the Fonz or Fonzie.

> **A side note**: I had this passenger on one of my tours. This person went on several tours and insisted he dress like, talk like and be called the Fonz or Fonzie. His name was Alan. Which name, do you the reader like better?

Max goes on with the "Fonz" tour to WA.

> "There was a group of **TOUR MEMBERs** that liked to dance in the aisle. Seeing the Dog Rock in Albany (which is where all direction to Albany locations started) "and climbing the Gloucester Tree were highlights of this trip south of Perth. The day trip to Rottnest Island was met with very bad weather.
>
> The boat was heaving and pitching around 12 feet (3 to 4 metres) in very rough seas and many people were turning green, I said to a group of our people 'I'm hungry I feel like a pork chop', which was greeted with groans and a rush for the railing
>
> On our return to camp, we found all but 2 tents flattened by the storm. There were long hours and much struggling to fix things up with lots of trips to the laundry to wash all our clothes.

Central Australia – the middle of nowhere

Max Watson recalls one of the characters he met in Central Australia while leading tour:

> "One of the joys of being at Uluru (formerly known by its non-indigenous name of Ayers Rock) in those days was **Lofty** who led tours of

the area while telling stories of the bush and "The Rock'. His real name was **Herman Zanker**. I was very sad to hear in late 79 that he had passed away. Lofty loved "The Rock" and he loved the old hymns. The **TOUR MEMBERs** went into the Cathedral Cave and sang for him. The cave had excellent acoustics and standing on the ground he could hear perfectly".

Max penned a poem on hearing of the death of Lofty on 25/10/79

Lofty

"He was Christened Herman Zanker, bushman true and bold,

He had no claim to fame, so the story is told.

But regardless of how unknown was he or how obscure as one old man,

He will always be famous to me, and in my heart hold a position grand.

The Lord is his shepherd. He shall not want.

Known simply as 'Lofty,' his manner was rather nonchalant.

And of all the species of flowers, he could tell you their names, every bud,

Of Aboriginal myths and legends and wise cracks he'd bring down with a thud.

In teaching city dwellers, he revelled and enjoyed,

> Of showing us "The Rock" he loved, in this was he employed.
>
> To life-long studies of the wild, his knowledge was so vast,
>
> But as to senseless vandalism, he was left aghast.
>
> The desert country was his home he loved it with his life,
>
> He would speak no bad of it, or of the afterlife.
>
> To God I prayed he trusted, and had 'the faith' in Him,
>
> So the 'Rock of Ages' I believe, he is abiding in."

Ros West has memories of:

> "Having to push a broken-down coach at one stage on a 1978 Central Australian Tour led by **Geof Hyde**"

John Grinsell also has memories of broken down coaches and of other tours

> "I went on the **CYTA** tour to Central Australia as a **TOUR MEMBER**. I remember the coach broke down 120 km from Tenant Creek. An empty road train towed us into Tennant creek for 3 days there. It was a great tour of fun and fellowship. From there I joined the **CYTA TEAM**.
>
> I was privileged to lead tours including snow, Central Australia, Barrier Reef, Western Australia, Tasmania and Fuji. It was great time of

fun and fellowship on these tours. As well as many people impacted in their faith and even couples meeting each other and getting married. These tours certainly provided a great alternative to touring Australia and the world".

Max Watson remembers,

*"In July '79 I led the Central Australia tour, with **Anne MacDonald**. Great trip, camel rides the works. I had the saddest moment in my **CYTA** time when Kev rang me on Boxing Day to tell me that Anne had been killed in a car accident."*

> **A side note:** The story of, and postscript to it of the tragic death of **Anne Macdonald** appears in the chapter that covers: **Death comes to the TEAM.**

Fiji not all it's cracked up to be
Ross Killick toured to in Fiji.

"In the summer 1972-73 I led a tour to Fiji. The travel group consisted of about 20 females and 10 guys. We bought meat from a shop in Nadi which had no refrigeration. The meat went quickly on to ice.

When we stayed in a village near Sigatoka we drank kava with the chief, danced with the chief's wife, watched a pig being prepared for Hangi. We stayed in school accommodation where half of the group got diarrhoea. Possibly due to the Hangi the day before which made its presence felt long after finishing the meal. I was one of a few who did not suffer, so I borrowed the school's vehicle to get to the island hospital to get assistance.

We went reef fishing off Nananu-i-Ra Island near the north coast. Though this was a great experience we got seasick from the fumes in the small boat in which we travelled."

Tours – short comments on assorted tours
The good the bad, and the unusual
Steve Castle "remembers on one trip he was on.

"That the **TOUR LEADER** miscounted the number of guys and girls, resulting in not enough tents to allow people do the normal which was sleeping two to a tent, boys, segregated from girls. On that trip the **TOUR LEADER** had an assistant leader, so we both bunked down in the cook tent which was a three metre square marquee that we stored all the food in. In the middle of the night I heard a rustling sound, looked around and saw a possum attacking the tomatoes. My assistant picked up a thong, threw it at the possum and we both promptly went back to sleep.

Longer trips meant the leaders were responsible for organising day excursions and purchasing fresh fruit and vegetables, the menu and shopping list for the entire trip having been preplanned by Jan Craik who was also a qualified nurse."

Yvonne Bubb recalls:

"I remember Lightning Ridge trip. We slept on air beds that were on some sort of matting. There were rows of bedding. Sleeping in very cold weather but not sleeping much. I took a friend from work with me and we shared my blanket to keep us warm, but Jacqui, my friend pushed it away from her so I had double layer. It was still too cold.

Other than the cold, I remember it was a great trip! Also another mystery trip where we ended up sleeping in a sheep shearing shed, in some sort of pens. These were great memories."

Max Watson posted on the **CYTA** Facebook page that on one overseas trip that:

"..Marilyn Lee and Steve Castle slept in the cook tent and got raided by a possum in the middle of the night".

"I threw a boot at it. We told the **TOURS MEMBERS** it was a bear."

Rossanne Hyde wrote on the **CYTA** Facebook page in April 2020 that she and Geof's trip into COVID quarantine reminded her of the **CYTA** mystery tours.

"Yesterday as we hopped on the bus at the airport for the trip to our hotel for 2 weeks isolation I said to Geof- this is like the old **CYTA**

> *mystery tours. None of us or the bus driver knew what our destination was."*

> **Everything old is new again**

Serious problems

A **TOUR LEADER** that had some monumental problems. **David Joyce.**

> "On the dirt road leaving Mt Isa in Central Queensland the rain starts bucketing down. We pass many others stranded in the mud. Later, a detour took us off the road through deep water and the Hino was struggling until it was about to stop, when we got back on the sealed road. On we drove in the darkness until suddenly after crossing a single lane bridge the bus came to a sudden stop, bogged in mud. Despite the valiant effort of **TOUR MEMBERs** trying to dig us out and put logs under the wheels, there we stayed in the middle of nowhere. Many of us prayed and God provided of all things, a 3-trailer road train that was able to reverse just enough to tow us out, getting some wheels back on the road.
>
> A **TOUR MEMBER** was coughing and struggling to climb the trail at Lake Louise in Canada. His pulse was very high, so he was asked to make his way very slowly down the trail and wait for us. When we returned, he seemed OK but that night he continued coughing. I promised him that we would get him checked out the next morning.

After taking him to Banff Hospital I was informed that he would not be continuing with us on the trip, as he would be flown immediately to Calgary Hospital for open heart surgery! Praise The Lord the surgery was a success.

Driving on the Motorway in France we see an approaching car lose control of the boat he is towing at high speed. It sways side to side and flips the centre divider and lands spinning just behind our coach, just seconds away from a direct hit into the coach windscreen.

Asking the **TOUR MEMBERs** to stop and have a rest as we climbed The Rock, I said there is nothing to prove by overdoing it, like him, pointing at a middle age, overweight guy pushing himself too hard. We were shocked to find the same man had passed away once he had reached the top.

After pulling into the Carnarvon Gorge QLD campsite, the **HOSTESS** came up to me and said, "Dave, the door to the trailer is open and there is no food or equipment." A **TOUR MEMBER** and I started the drive back to see what we could find. Fortunately, the door had opened when we hit the cattle grid at the entrance to the park and all the missing items were littered along the road.

On a lighter note, going to bed, I found half a frankfurter in my sock after having a wrestle that day. I didn't need a midnight snack.

There was the kind girl who volunteered to wash some clothes for me, but with her new pink pyjamas. "They were my favourite grundies!" I shouted. Next thing I know I am presented with a new T-shirt saying, "I AM WEARING MY FAVOURITE GRUNDIES!" And yes, I wore it.

Spiritual highlights included, reading together St Paul's speech to the 'men of Athens' on Mars Hill looking over Athens. Also, reading the Beatitudes on the Mount near the Sea of Galilee.

Many **TOUR MEMBERS** *came on tour at a pivotal moment in their lives. Many of the* **TOUR MEMBERS** *were people who were either looking for a new start or seeking friends and fellowship. Some were able to make objective decisions that would affect their lives, whether it was in regard to their job or related to relationships, a commitment to Christ or rededication, or just understanding more about, for example, discipleship, spiritual gifts, or assurance of salvation, from the devotion times.*

Tour Reflections from the Desk of Kevin Craik

A roll over

"*Arthur and Bev Rickersy's* tour of New Zealand saw the coach roll-over. They were travelling along the narrow and unsealed Western Road towards Greymouth. Passing an on-coming vehicle, the weight of the coach caused the side of the road to give way, the coach rolling down a small embankment. Newspaper headlines: "4 Australian **TOUR MEMBER**S in hospital" A bit sensational as they were in hospital only overnight."

Almost a drop in the ocean

"On **Kevin and Jan's** Tasmanian tour the coach was travelling along a narrow road near St Helen's, on New Year's Day, following torrential rain the night before, the coach paused to view the ocean. The coach slowly started tipping towards a huge drop to the water below. The coach could go neither forward nor back. How to get out of trouble?

Just around the previous corner, the electricity people, with their big crane truck, had just finished repairing fallen wires. All **TOUR MEMBERS** were gingerly and slowly extricated. After that, the electricity guys hooked up to the front of the coach and fortunately got it back onto solid earth, thus avoiding the danger of the coach falling into the ocean below."

A view from the bridge

"On **Peter and Margaret Croft's** Cairns Tour in 1968 Cliff Warburton drove the coach for many kilometres along the Port Douglas beach. He turned off onto what appeared to be a bush track and took the coach over a wooden bridge, slightly narrower in width than that of the overhanging width of the coach. It was about 5m above the river below. Cliff stopped the coach about mid-way over the bridge for photographs and said to the group:

"Look it's only a Cyclone"

But the ticket says

"On the 1976 USA tour **Bob and Wendy Dierikx** tour flights to Australia from Honolulu left between 11:30pm and midnight, so it was easy for dates to be misunderstood. Upon arrival, the **PAN-AM staff** said,

"Guys, you're not due here till tomorrow night!"

"However, all the tickets said tonight! PAN-AM had written the tickets. The airline kindly gave the group – at no expense – another 24 hours for their tour. This included a stay at a four star hotel."

"Yes I am staying at the YMCA."

Jan had many hair-raising stories – this was just one of them. Jan had just flown in to San Francisco to join this tour, from a music seminar in the Rocky Mountains that was the forerunner to the **AUSTALIAN CHRISTIAN MUSIC SEMINAR**.

She caught a cab from the airport to the YMCA hostel and a surprised **cabbie said**,

"Are you sure that's where you want to go there?"

The **YMCA** *was not in the nicest part of San Francisco. Upon arrival at 1am, everything was locked up and boarded. The cabbie drove off quickly, but no-one would answer the door. Eventually Jan was asked from behind the door, what did she want? She replied,*

"I'm booked in!" - "No you're not, madam!" came back the **retort of the manager.**

The problem was that the group booking was not in her name. The group was booked in as Bob Dierikx's group. Eventually the clerk got Bob out of bed and solved the problem.

Hoppy to the rescue

Kevin relates this story. **"Graham Parkinson** led a tour to Western Australia in 1985. The **CYTA** mini-coach – the Hino – on its eighth trip to Perth safely travelled to Perth with 19 **TOUR MEMBERS** and returning to the East Coast, blew up the motor near the gold-mining area of Coolgardie.

Graham and Alan Hale, by the good providence from above, were able to get a coach and trailer from the Hertz rental car company. The Hertz franchise was willing to let them take the coach and trailer home on a one-way trip to Sydney,

> whilst the Hino came home, minus the roof-top luggage rack, on two flat-top rail cars.
>
> A good friend of **CYTA**, Graham "Hoppy" Hopkinson of Hopkinsons Coaches, arrived at Clyde goods yard, arranged for a tow-truck to take the coach to his workshop and had his mechanics refit a replacement motor, remounted the roof-rack and got the coach back on the road in double-quick time."

A sad sight

Kevin Craik relates a story told to him:

> "Any Overland tour from Kathmandu can have serious problems. This is a sad commentary on one country through which **CYTA** tours travelled. On one tour, children in Pakistan were throwing themselves against the side of the moving coach. Parents of the children demanded the police to take action and a ransom (a bribe) was paid to free the driver from his 6 days in jail."

Surprise, Surprise

Kevin Craik was and probably still is a true romantic at heart.

> "There was a surprise romantic rendezvous I organised in the French Riviera for two **TEAM MEMBERS**. In 1986, I arranged for the full-time **CYTA TOUR LEADER Jeff Robinson** to fly into Nice, to meet up with his girlfriend **Karen**, on route to him leading the 33-day Scandinavian 'Nordic Explorer' tour.

Karen was travelling on the 54-day 'Grand European', Tour at the time, quite oblivious to what was about to happen. Jeff recalls his sense of excitement and anticipation growing as his flight approached France. He made his way to the rendezvous point on a certain street corner and waited eagerly until the tour coach pulled up for lunch.

What a surprise Karen - and all the other passengers on the Europe tour - got, when the coach pulled up and Jeff boarded the coach in the middle of Nice. There was much excitement along with tears of joy! Jeff was able to spend the last week of the Europe tour with Karen travelling through France, Monaco and Spain, before they separated again, with Jeff going on to lead the **CYTA** Scandinavia tour and then the mini coach tour of England. When they were reunited in Australia later in the year, Jeff and Karen announced their engagement and were married the following year."

Two coincidences of timing
Coincidence One- Kevin catches Geof changing gear

Geof Hyde was leading a USA tour when the coach that was transporting **TOUR MEMBERS** had motor problems. The tour was delayed 2 days for repairs.

Kevin called the repair shop to be told Geof had just left and believed to be heading towards to a

> campground. Kevin referred to a USA Campgrounds Guide as this camp was not in the itinerary. He called the first listed camp to be **asked this question**:
>
> **'Is he driving a Chevy van that is fawn coloured?'**
>
> Believe it or not, Geof was just driving up the driveway at that very instant! Kevin got all the up-to-date information on the tour."

Coincidence Two - **Near at hand**

> "**David Joyce** was leading a Europe tour when Kevin needed to contact him. Upon calling the campground and while asking the manager to give David a message, the camp ground manger said:
>
> "Here, you give it to him directly!"
>
> "He handed the phone out to David out the office window."

Max Watson summed up his reflections on tours long and short by when he described what **CYTA** was all about as follows:

> **"The most significant reflection I have of tours with CYTA is the number of people won for Christ. There were more than just a few."**

Let us move onto the fluffy white, wet snow tours.

Going places - CYTA

24. Snow Weekends

The previous chapter mentioned the non-snow tours. This chapter provides some reflections specific to those cold, wonderful, wet snow tours.

Why a separate chapter?

The Snow tours were the start of CYTA and as far as tours went represented pretty much the end. Snow was the backbone of the tour operations of **CYTA.**

Andrew Wardle remembers **CYTA** from the days that the organisation used the Cooma Salvation Army buildings for accommodation.

> *"I first heard of* **CYTA** *when I was asked by my sister if I was willing to make up numbers on a Scripture Union staff snow trip in the winter of 1969. I had recently been discharged from two years of National Service.* **CYTA** *was using the Salvation Army facilities for accommodation. I became involved after the Cairns-Cooktown 1972 tour with* **Graeme Leishman** *as Leader and* **Lois Reilly** *was* **HOSTESS** *when they talked about potential volunteers for the* **TEAM**.*"*

Kevin Hastie recalls the snow tours.

> *"The Snow tours started on Friday. Load a coach after dark, leave at 9pm, generally no sleep until midnight Saturday. Up at 6 on Sunday, and home about 11pm. Back to work Monday morning for a rest. Those were the days, loved it."*

Going places - CYTA

Steve Castle describes snow week ends

> "The snow weekends meant leaving Sydney at 8pm on a Friday, sleeping (or trying to) on the ten hour trip (with rest stops. The roads were a lot worse back then) to Cooma. Before **CYTA** purchased the Cooma **LODGE**, breakfast was at a café in Jindabyne, later it was at the lodge. Saturday was spent on the ski fields. It seemed to take "hours" on the gas rings to heat water On Sunday there was a long drive back to Sydney, with a tour of the sights of Canberra, arriving back around 9pm, being totally exhausted for work on Monday!"

Max Watson recalls his first snow trip and his decision to join the **CYTA TEAM**

> "My first experience of **CYTA** was a snow trip in 1971. I simply can't remember how many snow tours I led. Cooking hotdogs in blizzard conditions, near impossible.
>
> After my first snow trip I joined the **TEAM** and immediately got involved in Tuesday night's maintaining the gear at Everton Road."

Colleen and **Vic Barrington** were involved in the early snow tours, where they had to turn down a request from the general skiing population:

> "While we were cooking lunch for our coach load of hungry skiers, when other skiers came of the slope and begged us to sell them whatever we were cooking. We were tempted but not wanting

> to face the wrath of our coach buddies if we ran out before everyone on tour had, had enough we had to say no."

Early catering for the **TOUR MEMBERS** was sourced from on snow outlets such as the Smiggins Hole Hotel. But why not cook it yourself.

James Gow remembers a late phone call.

> "Then there was the phone-call asking":
>
> 'What are you doing at the end of this week? Can you lead a snow tour?' It was Kevin.
>
> "Sure, I replied how hard could that be? 40+ "Egyptians" on a Hopkinson coach. But aside from the opportunities, skills and stories and of course there are plenty of stories behind these short reflections, I was taught the power of placing trust in someone younger and providing them with opportunities to serve. For me, it built enormous confidence as I moved into adult life.'

A side note: James Gow has suggested that you should never lean your skis on the side of the coach. They could fall and be broken, run over by coach as it takes off or stolen by a passer-by. Some wise words of experience?

Once coaches started to operate they did not at first stop at the **LODGE**, on the Saturday, as there was no **LODGE** except of what could be in the minds of the original Directors. Even when the Lodge existed the tours did not stop there for breakfast for some years.

Going places - CYTA

Coaches went straight to a Jindabyne café who supplied the tour groups with breakfast. The breakfast was comprised of steak and eggs and sides. *"Johnny"* the proprietor, took great pleasure in opening the freezer and showing what must have been hundreds of frozen steaks he had purchased before the start of the season.

Johnny trusted Kevin with the bill for the season's breakfast being paid at the end of each snow season. Over time the Lodge was better prepared to offer breakfast and coaches stopped there for breakfast. Johnny also supplied 35mm film to **CYTA** that the early **TOUR LEADER**s sold off **TOUR MEMBERS** at cost.

Dinner on the way home from the snow was a boxed chicken meal in Goulburn on the early tours. **CYTA** decided to try an alternative approach during the 1970's of stopping at a working sheep station, Pelican Sheep Station, for dinner. Pelican Station which is around 10Kms from Goulburn offers accommodation and meals.

Sunday night dinner for **TEAM** and **TOUR MEMBERS** became a sit-down meal at a table rather than chicken boxes sitting on wet grass in the park. Seating was often regimented for coach groups with strict uncompromising instructions given on where to sit. However, the food was good, and you did not need to try to find shelter or run for the coach if winter rain began to fall.

For *Marilyn Lee*, Pelcian is remembered as a special place

> *"Remember it well. **Gary Lee** and I had our first walk together"*

Going places - CYTA

A great finishing point as Kevin wanted a chapter on the European Tours, which is coming up next.

25. Grand Europe Tours

Kevin requested a separate chapter dedicated to the Europe/Grand European and Overland tours. There are a few comments on Europe tours in an earlier chapter but this chapter gets to the heart of several Europe and Overland tours.

Extended tours offered more time to extend relationships, a greater likelihood of long-term friendships and time for a possible moment of or even a lifetime romance as well as to hear the message of the sacrifice of *Jesus Christ*.

Overland 75 the trip that is still going
*From **Kathy** who was a **TOUR MEMBER** on the Overland trip of 1975*

> "The Overland was a life-changing experience in many ways. As a 24 year old in 1975, it was the first time I'd had the opportunity to observe and experience other cultures and religions. Having only experienced a mainly Christian/Western culture up to this point, the trip expanded my horizons in many ways. For this I will be forever grateful.
>
> Travelling with a group of other Christians through many of the locations mentioned in the Bible was a unique experience. It made visiting places such as Ephesus and Laodicea, much more meaningful when seen in the Biblical context, particularly having known about them through Scripture. Our group often had a devotional time at places of Biblical significance.

The Overland trip had a significant impact on my personal and spiritual growth thereafter. This was largely due to the experience that only such a trip can provide, particularly with a group of likeminded fellow travellers. Our (now) biannual Overland Reunions reinforce the value of the trip, in the friendships we have made, the fact that we can still recall many aspects of the Overland itinerary and the impact it has had on who we are today. The impact that the trip had on my life, takes on even greater significance over 46 years later! I often thank God for the amazing travel opportunity that was provided for me all those years ago."

Warren Wimble was also on the memorable Overland trip of 1975

"This was the best 3 months of my whole life.

Needing a fresh start in my life I heard from a friend who had been on a snow tour about this adventure, so I went along to the information meeting. From the outset I felt that this organisation was well-managed and led by God's guidance.

Travelling through countries where personal safety was not guaranteed troubled me a little. However, we were convinced by those who had travelled on previous tours that every precaution would be taken. We felt assured.

I had one dilemma, whether to take my piano accordion. The instrument and I had been inseparable since I was 11. (It was not particularly heavy, and I did have two hands.) After much soul searching, I decided to take it and it turned out to be the best decision I could have made. I played, and we sang, at several Christian fellowship gatherings in Kathmandu and India, brining joy and encouragement to struggling Christian Churches. It was magical to sing "Jesus Loves Me" with their native tongues overlaying our voices. We were praising God together, as one. It was also good to accompany daily devotions, singing around campfires, and lifting spirits during long breakdown stoppages.

Each day began with devotions. People on the tour took a turn to share. I felt God was with us no matter what confronted us. We did have several challenges where we prayed 'a lot'. Crossing the lawless Khyber Pass and several other unfriendly border crossings concerned us. We were constantly aware that we were suspected of trafficking drugs.

Travelling with fellow Christians was comforting as one could just "be you". We felt accepted and loved. Several of our group were new Christians and the witness of those more experienced, cemented their faith. The bond of our friendships is shown by our reunions every 2 years. Only 2 of our 28 are not contactable. Those who can attend, do.

Much laughter emanates as we view films and retell stories. Our Sundowner driver, **Ed Hall** *and* his wife Judy also attend our reunions. Ed has branded our group as one of his best.

I want to finish with a heart-felt "thank you" to **CYTA** and the behind the scenes support. Such support enabled us to grow as Christians, which carried through my life. From the comment sheets the office received after this Overland Tour, "the piano accordion playing" was what brought the group together."

> ***A side note:*** Warren with his trusty piano accordion also attended several **AUSTALIAN CHRISTIAN MUSIC SEMINAR**S.

Rick Gribble the overlander

"As "Overlanders", we used London as a base for further European travel. We attended All Souls Church in Langham Place and sat under the teaching of The Reverend John Stott. For a midweek young adults meeting there one night I arrived a little late to find a film already started and being unable to locate my friends I took the nearest seat available.

As the meeting finished the girl in the next seat shared how she had just come from this place called L'Abri, a Christian community in Switzerland. I couldn't believe it!

My brother had said to me, 'the Lord has better plans for you.' He had encouraged me before I left Australia that I should go to L'Abri. I mentioned that I had read one of Francis

Going places - CYTA

> *Schaeffer's books but the second one I didn't finish finding it too intellectual.*
>
> *The tears of the girl, who I sat next to at the meeting, welled up in her eyes. Oh no she said it is not like that. The Schaeffer's with compassion had taken her into their family home for the past 18 months when no other country would recognise her Rhodesian passport.*
>
> *"You must go to L'Abri" she implored and proceeded to write down in detail directions all the way to the front gate of L'Abri in Huemoz.*
>
> *Our God creates/uses circumstances co-ordinating the people who cross our path and even providing the seat we sit in. The seed sown in my mind before leaving Australia was sure being pushed along but for now as a small group of Overlanders we were booked and heading to Israel. From there I went to Nepal"*

Robyn was also on the memorable trip of '75

> *"I believe that the **CYTA** Overland trip had a profound effect on the person I am today. Besides being an ultimate adventure, with God as our Guide, the daily devotions kept our focus on who I was, a faith filled believer. Every day was a reminder of who God is and his masterpieces of creation, whether it be mountains or deserts.*
>
> *Three main experiences that grew me as a Christian are:*

Going places - CYTA

- At the Sunday service in Kabul, we met with American Christians who had the sign of the fish (ichthys) on their gate, as it was forbidden to have Christian churches. We had a fabulous time of fellowship and a great Praise and Worship.
- The visit to Ephesus saw me imagining and still I imagine the Apostle Paul standing on the hill and preaching to the masses. He was there proclaiming the Good News, the gospel of Christ.
- In the Goreme Valley I stood trying to understand that many had to flee from persecution, all because they believed in Jesus the Messiah. 1400 years later their stories are still being told. Such courage and commitment they had. "

Robyn finishes with a tribute to impresario Warren Wimble.

> "Warren Wimble, with your talent on the piano accordion and piano made praise and worship just that bit more special. Each person on that bus has helped me grow into the person I am".

Pam another **TOUR MEMBER** was also there in '75

> "Just before we left Sydney on the trip I'd been saving and planning toward, for about five years, Mum gave me a gift of a small New Testament. In the inscription she wrote the Bible verse:"

'**Joshua 1:9**. "Be strong and courageous. Do not be afraid; do not be discouraged for the Lord your God will be with you wherever you go."

Going places - CYTA

> "I guess she was concerned for me, setting off by myself on such an epic adventure, the first of my family ever to travel overseas. I know she was happy that I was travelling with **CYTA**. I had been to several meetings where I got to know some of the other travellers who would also be on my coach. I was blessed with a beautiful group of like-minded travellers in whose company I felt very safe. I remember daily devotions that we took in turns to deliver. It was a wonderful journey where we were well looked after by our drivers and able to see places that today would be too dangerous and too difficult to navigate.
>
> God's promise to be with me wherever I go was good for then but has continued throughout my life."

> *A side note:* I did change one word in Pam's reflection. She called the vehicle they travelled in a "bus", not a coach. Money in the jar please, Pam.

Lyn remembers that trip.

> "I was a relatively new Christian of only a couple of months when I joined the Overland trip. I had grown up in a Christian home but had avoided the hard decision, knowing it was all true but believing that my fun would stop. Therefore, the trip was a major opportunity for growth. I learnt on the trip via other Christians the importance of friendship in evangelism, the radical difference our words and actions can make to others and

the value of immersing yourself in the historical truth of the word of God. I saw how being a Christian resulted in true freedom and had opportunity to see in the lives of those around me, the true value of a walk with Jesus. Thus, from a Christian perspective no individual incident stands out but rather the impact of the individuals on my new walk with the King of Kings and Lord of Lords."

Brian West, recalls the bad that was really good on a trip to Europe

"The bus started blowing copious amounts of smoke from the second day of the tour from London, putting it out of commission on the following days while in Amsterdam. After a spare part was fitted, we then had to push start the bus to continue our journey to Cologne. It was exhausting (pardon the pun) work especially since there were so many, speed- humps in the camping ground.

The problem redeveloped after another 3 weeks, limping into a crowded camping ground in Florence late one evening. This time the brakes failed (fortunately only at low speed) and we managed to roll into a tree, saving us from plunging over a 4' drop.

We needed to get to Nice to pick up a replacement part (again) but only got as far as the border between Italy and France at Ventimiglia where we had to push the bus

> through the Italian checkpoint. Gave it one more try to get through the tunnels to the French side but got no more than 100 yards into the first tunnel before the crankshaft blew up and we somehow managed to back out into no-man's land, spending the night on board before another bus rescued us the following morning. In the end it was just a small part in a big adventure. We still had lots of fun with a friendly bunch of Christian travellers"

Rick is off again now to Nepal

> "In December 1975 the first **CYT** Nepal Trek had been planned well in advance. However, the original **TOUR LEADER** appointed was unfortunately involved in a motor accident six weeks out from the tour suffering a broken leg. As a replacement call-up to lead the tour meant getting fit quick. Nepal has two ways to hike, up or down.
>
> Each available weekend I drove to Govetts Leap Blackheath and donning my Swiss mountain boots ran down the mountain to Blue Gum Forest in the Grose Valley, an old campsite from Boys' Brigade days. More wearily I retraced my steps back up getting stronger each excursion.
>
> The Trek tour group enjoyed Nepal immensely. Some memories: Exposure to the Himalayan culture was a shock for many. The daylong bus trip to Pokhara accompanied by chickens and the narrow mountain roads without guideposts

> and 1,000 metre drop offs. Being directed to the Australian nurse at The Shining Hospital in Pokhara prior to the trek with her insisting we carry emergency medicine she offered – this turned out to be the overnight saving remedy for our incapacitated trekker who miraculously walked out to continue the trek the next morning.
>
> The cooks were going ahead on the trek to purchase a yak for dinner. We cared for those who struggled at the back of the trekking group. The beauty of the mountains was unforgettable. We enjoyed a meeting in a secret room with a Nepali Christian businessman who had earlier been imprisoned for some years because of his faith. Visiting the Leprosy Mission in Kathmandu and seeing the beauty in the smiling face of a patient who had accepted Jesus. We met a missionary who had been rejected three times for service only to study for yet another required qualification each time until he was finally accepted for the Lord's work in Nepal. There was so much to see and to change one for good."

The Tour of '76

Geof Hyde recalls several tours.

> "In 1976, I led the Overland trip. Some of the tour group still meet each year. Devotionals on this trip reflected the Biblical times of the areas in which we were travelling or the difference between the religions in each local area. Over the years I was fortunate to not only lead tours in Europe, Overland to London, North America,

Going places - CYTA

*New Zealand, Fiji and Australia. I was fortunate to be able to be involved with a few US tours with my wife while living in Canada. During my time with **CYTA**, I've been fortunate to see people become believers, and have had letters after saying they had become a Christian on the tour. It was a privilege to be able to baptise one new believer on a tour. On one tour a couple became engaged.*

*It was a privilege to be a part of this ministry for our Lord both as a **TOUR LEADER** then later working in the office. Another aspect of the ministry that I was privileged to be a part of was the **CYTA** concerts.*

*In the period of ministry with **CYTA** (1973-1984), I was fortunate to lead tours to Barrier Reef Queensland, Central Australia, Western Australia, Tasmania, New Zealand, Fiji, and Overland to Europe, Grand Europe and North America/Canada.*

*Who would have thought a hitchhiking trip in north Queensland and meeting Kevin on a corner would lead to many fulfilling years of ministry with **CYTA**."*

Steve Castle recalls:

*"1976 saw me take an eight-week camping trip with **CYTA** through Europe. I had only just started going out with Jenni two months earlier, so being away for eight weeks was tough on both of us. That trip was a load of fun, but*

relatively uneventful except for our coach being broken into and a lot of our belongings stolen.

Our **TOUR LEADER***,* **Geof Hyde***, (called Courier in those days) had advised us that leaving valuables in our tent in that area (Nice, on the French Riviera) was not advisable. This was because thieves often slashed open tents and sleeping bags with people still in them to look for valuables.*

Consequently, we left our valuables in the coach which was then parked in a secure coach parking area. The next day we were informed that all coaches in the parking lot had been ransacked overnight by professionals who had used graphite grease to break the locks. I had a movie camera, still camera and travellers' cheques stolen. Passports were not taken. A passenger in one of the other coaches had purchased a set of glass beer steins in Germany; these had been picked up and smashed all over the coach floor.

I was unable to replace the cheques for 2 days so was a bit short of cash for a while. A replacement movie camera was purchased later in the trip, the still camera I had borrowed from a friend at work. It was later replaced from a payout from the insurance company."

Another oft discussed trip in 1981
Rod Derley was the **TOUR LEADER** on the 1981 Grand Europe tour that in 2021 had a forty-year reunion. The group hold a reunion every two years.

> *"For 45 young Aussies embarking on camping tour through Central Europe visiting 14 countries/principalities was the adventure of their lifetime. And this 1981 **CYTA**/Sundowners trek did not disappoint. Our tour consisted of 3 married couples, 34 single ladies and 5 single men. Apart from a few who had travelled with friends, we were all mostly strangers who became a temporary family. We laughed together, cried together and watched over each other.*
>
> *There were many **memorable moments (#)** on tour, far too numerous to include them all, but below are a few stand outs.*
>
> *#1 – Each day began with a devotional. We managed to cover the entire book of Romans on tour. Through our witness and love, one tour MEMBER committed her life to Jesus on tour.*
>
> *#2 – Two of our **TOUR MEMBERs** who met on tour, struck up a romantic relationship. They celebrate 40 years of marriage next year.*
>
> *#3 – We took part in the Tour Coach Challenge at Seven Hills Camping in Rome. We performed two skits and sang "With Christ in my Vessel." As you can imagine our performance was mild*

compared to others, yet we managed to win second place.

#4 – The ground at Venice campsite was so hard it bent the tent pegs. The guys were quite busy at that camp setup.

#5 – In Vienna we attended a ballroom dancing evening. One young Austrian man, dressed very formally, asked one of our young ladies to dance to lots of cheering from our group. Our guys were very busy dancing that evening, and the girls were very patient.

There have been many wonderful memories over the last 40 years since returning and also some sadness. Many marriages have produced over 30 children (that we know of). Sadly, we have said goodbye to two of our **TOUR MEMBERs** and lost contact with a number of others. But for those of us who remain in contact, we are still family".

A side note: This is not the end of 1981 Overland trip. They will be meeting again. For the two people who cannot be contacted, if you read this book, then I am sure they would love to hear from you. If you have no point of contact you might look at Rod's Facebook page. You can email me, reidmess234@gmail.com. I will pass it on if you do not have any details of other former **TOUR MEMBERs**

Brian West recalls:

'Probably the most significant tour was the '87 Europe tour, the head count was wrong on Day 1 leaving a passenger behind in London. The passenger had snuck off to the toilet as we departed. They had to catch us up alone and found us in Belgium a few days later.

My wife found out she was pregnant with our first child. She had this confirmed in an Athens hospital. We still had 3 months of leading the tour in front of us to go. Not how you would plan it but God had us covered with medical passengers and even a midwife who is our adult daughter's namesake."

And here we leave Europe, the home of the classical, well everything and all the tours to go to the music of **CYTA**.

Going places - CYTA

Part Five - The Music

Going places - CYTA

27. CYTA Music – The Internationals

The challenges of bringing high profile overseas artists and speakers to Australia were numerous. The decision on who to invite, planning for, and management of an extended tour, and accommodation suitable for each person who came to Australia took considerable time. There were also the financial ramifications of tours to consider for **CYTA**.

Opera House Opening

In the words of Joe Cahill, the premier at the commencement of the project in 1954, the Sydney Opera House was being built to "help mould a better and more enlightened community," Completed on October 20, 1973 what better place for **CYTA** to host a concert of Christian music.

CYTA was part of the official first six weeks of the opening of the Sydney Opera House, which was built on the site of old tram sheds. **CYTA** had secured a two night booking for a total of 2,700 seats in the Concert Hall. Kevin had spent the previous five years securing the prized booking. The first enquiries in relation to the use of the Opera House by **CYTA** were made in 1968.

With about 5 months to go to the opening of "The House", there was no suitable artist to use on the first available Friday (November 3), and Saturday night available (December 1), in the Opera House. *Brian Willersdorf* (a regular CYTA snow tour chaplain mentioned in a later chapter) suggested **CYTA** contact **Andraé Crouch and The Disciples** as they were big time in the USA at the time.

The **CYTA DIRECTORS** acted immediately as they had less than 6 months to have a programme worthy of the Sydney Opera House and with *God*'s help, they did it! Kevin was asked to go to the USA to listen to and talk **to the** group after a huge concert in Houston, Texas Astrodome.

The result was that **Andraé and The Disciples** gave the first two Christian concerts in the Sydney Opera House, compered both nights by Brian Willersdorf. Brian's suggestion was prominent in helping change the face of Christian Worship in Australia.

The schedule for the first tour was:

C.Y.T.A: presents: Andraé Crouch and The Disciples
FRI 30 NOV 1973 SYDNEY OPERA HOUSE
SAT 1 DEC 1973 SYDNEY OPERA HOUSE
SUN 2 DEC 1973 MELBOURNE, DALLAS BROOKS HALL
MON 3 DEC 1973 MELBOURNE TOWN HALL
WED 5 DEC 1973 BANKSTOWN CIVIC CENTRE

The Internationals

Overseas acts started with the Opera House but rolled on for some years. ***Andraé* Crouch and The Disciples** made further appearances at the Sydney Opera House in 1975 and 1976 and toured Australia on multiple occasions. Besides the concerts they played at the "House", Andraé and the band also played concerts at

Going places - CYTA

the Sydney Town Hall and **CYTA *LODGE*** and in most capital cities in large auditoriums.

Kevin Craik reflects on the work of Andraé Crouch and The Disciples

> "Andraé Crouch and The Disciples played in various venues in Australia from high school auditoriums to outdoor tennis arenas, to the Sydney Opera House and the old Sydney Entertainment Centre, plus many major entertainment centres throughout Australia.
>
> I along with the other directors, are sure **Andraé** Crouch and his group's impact on Christian music around Australia was immense. **CYTA** was privileged for the friendships that were formed then and still continue to today"

Perry Morgan – a band MEMBER of ***Andraé Crouch and The Disciples*** reflects on his experience of Australia an experience very different from back home.

> "Born in 1944 in Los Angeles, at the age of 5, I was sent to a small town in Texas, along with a sister to be raised by a Great Aunt. Texas was considered the "South" where there was segregation which in essence was a separation of the "Whites" and "Blacks" in everything including schools, churches, neighbourhoods, down to separate public toilets and drinking fountains.

Going places - CYTA

At that age I didn't understand any of it and why my Black family and friends were treated differently from the "Whites".

*At the age of 17 I graduated from high school and returned to Los Angeles to live with my mother and continue my education. Soon afterward I met Andraé Crouch who witnessed to me about Jesus. Later on we started singing together along with Bili Thedford and Sherman Andrus as "The Four Disciples" which later became "**Andraé Crouch and The Disciples**".*

*One of our many tours with Andraé Crouch and The Disciples was to Australia, which excited us because we were the first Christian artists to be featured in the recently opened Sydney Opera House. This was in November 1973. It is here where we met the Directors of **CYTA**.*

We had never met people who were Caucasians, who showed so much love for a group of African Americans. Being from the Deep South, as they called it, I had never experienced people loving me just for being a human being who loved the Lord. At first I was a little perplexed, until I felt the Lord explaining to me that it was His love that the people of Australia showed me. The Lord reminded me His Word says, "If you are going to be my Disciples you must love one another". I will always remember our trips there and the people of

> Australia and cherish those whom we met. I will always love and appreciate Jan, Kevin and all the **CYTA TEAM** for their love and the wonderful experience they showed us.
>
> I was blessed to play in Australia. I went to a private golf course, not realising it was private and asked the secretary who was middle-aged if I could play. She asked if I had clubs and I said no. She then asked if I had shoes, and I said no as well. She then said, "Let's get you some". She brought clubs, shoes and a buggy, for which I didn't have to pay. I had the best time I had never experienced such kindness before or since on a golf course. "Aussie hospitality"

Thirty years after their last meeting, Jan Craik received a phone call from **Perry**, reflecting back on the times he was in Australia. He thanked Jan for the way he and other MEMBERS of The Disciples were treated.

What Perry was alluding to was that the group of Afro-American musicians were treated just the same as everyone else, as individual people. Facing discrimination in America, non-whites had to enter buildings by a separate entrance to the white population, use separate toilets and racially segregated drinking fountains. Perry and his fellow musicians while in Australia were treated just as everyone was treated. No special discrimination in favour of or against them.

Going places - CYTA

Fletch Wiley, early in 2021 passed on this comment on the time he spent with **CYTA**

> "Everywhere I went in the world I told people about **CYTA**. Kevin and Jan never did ANYTHING half-way. **Travel evangelism**. You want to go overland from Sydney to London? No problem; we'll be camping in Iran on the way. The Seeds of the Kingdom were scattered worldwide. And their music seminars were the best ever. Everyone mingled. We got short-sheeted which is a badge of honour!! So much love."

Evie Tournquist was born to Norwegian parents in the United States. She was the Dove Award recipient for outstanding work as a Gospel Artist of the Year for 1977 and 1978. In November, 1978 she became he first gospel artist to receive a gold album in Australia for the album "Gentle Moments".

Evie toured Australia with **CYTA** as the promoter on several occasions. **Evie Tournquist** toured 1976/77/78 including appearances at the Sydney Opera House. She also did concerts as adjunct to the 1979 Billy Graham Sydney Crusade.

There was a memorable concert at *CYTA LODGE*. The songs that **CYTA TEAM MEMBERS** considered their favourite Evie songs included:

> '***Give them all to Jesus, Four feet 11, Broken Up People, and Part the Waters***

John Craik an original **CYTA** Director travelled overseas to meet with Evie Tornqist and her parents,

Willy and Inge, to discuss the first visit of their daughter to Australia. Inge accompanied Evie on her first tour of Australia.

I remember Evie going on the Saturday morning music show – **Sounds**. *Evie* was supremely confident on stage but due to an unfortunate incident while appearing on a live music television show in Europe which occurred before touring Australia, she was reluctant to appear on television in music talk programs. Evie was booked to appear on the program **Sounds** which was hosted by Donnie Sutherland, a popular Sydney radio and television personality at the time.

In between segments Sutherland was chain smoking and gave the appearance of being tired and agitated. Evie was asked questions about her music. Donnie Sutherland kept the questions relevant and allowed Evie to answer in her own time and in her own way. It all went well.

Channel Seven, who screened the Sounds program, had made a special with Evie during the week before her live appearance on Sounds, which was shown in mid-week prime time in the week after the Sounds appearance."

Evie was a **TEAM** favourite as *Donald Hunt* recalls on the **CYTA** Facebook page.

> "Still have my Evie Albums (Vinyl) of course autographed by Evie when she sang at the lodge. Evie was great. What memories. Think it was an Easter weekend or January, my memory fades. I was on cushions right in front of stage.

Going places - CYTA

> *Evie was my idol, came down on coach from Sydney. Her stage was meeting area adjacent to the Dining Room of LODGE"*

I wonder if Robyn, Donald's wife knows that Evie was Donald's idol

Roger Vincent King recalls:

> *"I was her (Evie) chauffeur when Beth and I helped manage **CYTA** in Melbourne. I still have her albums. I have great memories of a lovely person. We took her to the Swedish seamen's church in Toorak while she visited us in Melbourne."*

> *"She also had a song "Special Delivery" and in a song session I used to do at Berwick Church of Christ. I played it and we announced that we were pregnant with our first child, Ruth, who was born in 1980."*

Evie is still a friend to so many. Even after 45 years, many of the people who were **CYTA TEAM MEMBERS** remember the opportunities they had to talk with Evie on the first tour and also in 1977 and 1978. The **CYTA TEAM** were also involved when Evie visited Sydney, for the 1979 Billy Graham Crusade.

Evie albums are still available today. Evie is a "Word" artist distributed by Sacred Productions Australia within Australia. You might check their website as there has been a special packaging released for Evie's albums

Ken Medema as well as well as being the key not presenter at one of the Comma Music Seminar's toured

Going places - CYTA

in 1979 and 1981. Information on him appears in the chapter on the **AUSTRALIAN CHRISTIAN MUSIC FOUNDATION**.

Barry Maguire was a one hit wonder, but what a hit. "Eve of Destruction", his biggest hit, recorded on a Thursday morning with lyrics scrawled on a piece of paper by the writer Phil Sloan, became the longest running protest song on the United States Billboard charts. The song was recorded in one take. The song was a protest against the registration of American youth for military service. It charted in various countries in Europe after being number one in the USA. It was on the radio the Monday following the week of its recording.

Kevin fills out the story pf *Barry Maguire*

> "Barry became a born-again Christian in 1971, influenced by Arthur Blessit, the cross-carrying evangelist. Barry made a surprise visit to **CYTA LODGE** on the long weekend in June 1976.
>
> In December 1985, he was the special guest at the Adelaide **AUSTALIAN CHRISTIAN MUSIC SEMINAR** and at the Cooma in January 1986. **CYTA** was the promoter of an East Coast Tour by Barry in 1987". He also appeared at the **AUSTALIAN CHRISTIAN MUSIC SEMINAR** as a featured artist."

Colleen and **Vic Barrington** were the Queensland managers for **CYTA**. They set up an office in their home. Colleen recalls the Queensland team involvement with touring artists:

Going places - CYTA

> "**CYTA** expanded into concerts and we did everything from planning venues, to selling tickets to taking artists to radio interviews, to ushering on the night on the night of a concert, to catering, to cleaning up as well as counting and banking the money from merchandise sales.
>
> Vic and I along with our small Queensland **TEAM** were privileged to have the responsibility of hosting, Andraé Crouch, Evie Tournquist, Barry McGuire, Joni Eareckson Tada, and Sandi Patti to Brisbane, as part of their Australian concert tours. They were fun days."

Surprisingly there were no contracts signed between **CYTA** and **Andraé Crouch** and or other overseas artists, till the third and final trip Andraé made with his band to Australia.

Despite being pursued by many international artists, the Directors only invited those who they felt lived their Christian lives off-stage as much as they came across on-stage. Jan Craik met with most of these artists in advance to ensure that from the stage these artists would present a faithful Christian message

27. CYTA Music - the locals

The beginnings and the locals

This music ministry is my favourite part of my involvement with **CYTA**. Music was always part of **CYTA**. **CYTA** in promoting and supporting the provision of all forms of Christian music seemed to be everywhere. Even in the early days of **CYTA** major concert events featuring Christian local artists as well as soloists were giving concerts sponsored by **CYTA**.

Every snow weekend there was a musical group giving a concert at the **CYTA LODGE**. Different musical groups, duos and soloists, appeared every weekend. I spent several years going around Greater Sydney, hearing groups play and practice and working out a schedule for the "next" snow season. The first end of year function, for those who had toured that year, became an annual event where music became a highlight of the program.

CYTA LODGE Saturday night concerts for snow tours, the **AUSTALIAN CHRISTIAN MUSIC SEMINAR**, *True Colours* a simulated night club environment which offered an alcohol-free night of entertainment were all part of the musical fabric of **CYTA**. Small concerts were staged around Sydney and in country NSW which featured local artists.

Even the early days of **CYTA** and the organisation's promotion of Christian music, the Directors were always willing to embrace new ideas appealing to young people of the day. One thing that was evident was the encouraging of individual Christian artists and groups who desired to witness about Jesus through music. **CYTA** always attempted to help and encourage local individuals and groups.

Foundation was one of these groups. It was a twelve-piece band with a very good tight professional big band sound. Others were encouraged and given opportunity to be part of many **CYTA** events. Some of the early bands were *Country Sound*, *Gary and Ray*, *The Wanderers* and *Just in Faith*, among others. Most probably these names are just but a memory now but at the time, bands such as these contributed strongly to the ministry of **CYTA**.

Many musicians/groups have not been mentioned but be assured, they played a great part in making **CYTA** right for its time. **CYTA** was indeed are thankful for their partnership with all praise being given to our *Lord* and *Saviour*.

Concerts, tours of Local Artists

Along with weekend bands and solo artists appeared at the **LODGE** each weekend, the CYTA DIRECTORS made a conscious decision to ensure that local Christian talent was featured on the same program as overseas touring artists. This allowed Australian Christian performers to experience playing in front of larger audiences than they might otherwise experience and provided an opportunity to grow a larger following.

Country Sound was a prominent local country band, playing Christian music. **CYTA** took a prominent role in promoting the band. The first album recorded and released by *Country Sound* was recorded on a snow weekend at **CYTA LODGE**. The exposure the band got through its links with **CYTA** gave them a wider audience and increased bookings for concerts.

True Colours the Voice

With the move of **CYTA** to Silverwater a Friday and Saturday night program known as *True Colours* later renamed *The Voice* was launched. This was a program of music, held at a place where young people could just hang out on Friday and Saturday nights. Youth groups from around Sydney came to the **CYTA SILVERWATER CENTRE**. As with almost all **CYTA** activities it was staffed by a voluntary group **TEAM MEMBERS**.

> **A side note:** There is more on the establishment, rise and fall of True Colours later named The Voice in a later chapter which helps illustrate in part the changing role of CYTA as time moved on.

Sunday Sing

Especially popular in the seventies was a concert series called *Sunday Sing* held after evening church service times at **Strathfield Town Hal** with up to 200 people attending each evening.

First Concert

CYTA intended music at first as a form of promotion for tours, or as a reward for **TEAM MEMBERS**. I have a memory of attending my first **CYTA** concert:

> "The first **CYTA** concert I attended was at the Alexandria Basketball Stadium. I remember the music was not to my taste but you got caught up

> in the music of the band and the singing. It just overwhelmed everybody. It was a great night with about 400 to 500 young people all in the one place. I knew for sure now that CYTA was going to be home for me, for a few years at least."

Kevin provides some background to **MY** first **CYTA** concert.

> "The original artists were to be The Proclaimers. This was a big band group of exceptional talent from Melbourne. Due to a transport strike they could not travel to NSW.
>
> With less than twenty four hours till 'curtain up', a program worthy of any concert stage was put together by the **CYTA DIRECTORS** with Vic Barrington as the compere."

It turned out to be night enjoyed by an excited audience.

Short tours by local artists

CYTA decided to promote its tours through having artists give a concert in country centres. I was given charge and free rein to organise venues, local support in the locations where concerts were held, artists, and **TEAM MEMBERS** to make these concerts happen. Though Kevin suggested these short musical trips were to promote **CYTA** tours it was clear over time that a music ministry was an evangelical ministry in itself.

Several carloads of **TEAM MEMBERS**, musicians and support crew headed off on a Friday night to country venues for a Saturday night concert followed by appearances at churches around the area on the Sunday. When it was over then there was the long trip home. Rural locations where Sydney artists were featured included several trips to Newcastle and a trip to Wagga Wagga.

Sydney concerts included a concert held in the hall at Granville TAFE College and in the auditorium at the Methodist Ladies College (MLC) at Burwood as well as other private school auditoriums. A concert often followed by a fried chicken and cider supper was a sound proven approach for **CYTA**.

Not all concerts featured a chicken and cider supper such with the Wagga, Wagga sojourn. For everyone to get to Wagga, Wagga, set up, hold the concert and break it down, followed by church and the trip home on Sunday was more than enough. Chicken and Cider would have proved to be a monumental problem.

The concert held at MLC offered particular logistical problems. The piano was on the auditorium floor off the stage. I made a request to move the piano onto the stage and return it to the floor at the end of the night. This request was denied by the school representative with the reason given being that at any movement the old piano may see it fall apart. It was certainly a fragile piano.

The band was on the floor level with the audience. The lead singer was on the stage. It looked odd but it worked out.

Going places - CYTA

The night band members catch a felon
This is an unusual one.

*"For several years I, Howard recruited bands, groups and solo artists to appear during snow season on the Saturday evening at the Lodge. After establishing Saturday night **LODGE** line ups over the first few years Kevin decided he would like to meet the artists' sound engineers etc. who made up our weekly contingent.*

A night was set aside for representatives of the various groups and soloists to meet at CYTA Centre Homebush to meet with Kevin. More than fifty musicians turned up with some groups bring a full compliment. As the room filled I moved further back greeting people as they walked in. With the seated area being filled a large group of artists were left standing with some just inside the front door way. As Kevin spoke, I pushed any latecomers in the door and who were up on to their toes on the front step. Eventually I stood in the street, not hearing the no doubt inspiring words.

About halfway through the evening I heard a woman scream and turned to see a woman being assaulted and robbed while making at telephone call at a public phone a little way up the street. The assailant ran onto the road crossing it as he ran. I ran after him, though I realised afterward I was not sure what I would do if I caught him. Pardon the nature of the simile but it was like the demeanour of a greyhound that catches the lure and finds out it is not a real animal and does not know what to do with it. Apparently, those dogs never race again.

What would I do if I caught the assailant?

I was catching him quickly (a great surprise to me) when he dropped the change he had taken and stood facing me across the road daring or maybe worrying about me coming closer. As we stood facing each other, several of our artists grabbed the assailant from behind and held him till police arrived. He was arrested and statements were taken. The coins were collected off the road and returned to the woman.

Police visited each of the three or four people involved in the capture offering them commendations which I believe may have been declined.

Not only could our artists sing and play they were pretty handy at catching "crooks". Oh, and I am sure Kevin's talk was great, whatever he said.

A side point: *"At that time, I worked in the city centre and I sometimes parked at Strathfield to travel into the city for work. One morning some six months after the above assault and robbery, I walked past a service station towards Strathfield Train Station and the assailant of that night was sitting in a car while the driver was getting fuel. We looked at each other, and it was clear as I recognised him, he recognised me, and……"*

Talent in the TEAM

One of the **TEAM MEMBERS**, a singer, *Jenni Plumb* was given an opportunity to tour with **CYTA**. A short tour, with venues in Sydney for four concerts were arranged and played. Jenni was an unknown so audiences were sparse.

Steve Castle recalls the concerts.

> *"I ran lighting at The Kings School concert. The school would not let us use their control console, so we had to do it all using back stage controls. I had one guy at the back of the auditorium with a two-way radio telling me which lights to turn on and which to turn off."*

Jenni's concerts were promoted ahead of Evie's first tour. This initiative with Jenni Plumb was one of the examples of **CYTA** as an organisation supporting **TEAM MEMBERS** and allowing individual **TEAM MEMBERS** to develop their skills.

Concerts and Costs

Just as Kiah Ridge posed financial issues for **CYTA** so did concerts from time to time. One international concert series had to be cancelled before it begun resulting in a consequential loss. **CYTA** was always aware of the downside as well as the upside of everything the organisation attempted.

Within the **TEAM** was other musical talent. Scratch bands formed at the **LODGE** from **TEAM MEMBERS**. I have been prevailed upon to mention one such group.

Going places - CYTA

Apparently, there was a group of undiscovered unknowns who could hold a tune and would have taken the world by storm if they were discovered. I worked in the music industry for several years before securing a "real" job. Why didn't you call?

John Grinsell both manager and rhythm guitarist of the band fills us in on the undiscovered phenomenon.

> "One of the top bands to emerge from the **AUSTALIAN CHRISTIAN MUSIC SEMINAR** was **Terry Towelling and The Dishwashers**. The original band members included Mark Bradley, John Grinsell, Tom Bishop and Rod Derley. At their second gig, Tom Bishop was replaced by Paul Cleasby as Tom decided to go solo
>
> The band went on to perform on some top stages at the **CYTA** centre and at the **CYTA** 40-year anniversary big reunion. The **CYTA** One Last Time reunion featured all the great songs of the band and a full cardboard cut-out of Jan Craik.
>
> The managing director, Kevin Craik, stated that one of his disappointments was that the band could not tour alongside **CYTA** artists such as Evie, Ken Medema, and Andraé Crouch. Kevin felt the band should have played alongside Evie at the Sydney Opera House. They are still awaiting further bookings in nursing homes, retirement villages etc.

Going places - CYTA

> *If you missed the band's performance, please contact the band's archive manager, **Kevin Craik**. Copies of the performances are located in Kevin's garage... in a fruit box. For bookings, please contact manager John Grinsell, who is now taking guitar lessons..."*

Ok, so let's move on to what I think is the most significant development in Christian Music ever in Australia, authored by **CYTA**.

28. Australian Christian Music Seminar (ACMS)

Foundation to Seminar

Initially an Australian Music Foundation was established by CYTA though it was not a traditional foundation. It had no discrete wealth which is the basis of most foundations. Usually the wealth of a foundation is distributed to those people, (beneficiaries), who are central to the focus of the foundations work. The work of the foundation was to support artists in their development. The first CYTA Christian Music Seminar was given the name of the foundation.

However, the idea was to hold a Christian music seminar. It was decided to register an appropriate name for the seminar. The second year it was called the **CYTA - AUSTRALIAN CHRISTIAN MUSIC SEMINAR (ACMS)** after the initial request to register the name of the Australian Gospel Music Seminar was rejected. (A great decision as Gospel music differs from Christian music)

The **CYTA** Board at the time acknowledged and agreed that a separate organising committee would need to be established to plan and operate the **AUSTALIAN CHRISTIAN MUSIC SEMINAR**. I was fortunate to be asked to be part of the initial organising committee.

We were blessed over the years of the **AUSTALIAN CHRISTIAN MUSIC SEMINAR** to have a committee of experienced people to be invited in the organising and conducting of the Seminar. The chairman of the committee was a significant person on the leadership **TEAM**. The first chairperson of the **AUSTALIAN CHRISTIAN MUSIC SEMINAR** was Fred *Grice*, followed by *John Waller* and then *Barry Starr*. *Fred Grice* was a knowledgeable Chairperson who took the seminar to Adelaide for several years.

John Waller was notable for his youth work on the northern beaches and the musicality of his family. His wife Loris released an album and one of his sons, Randall Waller is well known in the local music industry for his own music and featuring on tours with local and international artists.

A committee made up of musicians, promoters, logistical people and event organisers supported each chairperson. Each year the committee would offer up to 10 scholarships which, depending on the circumstances, gave the recipients free registration and in many cases, free meals and accommodation as well.

To pull together all the aspects of a successful seminar required much planning ahead, whilst the day programs of the seminar were set in the 24 hours prior. Much thought was put into the planning by the organising committee personnel.

Over the years the committee changed but we pay tribute to the leadership of *Fred Grice* 1976-1984, Adelaide 1984-1986, *John Waller* 1985-1992 (no seminar in 1984) and *Barry Starr* – 1993-2003 (no seminar in 2001).

Kevin was quoted as saying,

> "The **(ACMS)** provided an opportunity opened many doors in their music / arts careers / ministries engagements."

The Seminar was the response to a challenge issued in 1975 by a member of the **Andraé Crouch** Band. **Fletch Wiley** made the suggestion that **CYTA** should conduct a live-in music and arts conference/camp at **CYTA LODGE**. Fletch went on to be the key-note speaker/presenter at two seminars

In response to the suggestion from Fletch, **Jan Craik** one of the **CYTA DIRECTORS** attended a Christian Artists Seminar in 1976 at Estes Park Colorado, USA. The **CYTA** Board was enthusiastic to take up the challenge of Fletch Wiley by launching the AUSTALIAN **CHRISTIAN MUSIC FOUNDATION** in January 1978 and then subsequently the seminar was called the **AUSTRALIAN CHRISTIAN MUSIC SEMINAR**. It ran annually till 1984 and then again till 2001 when the Music Seminar was not held given it was close to the September, Sydney 2000 Olympics when many of the attendees were involved. The music seminar ran for the last time in 2002. There were twenty two seminars held annually during the life of **ACMS**.

Promoters and recording company representatives who attended the seminar were not to approach artists while the seminar was on.

The Music Seminar did travel. It naturally went to the home of WOMAD (world of music festival) and the leading Australian Fringe Festival, Adelaide.

Going places - CYTA

Fred Grice a musician, a founding committee MEMBER of the seminar organising group, after the first seminar took on the role of Chairman of the organising committee. Fred later on took up a position as an Associate Pastor at a church in Adelaide. The church found a school where the seminar could be held. The music seminar was held for three years in Adelaide.

Have seminar will travel.

A time slot for the seminar came about after the failure of summer camps to attract attendees. **ACMS** filled the summer void of bookings at the **LODGE**.

The **CYTA** Board were always concerned that the seminar ran at a loss. However, the seminar proved to be a "loss leader" for the accommodation sold to people attending the seminar. Accommodation was charged out at full rates.

Most of the sessions for the seminars were held in the local high school as the **LODGE** could not cope with the level of enthusiasm of attendees. Large numbers of people attended the music seminar every year it was held.

Kevin recalls the trust placed by the school principal in CYTA and one individual in particular to ensure the school was kept in and returned in good order.

> "Each year, the principal of Monaro High School (MHS) made available the full facilities of his school campus. Our facilities manager, **Arthur**

Going places - CYTA

> *Rickersy* (OAM), a very experienced high school maths master, understood the needs of the seminar using the school campus and the security needs of the school. He was trusted with the master key, which gave him all-areas access.
>
> The support of the Monaro High school staff was invaluable. Without their total support and offers of assistance, the seminar would not have been possible to be successful and worthwhile over a period of twenty-two seminars."

The seminar saw the Craik's take on differing roles from what might be anticipated. Kevin took charge of logistics and operations. Kevin believed he was on holiday once the seminar started. His job was done.

Jan on the other hand was the Coordinator of the teaching sessions and the seminar. She also took charge of the evening concerts. She had a prior and continuing role with the seminar.

Jan also managed other musical activities away from **CYTA** and with other organisation such as *Fusion* who sponsored a pre-Olympic Christian rally for around 30000 people held at the Sydney Olympic Stadium. She was named at one time as the International President of the Gospel Music Association (America).

The **AUSTALIAN CHRISTIAN MUSIC SEMINAR** was ably supported each year by a group of up fifty **TEAM**

MEMBERS, setting up and pulling down venues, cooking, cleaning and providing back stage support.

A Children's program at ACMS

A children's program was offered during the seminar. The children who were twelve years or older delighted everyone on the Saturday morning of the seminar with their own presentation of what they learned during the week.

Kevin remembers the program Director, *Tanya Inder (Née Pywell)*

> *"Tanya was invited to a youth leaders' dinner, held at the Homebush Centre. She was looking for an opportunity to serve and found excitement in serving God through her involvement with CYTA. She became a most capable and reliable hostess on Snow tours and extended camping tours.*

> **A side note:** A bonus at the dinner that Tanya attended was that she met her future husband **David** Inder.

Tanya takes up her own story.

> *"I was blessed to go to the 3rd music seminar as a "normal" person, a participant. My friends had filled in the form for me and all I had to do was mail it. I came back inspired, but never noticed a kid's program.*

> *The next seminar I attended I went to music seminar as a **MEMBER** of the **CYTA TEAM**. I served lots of meals, worked in the "record" shop*

*and had the privilege of cleaning every toilet in the **LODGE** every day for a week.*

*II didn't see any children's program, but I did love the night-time concerts and the fellowship. One December day Kevin Craik asked me if I was doing anything after Christmas and would I be interested in helping at **ACMS**. I said only if it is a real job. He asked me to establish and operate a children's program at the next seminar.*

I started in the old Baptist church. It was small but had a big outside playing area. We always started the mornings with a story and devotions. We had different people coming in to perform music, stories and puppetry. We played lots of games and did an enormous amount of craft. The days were long, and the parents would return at the end of the day visibly blessed.

After a few years we moved into the new Baptist Church near the high school. It was huge. I even managed to lock the pastor in one day and turn on the alarm, not knowing he was inside!

*There were so many highlights of **ACMS Cooma Kids**. One day while walking down a street in Cooma with 35 children, an elderly lady raced out of a property and said, "You are just what I need". I wasn't sure if I should, but I went in. She had an apricot tree full of fruit. She told the kids to pick the fruit and eat it. I have never tasted anything like the apricots we ate then. They were so full of flavour*

Going places - CYTA

> We had a swimming afternoon in Cooma Pool, every year. I stole the kitchen staff for the afternoon so we could match every child to a young adult. Both kids and young adults were instructed they had to stick together the whole time they were there. I'm not sure who had the most fun!
>
> I spent a year preparing for the one week of **ACMS Cooma Kids** and my car would be so full of equipment, that my own children had boxes on their laps for the entire trip down from Sydney to Cooma. They never complained as they, too, loved every moment of being there.
>
> Many of the children made decisions to follow Jesus at Cooma Kids. I have met up with some of them and they are still faithfully serving our Lord." I felt so blessed to be part of that. As the years went on, many of the children have been in contact with me and they have continued in their faith. Some have gone into full time ministry while others have chosen to follow active rolls in their churches.
>
> I spent 10 years running **ACMS Cooma Kids** and was blessed to have many amazing helpers along the way. It was a time of blessing for both me and my family.

Kevin reflects on the children's program **at AUSTALIAN CHRISTIAN MUSIC SEMINAR**

> "The Children's program from the outset of ACMS was blessed. It was coordinated by

trained leaders and keen voluntary input from many of the parents. Tanya Inder, an infants' school teacher of some 37 years of experience, and the coordinator for ten years of the children's program is and was a wonderful Christian woman who has been blessed as she has seen her "Cooma kids" grow into fine adults""

Notes of thanks from ACMS

Thanks for:

- A musical was printed on the final day of the seminar that had been practised during the week.
- The program team under the leadership of **Jan Craik** ably assisted by **Judy Firth** and other committee members, with committee meetings held after supper to arrange the next day's program. It sure was a pressure-packed week.
- The organising committee were extremely thankful for all the technical staff, who, without their whole-hearted effort and financial assistance, the music seminar would not have achieved the production support it gave every year. In addition to their responsibilities, many of the technical **team** also were engaged in afternoon electives as leaders.
- The organising committee were extremely thankful for the Technical team, who without their wholehearted assistance and financial contribution, the Seminar would never have achieved it's the level of success each year.

- The children's program discussed earlier presented by **Tanya**.

As the week progressed, registrants under the guidance of the technical **TEAM** were involved in sound, lights and stage management. Particular thinks is due to the:

- PA People, Lots Of Watts,
- PA People Melbourne,
- Seventh Day Adventist video unit and the
- Wesley Central Mission video department, the technicians also presented afternoon electives.
- Max and Morna Harding for recording of the auditorium sessions for distribution to attendees

We now turn to the visiting artists who helped shape ACMS.

Going places - CYTA

29. ACMS - Featured artists and speakers

Each year the Seminar ran there were featured artists, presenters and speakers.

Jimmy and Carol *Owens* were featured artists at the second music seminar. Jimmy was a pianist, singer conductor and music producer. He continues in ministry with his children in his family ministry in Baton Rouge Las Angeles. As a prequel to the second Music Festival Jimmy Owens over three days gave instruction to a small group of 30 people who were scholarships winners that attended the pre-seminar workshop at no additional cost to the payment required to attend the music festival proper.

Ken Medema – is a musician who was blind from birth. He has only had enough sight to tell dark from light. After completing a degree majoring in music therapy at Michigan State University, he worked as a music therapist. During that time, he wrote songs to support teenagers affected by injury or trauma.

His song writing led him to decide to write songs about his Christian life. Playing piano and singing, he often modified the lyrics of songs to fit in with sermon outlines, suggestions from the audience or to publicise social issues. Ken Medema was a favourite on tour in Australia and at the **AUSTALIAN CHRISTIAN MUSIC SEMINAR.**

Going places - CYTA

Subsequent to his appearance at the music seminar, Ken toured Australia with **CYTA** as the promotor. On his first night in Australia which was at the smaller auditorium at the Bankstown Town Hall, which holds a crowd of just over 300, his supporting artist(s) were a young ensemble from Castle Hill Baptist. The young peoples' choir of Castle Hill Baptist were asked to do a performance of a musical written by Medema: ***The Story Telling Man.*** **CYTA** sponsored a weekend of training for the over 50 members of the choir.

Ken Medema still does concerts and can be seen on YouTube each Friday. Kevin Craik is unavailable at that time.

Fred Grice was the conductor of the choir and also a chairman of six music seminars and in particular the coordinator of three seminars held in Adelaide.

Martin Joseph, a welsh singer and guitarist is said to focus his music on his lament with state of society. Winner of the best male singer category in 2004 at the Welsh Music awards along with a series of other music awards he has campaigned for justice. He was sponsored by **CYTA** to attend and be involved with **(ACMS)**

Sheila Walsh, describes herself on her website as, "*first a wife and mom and in her spare time she is an author.*" As an author she has written "*It's Okay Not to Be Okay*". In February 2020, she released her newest book, "*Praying Women, How to Pray When you don't know what to Say*".

Born in Ayr, she became a Christian singer after studies in theology at the London Bible College (now the London School of Theology). A popular key-note artist at the **AUSTALIAN CHRISTIAN MUSIC SEMINAR** she became the co-host of the television talk-show, The 700 Club.

Barry Maguire was a welcome guest at (ACMS) in 1998. His ministry is discussed in a previous chapter dealing with CYTA and visiting International musicians in a previous chapter.

Fletch Wiley from the DISCIPLES. His story is reflected in the chapter 'dealing with the Music-Internationals. He pops up through the chapters on **ACMS**. He was a guest presenter at ACMS twice.

Sister Eleanor, a catholic nun, who had a charting single of the Lord's Prayer, attended the seminar as a vocal coach

Steve Taylor, an American who popularised the musical concept of *Christian alternative rock*. In this form of music the emphasis was placed on the musical style over the lyrics. This was contrary to other Christian artists and song writers who placed the emphasis on the message of their songs. Taylor also produced, directed and acted in short films and feature films and continues to work in films today.

Steve Taylor's presentation to the **AUSTALIAN CHRISTIAN MUSIC SEMINAR** placed the emphasis on musicality first before lyrics. He believed that audiences need to enjoy well-written and well-performed music. Such enjoyment enhanced the message. This is a sentiment with which I concur.

He has a long list of musical videos he produced. His first single was in 1980, "I Want To Be a Clone" with his latest album at the time of writing this book being, "Ecstatic Delight".

Rick Powell was the first guest for the first **ACMS** held at **CYTA LODGE** in 1978 was Rick Powell. He returned for the fourth seminar with his wife **Sylvia**.

Rick was a well prepared and dynamic speaker. He with his wife Sylvia formed a harmonised team. Rick taught on praise and worship while Sylva had a background in children's television.

Rick Powell produced and arranged more than 200 mainly Christian albums and had, had thirty five choir books published. With Sylvia the collaborated on numerous music programs, such as shows specifically designed for children and Pat Boon Christmas Specials amongst other activities.

Jan Craik met Rick at the 1976 Estes Park Seminar in Colorado. She states that:

> "I was immediately drawn to him, as I observed a Godly Christian man. I immediately suggested the possibility of him coming to Australia, which eventuated in the 1978 invitation. I recall that Rick's wife Sylvia said to me at one time that she

> loves being involved in a ministry to children because of what she described as their sensitivity to spiritual things.

Kevin remembers the volume of reference books in Rick Powell luggage. Well used reference books as Rick and also Sylvia left a lasting impression on many of the seminar participants who attended these early **AUSTRALIAN CHRISTIAN MUSIC SEMINARS**.

Robert Ferguson – Originally from England, Robert Ferguson has been a pastor and teacher at Hillsong Church in Australia for over thirty years and is passionate about teaching people:

> "How to live in order to please God"

In this capacity he was invited to speak at the 1994 and 1995 Australian Christion Music Seminar.

Mike Frost – on his website calls himself an Australian *missionologist*. He is said to be one of the leading voices in the missional church movement, where churches are mission-centred rather than just preaching to church attenders.

For twelve years, he was the weekly Christian columnist for the Manly Daily, and has had articles published in the Washington Post. He is the author of books that are required reading in some ministry training colleges. He was a speaker of note for two years at **ACMS**. Frost is the founder of the *Forge Mission Training Network*. He is the founder of the missional

Christian community, **smallboatbigsea**, based in Manly in Sydney's Northern Beaches.

Graham Kendrick – is an English Christian singer, songwriter and worship leader. Probably the best known song among the various songs he has written and performed is the song, "Shine, *Jesus*, Shine" Kendrick is a co-founder of the "March for *Jesus*", probably best illustrated in Australia through the march held in Sydney (and other locations) over the Easter weekend where the march finishes with the marchers congregating down central Sydney streets in a formation that resembles a cross. He received a Dove Award in 1995 for his international work. Graham Kendrick was a well prepared speaker and worship leader for **ACMS**.

Barry Mc Murtrie grew up in a family that did not attend church. They lived in the steel town of Wollongong. He adopted Christ as his saviour in his teens.

After completing a degree in business he felt a call to minister for Christ. He was the pastor at Crossroads Christian Church in the United States were up to five thousand people attend each Sunday. When Barry Murtrie returned to Australia he was pastoring a church of forty or so people in country NSW. He is at the time of writing planting a new church in Wollongong.

Joni Eareckson-Tada had a permanently disability after she dived into the Chesapeake Bay after misjudging the shallowness of the water, became a prominent international Christian speaker and activist. She appeared as a speaker at the **AUSTALIAN CHRISTIAN MUSIC SEMINAR** in 1984. In the same year she spoke at Sydney Convention Centre to an almost full house with **CYTA** being the promoter. Amongst the crowd who watched her appearance at the convention centre were 300 disabled people and their carers all of whom were given free admission.

There were numerous featured Australian Artists at the **AUSTALIAN CHRISTIAN MUSIC SEMINAR** including, **Paul Colman** was a very young when he attended the early seminars. Paul Colman was a British-Australian pop-rock guitarist, vocalist, pianist, and composer. He started a Christian band the, Paul Colman Trio in Melbourne. The son of previous Associate Pastor at Melbourne's Crossways Baptist Church, he joined the Christian band, the Newsboys, and then pursued a solo career. He continues to work to this day with other artists as well as producing music for other musicians.

Some of the other featured artists that not only appeared at the **AUSTRALIAN MUSIC SEMINAR** but also toured with **CYTA** included:

- *Kenny Marks* in 1986.

- *Sandi Patti* appeared at the Sydney Opera House in 1982which was included in an East Coast of Australia and another tour in 1987.

- *Steve Taylor* toured in 1985 and 1987as well as featuring at the music seminar.

Going places - CYTA

- **Amy Grant** appeared in Sydney concerts in 1983 and 1984 arranged by **CYTA**.

Just a reminder that concert tours and guests presenters from overseas to ACMS, were not just about the promotion of touring overseas artists. All these major concerts and the seminars were supported by Australian artists who gained experience by being on a platform with internationally acknowledged artists.

Let's now look at the impact of **ACMS** on **TEAM MEMBERS**, attendees and artists.

30. Response to and Impact of ACMS

Food sleep and music

A feature of the Seminar was the meals presented by the **TEAM** and staff of **CYTA LODGE**. Meals were under the direction of the LODGE manager as well as for many years, the late *Joy Craik*.

With the support of the voluntary **TEAM** of between forty and fifty **TEAM MEMBERS** both in the kitchen and the dining room meals were presented on time every time. Upwards of 500 meals were served three times a day. There was always a choice of at least two main courses. The final night of the Seminar, a formal dinner for the participants was served to all in well under 90 minutes. This was due to no small effort of the **TEAM** "working together as a **TEAM**".

The **CYTA LODGE** provided the accommodation while **TEAM MEMBERS** volunteered their time to cook. *James Gow* remembers cooking at the **LODGE** and how it was to lead to his involvement in the **AUSTALIAN CHRISTIAN MUSIC SEMINAR.**

> "I was a young teenager back then, however people put their trust in me and I learnt a great deal – crack eggs in one hand, safely use a deep fry, count plates to assist with portion control, thinking through logistics and timing. It was also learning about doing jobs properly (I do recall Bruce calling me back to rebuff the whole dining

> room floor, my initial attempt being fairly average!) and serving with a humble heart.
>
> They were good lessons to learn and over the years my responsibilities increased. At the Australian Christian Music Seminar I was invited to M.C. lunch time concerts and then later, an evening concert. For someone in their mid/late teens this was a fairly awesome experience – learning about stage, production, microphones and run sheets and working with the differing needs of individual artists."

Gerard Thompson one of the **TEAM MEMBERS**, remembers with great fondness working at the LODGE in seminar week.

> "It was a pleasure and an honour to be able to serve as part of the **TEAM** for seminar week and to share with so many people over the years I was involved and to actually learn things that I have used in my Christian walk. Many memories of the seminar and life at **CYTA LODGE**"

One devoted seminar fan was Reverend **Ted Edwards**. (The first part of the tribute to **CYTA** by Ted appears in the chapter on the **LODGE** where he and his wife Jenny were wed). The final part of his tribute continues with his attendance at, and reflections on, the **AUSTALIAN CHRISTIAN MUSIC SEMINAR** from 1976 till 1980

"I still count it an immense privilege to have seen and heard highly talented visiting artists like Evie Tornqist, Rick Powell, and other local groups like Sanctus. I can still remember wonderful gospel truths spoken by Evie in

support of her musical presentations, such as, "When God forgives us our sins, He takes them out into the depths of the deepest ocean and buries them there, and then He puts up a sign saying, "No more fishing here." An amazing truth!! In fact, we still possess five of Evie's LP albums, with some of our favourites including the Christmas album, "Come on Ring Those Bells" and "Gentle Moments."

In the end, only eternity will best be able to tell the complete story of all that **CYTA LODGE**, and in particular, the **AUSTALIAN CHRISTIAN MUSIC SEMINAR** accomplished for the Kingdom of God during these amazing years."

Not just music

The **AUSTALIAN CHRISTIAN MUSIC SEMINAR** was not just restricted to music. There were also Christian dancers that made an appearance as a group at the second music seminar. Some attendees were interested in writing rather than performing while others were interested in staging events. There were also Christian comedians who attended the seminar. One attendee created a song about Bible characters working through the alphabet. When he got to Z he came up with 'Zany Zephaniah"

The Formation of the Christian Dance Fellowship

Mary Jones was an attendee at an early seminar. She was to incorporate many aspects of the **AUSTALIAN CHRISTIAN MUSCIC SEMINAR (ACMS)** into the

Christian Dance Fellowship of Australia (CDFA) Conference, which she was organising at the time. From that first (CDFA) Conference, the ministry has spread to over 37 countries. Mary continued for many years as a teacher in the ACMS Christian Dance elective.

Mary has not allowed age to diminish her enthusiasm for Dance and still travels the world encouraging existing Christian dance groups and assisting in the establishment of CDFA groups in new countries. She also was involved in a very important teaching role at the Wesley Institute during its existence.

A side note: Mary's tale of a moving seat

After an afternoon *ACMS* session for the dance group, dinner was served on a grassy section at the rear of the Flynn's wrecking yard near where the dance group were meeting. A port-aloo was positioned at a discreet distance from the diners. It was on a trailer and not unhitched from the utility that brought it down from Canberra.

At the end of the afternoon, and in an effort to get it back to Canberra, the driver jumped in the Ute and started to drive off towards Canberra with Mary still behind the closed door! The ensuing scene was hilarious!

> **A side note:** Mary Jones now with numerous degrees and other qualifications to her name is the founder of The International Christian Dance Fellowship and the former Dean of Dance at the Wesley Institute. She is currently Director of Cara Mayan and of the online course Diploma of Dance Ministry. Search for her online to find out more.

Impact in Worship

Starting in 1978 and concluding in 2002, the Seminar had a positive impact on the worship and fellowship in our Australian Christian churches – to which we give honour and praise to *God*. It wasn't only the music or the voluntary teaching cohort but the spirit of sharing and learning together about one another's gifts and talents which contributed to the seminar's success during and after its conclusion.

Pastors learned how to make more use of music and arts in their services. Teachers gave freely of their time in classes and major morning and afternoon elective sessions.

The Witness

Just prior to the 1979 seminar, Kevin had a phone call from a lady wanting to come to Cooma to spend an afternoon with Jimmy and Carol Owens, the special guest teachers. Not knowing who this lady was, Kev was a little taken aback, but said, "by all means, come". The outcome of the visit of this lady, *Irene Gould*, was the Australian production of "**The Witness**", which was written by *Jimmy and Carol Owens*.

Going places - CYTA

Many of the musicians and singers who formed the ensemble of the staging of the musical in Australia were selected after the organiser visited the music seminar. Irene was able to recruit most of the lead characters, some 15 people for the musical from the Music Seminar participants. These included Robert Colman who was in the lead role of Peter the apostle. Chris Foley was also cast as one of the disciples. No one was guaranteed any payment.

The Witness toured Australia and New Zealand seeking donations at each venue it played. No charge for seats. The touring group were living by faith. Tour completed. All accounts were paid with the tiniest of surpluses left over. The faith of Irene Gould and the cast were rewarded.

Irene later wrote of her relationships with Jan and Kevin Craik.

> *"I am greatly honoured to call Jan and Kevin Craik "my friends". They are two of God's specially chosen, gifted and giving servants.*
>
> *Over the years, they have unreservedly shared with me their professional expertise, wise guidance and assistance. This was especially evident during the set-up of the Gospel Music Tour "The Witness – The Musical", written by Jimmy and Carole Owens, which toured across Australia and New Zealand. In summary, Kev and Jan Craik are two of God's truly shining lights in this world.'*

God delivers on the efforts of the faithful.

Waratah Girls' Choir

An outstanding by-product of the **AUSTALIAN CHRISTIAN MUSIC SEMINAR** was the establishment of The Australian Waratah Girls' Choir. The basic tenet of the choir is to:

> "Sing to, sing for God, and sing of God".

From humble beginnings, the choir has cemented itself as one of the most renowned choral groups Australia has to offer; a rewarding result of hard work, dedication, discipline and a simple and common love of music." Founding Director **Wynette Horne** OAM was inspired to start the Christian girls' choir as a result of being challenged by **Jennifer Filby,** a Tasmanian music teacher who attended a number of seminars.

Starting with just 40 girls in her rumpus room and no choral training, she stepped out in faith to follow this 'call'. Her faith, enthusiasm, inherent musicality and catalytic ability soon brought to life the young voices of the Waratah Girls' Choir and in 1985 it emerged as the Australian National Champions – the beginning of many successes for the choir.

The Australian Waratah Girls' Choir still has the same core value at its heart more than 30 years later: Sing to *God*, sing for *God*, and sing of *God*.

Now under the inspired vision of Wynette's daughter, Lindy Connett, there are exciting new challenges ahead: engaging performance programs; local, national and international touring opportunities; recordings; cultural exchange and much, much more. Now in its fourth decade, the Waratah Girls' Choir is recognised as one of Australia's leading female choirs, having achieved local, national and international acclaim.

Wynette Horne, Founder Director of The Australian Waratah Girls' Choir – "more than just a choir" said in 1998 of the impact of ACMS on her and her future.

> *"I can't believe **ACMS** is now celebrating its 20th year (1998) of Christian outreach to thousands of people. Praise God, my life changed radically when I attended your 5th ACMS in 1982, and through the commitment and dedication to your programme, God was able to reveal to me His amazing plan for my life.*
>
> *Our God is truly an awesome God, but it has taken me years to appreciate just how awesome! He set me apart to do things beyond my understanding and ability. He has called me by name and has never left me nor forsaken me. He has advised and directed me all the way to unbelievable heights of success and spiritual fruition.*
>
> *Thank you all at **ACMS**! It was an inconceivable experience bringing my 'God-directed' choir back to its birthplace last year. Something I would never have believed possible 16 years ago! God bless you all abundantly as you continue to make yourselves available to Him. My prayers will be with you all – especially those who are*

> *really seeking God's direction for their lives. Expect the unexpected with God and you will not be disappointed! Never trust yourselves or rely on your own ability. Just be available and God will do the rest."*
>
> *Congratulations, good and faithful servants! May God grant you the physical and the spiritual strength to carry on HIS work".*

The choir has been featured on the ABC and performed in many major cities of the world on their many overseas tours. Ahead are recordings, performances and the possibility of international tours. You can see more of the wonderful achievements of this choir at

https://waratahgirlschoir.com.au/achievements/

Impact on Attendees

Greg Oates whose relationship with **CYTA** was solely through attendance at the **AUSTALIAN CHRISTIAN MUSCI SEMINAR** recalls Fletch Wiley.

> *"I'll never forget Fletch Wiley doing his finale on the instrumental piece Fiesta, with **Billy Neilson** on bass, Crabs (aka **Jeff Crabtree**) on keys, Steve Henderson on guitar. Great musicians back then"*

Bill Neilson a leading Australian Christian musician recalls,

> *"So rich memories, blessings and deep friendships made there* (at the Christian Music Seminar). *So formative in my life!!*

Going places - CYTA

Faith Ling who was for some years on the organising committee for the **AUSTALIAN CHRISTIAN MUSIC SEMINAR** and who taught at the seminar managed to secure a souvenir at the last AUSTALIAN **CHRISTIAN MUSIC SEMINAR**.

> "It's a pillow from the Lodge, gifted to our family at the end of the last ACMS. So privileged & blessed to be invited to teach over so many years. It was basically our family's annual holiday. The Seminar birthed a lifetime of worship and service in each of our 4 children, they carry the legacy. The pillow is now an heirloom! Dudley and I as well as Belinda, Christopher, Jenny and Pete are forever grateful."

Sallie-Ann Wilson (Craik) and J**ulie Everist** (née Prowse) came up with the idea of 'let's have the Wednesday night in The Cooma Jail', which was not in use at the time.

Another programme they organised was in the car wrecking yard 4 miles east of Cooma, towards Mount Kosciuszko. The management of the wrecking yard, first knocked back these two young ladies' request, but they then had "Uncle Kev" use his negotiating skills plus $1000 surety offered and got an agreement.

The owners' extended families came to the dinner in the yard after **John Smith** had earlier challenged people by illustrating how wrecked lives become new in *Christ*. They were amazed at what they were witnessing and were full of praise of how their yard had been used. The

$1000 surety wasn't needed! A highlight was the scratch bands who devised alternate instruments from bits and pieces they found in the yard.

Elaine Abrahams recalls the music seminar.

> "What special times they were. ACMS was on every January. Amazing experiences great interactions, seeing old and meeting new friends, great music and amazing speakers. Never to be forgotten moments."

The purpose of the seminar was to bring artists who were Christians together to participate in small group meetings on a variety of topics. Staging, sound, composition, writing, performance amongst many other topics were featured during the seminar.

Bill Nielson has a vivid seminar memory.

> "One great memory was Sister Eleanor, a catholic nun who attended the seminar as a vocal coach. She performed "Bad Habits" by Billy Field which bought the house down! I think at her instigation Kevin organised for the whole camp to go to the local theatre to see "Sister Act" which she hosted. She was genuinely loved by us Protestants and charismatics alike. It was glorious risk taking. She was the Bomb!
>
> Concerts were generally held nightly. Some outdoor concerts were staged in Cooma in the early seminars. The final concert was held in the school hall. Rehearsals for the Senior Musical

were held in the Cooma Musical Theatre which required liaison with the local theatre society. A seminar newspaper was a feature at the first two music seminars."

Some of the more memorable **ACMS** activities included a full concert program presented by our featured guest and coordinated by the platform team and the technical staff. Who would forget Ken Medema? A blind guy who not only kept the audience enthralled due to his musical presentation, but his jokes and antics on the side."

Random Reflections of attendees

The following reflections are from the privately established **AUSTRALIAN CHRISTIAN MUSIC SEMINAR** (ACMS) Facebook page.

Paul Matthews ACMS attendee and part of the technical team member at ACMS relives his time attending and contributing to ACMS.

"It is 1984 on a Friday night at Monaro High School hall Cooma. Assembled therein is a menagerie of Christians presenting the "best of" presentation of their week's activities at ACMS.

Up the back on the sound desk is a very young and green **Chris Dodds** who subsequently cut his teeth on the 2000 Sydney Olympics and became MD of "The PA People" in Sydney getting very flustered at how nothing seems to be working out.

> Jan Craik on stage however has it all under control. Meanwhile a 16 year old (myself) being responsible for all of the audio and video recording and tape duplication associated with the event, likewise cuts his teeth on recording the happenings on "state of the art" VHS equipment for the day, along with taking audio feeds from Chris's desk and mixing in audience mics.
>
> So much of the technology on display here was "cutting edge" for its time. Indeed the tape itself here nearly 40 years later was a serious restoration job just to get it to play. Enjoy as the time machine whirrs again."

Jacqueline Brown ACMS attendee

> I had the best experience at Cooma 2000. I went there not knowing a soul and made good friendships with members of the **CYTA TEAM** and my roommates. I took part in a major role in our creative arts group. They shot a video of me painting the world and they played in backwards in a production. I took the film back to my church to start performance art to be presented once a month in front of our church and the local community. I was really blessed that year by Cooma.

Deb Everist ACMS attendee

> "Cooma changed my life. We had the series on Esther.
>
> 'And who knows but that you have come to royal position for such a time as this? I will go to the

> king, even though it is against the law. And if I perish, I perish '.
>
> This has been central to my Christian life since then. To try and serve where I am whatever the consequences. I think these words come into my head 3-4 times a week. I have never been the same."

Fletch Wiley ACMS guest presenter and former Disciple and world class Christian Musician

> "One of my fondest memories is the two ACMS I did in Cooma. To say it planted something eternal in Australia (and my heart) is an understatement.
>
> May the Flame burn brighter!!! God's Peace, Fletch Wiley"

Future?

Greg Oates offers his hopes for the future

> "I pray God willing, that a new generation will relight the torch the Craik's once carried, and that such a seminar that includes hands on involvement and showcasing a week's learning, will again become the launch pad to take the gospel to the world through the medium of music
>
> "Is this a challenge? Will anyone take it up?"
>
> (I might be able to help)

Kevin believes the music ministry was worthwhile, particularly the work done to support the **AUSTRALIAN CHRISTIAN MUSIC SEMINARS**,

> 'The Australian Christian Music Seminars set the foundation for nearly three decades of leadership in Christian Music on the East Coast of Australia, not to mention it's influence on the West Coast churches worship **TEAMS** as well."

Was it worth it?

For **Kevin** and many others the answer is

> "**YES, YES and YES!** Though the last seminar was held in 2002, it is amazing that some of the stories are just coming to light now. Those who attended the seminar and those who were on "**TEAM**" at the seminar have spoken of how their Christian life and love of Jesus lead to service as a musician, a missionary and in other areas of Christian service. The friendships made and remain, the skills learned, and the use made of those skills in their local church are a testament to the fact **IT WAS WORTH IT!**

31. "True Colours" and "The Voice"

This chapter is part of the music ministry of CYTA. The story of **True Colours** which became **The Voice** is in many ways symptomatic of the changing appetite for the ministries offered for **CYTA**. The changing nature of demand for travel and the non-completion of the **Kiah Ridge** which was sold also indicate the changing nature of the ministry of **CYTA** went from an initiator and doer to an initiator and then handing on.

The move to create new ministries

CYTA CENTRE Silverwater had facilities for staging a weekend programs on Friday and Saturday nights. Paul Cleesby a **TEAM MEMBER** and later a **DIRECTOR** named the concert program **"TRUE COLOURS"** This initiative provided a venue for youth groups and individuals to have a great night out.

Kevin Craik recalls:

> "Each week a different band and/or artist was featured. A short devotional Gospel message was given. It was always a difficult operation number-wise, but we persevered with it for some four years.
>
> True Colours was initially managed by a student pastor from Morling College. Volunteers from the **CYTA TEAM** comprised the necessary staffing to make the venue work.

> *After each Saturday night event, the auditorium had to be set up for use by a church the next morning for a church service. This was achieved by the wholehearted involvement of the **TEAM** on duty.*
>
> *Sound equipment was one of the last items to be packed away. For many years we had the fruitful and faithful services of **Ken Bolden**, who continued in the sound business providing and operating sound equipment for international and local acts. A second sound provider, for some years, **Phil Lake**, also provided sound for the venue."*

Andrew Parkinson now **Rev.**
Andrew (Parko) Parkinson Rural Ministry & Training - Scripture Union NSW was the first manager/compere of **TRUE COLOURS.** He reflects on his early involvement.

> *"As a long-haired 22 year old theological student and amateur musician, studying youth ministry, the opportunity to be involved in a new initiative to set up Sydney's first "Christian Nightclub" (concert night) seemed too good to be true. I remember sitting around a table at that "first" meeting at the old Silverwater Speedboat Club. The smell of stale beer and cigarette smoke that pervaded the carpets, walls and furniture was palpable but the sense of excitement for 'what could be' was even greater. I remember suggesting that we needed a compere, a 'Darryl Sommers' type personality to be the face of TC's.*

Next thing I know, I'm there in a bow tie and cummerbund every Friday and Saturday night, praying with and for bands and musicians before their performances, standing on stage introducing them, welcoming youth groups, working behind the 'bar' and anything else that needed doing. It was such a privilege to be helping young Christians express their faith publicly through their music. Many went on to full-time Christian Ministry as a result of the opportunity to cut their teeth in ministry at TC's. It was also a privilege to host youth groups from all over Sydney every Friday & Saturday night at a place where they could enjoy Christian music done well in a safe environment and where they could invite their friends to hear the Gospel without the 'cringe factor'. For me, it reinforced my belief that Christian Youth ministry could and should be fun. After all (a quote from Andrew) **Jesus** *said*

"I have come that they may have life, and have it to the full." (John 10:10).

TC's (true Colours) allowed young people to enjoy music and dancing and fun without the dangers of drugs and alcohol, but with the added benefit of God's Good News. However, one thing I came to realise about myself throughout my time at TC's was that I missed the deeper relationships that come with church-based pastoral ministry. I saw groups and bands come and go each week but missed the opportunity to get to know them and share their journey.

> *I also realised that I loved the limelight and the potential was there for me to be motivated by self-gratification rather service. This led me to re-evaluate the trajectory of my own ministry and after 2 years at TC's I left to spend the next 30+ years in church-based youth ministry and pastoral ministry. Today I work for Scripture Union NSW, training and equipping a new generation of young people for creative Gospel Ministry and helping people realise their dreams to use creative means to reach young people for Christ. I will be forever grateful to Kevin & Jan Craik for the opportunity to be a part of this "out there" ministry."*

Kevin sums up his thoughts about this venture:

> *"I am forever grateful to all those who served week by week and made True Colours and later The Voice a worthwhile activity for the young people of Sydney and nearby country churches. It enabled each person to meet and enjoy the company of the people within the youth groups that attended. It was hard going most of the time and was never a money-making activity but the end result made it worthwhile."*

However, the timing of the plans for the program was at least thirty years too late. The weekends were draining funds from **CYTA**'s operations. A young Christian's approach to alcohol was not the same as that of many of their parents and young people wanted to experience a "night club", not a creation of one on a Friday and Saturday night. However, this did not stop new operators requesting that they take on the venture as **CYTA** decided to withdraw.

Going places - CYTA

Craig and Amanda Giles, who had conducted **TRUE COLOURS** on behalf of **CYTA** for some while, asked if they could take the responsibility to continue it under the new name of **THE VOICE**.

> **A side note:** This name **THE VOICE** was used long before the television program of the same name. Craig and Amanda continued with **THE VOICE** for five years, when they too felt the need to finish up.

Craig and Amanda Giles the new *operators* of the renamed *Voice* shared their thoughts on what was for them at the time a new venture.

> *"In the early 90's and newly married, we felt like God had given us a dream of running a Christian nightclub, where people could have clean fun and meet others in a safe environment. We then heard about **TRUE COLOURS** being run by **CYTA**.*
>
> *We visited to find that it was even better than we had imagined – really well run with great entertainment. We met Kevin and Jan just at what was known as True Colours as the **CYTA** Directors were considering closing it down to relieve the drain of cash on the organisation. We felt God was leading us to offer to run True Colours, carrying on the work **CYTA** had begun. We had the training to run True Colours and found Kev's mentorship a huge blessing in filling any gaps we had in our management training.*

Going places - CYTA

*At the same time, we were both attending Bible college fulltime as well as operating a refuge to help people who had escaped prostitution. The **CYTA** Board blessed us incredibly when they decided to pay our remaining Bible college tuition. We had enrolled for our second year in faith, not knowing how we would pay our tuition. God used **CYTA** to generously meet this need.*

*As **CYTA** finally decided to wind up **TRUE COLOURS**, we were grateful when they agreed to let us continue the ministry as the non-profit entity, **THE VOICE**. **CYTA** heavily subsidised the rent and facilities to help us make it work. Our young baby would sleep in a cot in the unused walk-in fridge as Amanda cooked in the kitchen.*

*Maintaining the values and principles established under **CYTA**, we saw God move in amazing ways. We saw lots of young people meet the Lord, some lives miraculously transformed and new friendships built. We were able to disciple a crew of around 35 people and 65 bands. The training **CYTA** gave us helped us to disciple teams in churches and in business and helped us to connect people with the Lord."*

A new operator, new enthusiasm, renewed faith and the ministry continued on but Craig and Amanda wre eventually called in another direction.

Kevin reports on the progress of Craig and Amanda since those days

"Since those early days of The Voice, Craig and Amanda have gone on to bigger things, which include television production for churches, and other religious and secular organisations. They are presently involved in producing a 50-episode series, which, is about all forms of modern slavery especially enslavement of women. It will possibly be aired on Netflix.

They have gone on to establish Central Coast Studios which is a $200-million initiative, in which they are partnering with local, state and federal government organisations. The planning for this venture will include the local indigenous community, the Darkinjung people. The studios are being established to attract big budget movies. It is hoped that the studios will attract work so as to create thousands of jobs and put around $1 billion into the community, during the first few years. It involves seven sound stages, with the biggest stage being the size of a water tank you would find in a Gold Coast Theme Park."

A side note: The **CYTA CENTRE at Silverwater** was available for a variety of functions. The centre was rented by groups, induvial and couples to hold private functions from time to time. But no alcohol was allowed. Wedding receptions were sometimes held in the Centre. Paid staff was used to supplement **TEAM MEMBERS** in catering those affairs.

31. Beyond the Black Stump

CYTA had a vision to run a big outdoor festival where the Narara Secular Festival was held on the site of the Old Sydney Town theme park, near Gosford, NSW. After inspection and early negotiations, the Directors agreed that it was too big an event for one organisation and put away the file.

Sometime later, The Baptist Youth Department approached Kevin to assist in their Easter camp in 1985, which was The Year of Youth. Kevin said,

> *"Wait one minute fellas!"*

Kevin went into his office and got the file out. His reply;

> *"Well if the Baptists were willing to be part of a larger group representing other denominations, then he would have the **CYTA DIRECTORS** consider taking on the task."*

Though essentially about music, speakers came from various Christian organisations to present the Gospel and represent their area of Christian activity and mission. Initially, **Beyond the Black Stump** was modelled on early secular music festivals. Kevin upon viewing the organisation and staging of the secular festivals believed **CYTA** with other partners could do a better job staging a Christian festival. They did.

Rather than just partner with the Baptist Church, Kevin representing the **CYTA** Board, approached what became foundation members of **Beyond the Black Stump** who were to provide seed capital, though they along with **CYTA**, never took ownership of the festival.

Going places - CYTA

He believed that more could be achieved in a group effort than sticking with just one Christian denomination. He was proved right.

The organisations who partnered with **CYTA** as sponsors were the Anglican Youth Department, the NSW Baptist Youth Department, Churches of Christ Youth Department, Scripture Union NSW and the Uniting Church Christian Education Department (NSW). Each sponsor was to provide $6 000 as seed capital to establish the festival. Each partner followed through on their contribution and eventually their share of $16000 shortfall for expected ticket sales that did not reach budget on the first festival. At first it was not easy to secure the cash.

> **A side note:** It should be noted that over-time thirteen other Christian youth organisations became affiliated with the Not for Profit company **Combined Christian Youth Activities Ltd**, which was the legally constituted company limited by guarantee. This company owned and operated the festival which operated with the festival title of **"Black Stump'**

Very few new ventures go as planned. Though, the various organisations who were partners with **CYTA** for the launch of the festival, had been invoiced for their share of the seed capital to stage the first Black Stump festival, there was no money in the bank with six weeks to go.

An emergency Saturday meeting was called with the then **CYTA** board. Kevin spoke to the **CYTA** Board.

> *"The best solution to minimise losses is to cancel the event. The partners that have pledged financial support have not delivered. The alternative is for **CYTA** to go ahead with the festival and attempt to collect later on promises made by the partners."*

After prayer and some discussion by the **CYTA** Board it was agreed that the festival should go on supported by **CYTA**, even though the organisation may suffer substantial losses by solely underwriting **Beyond the Black Stump**. It went on and the other partners did eventually paid up.

The first four years of its operation the Black Stump festival was managed by **CYTA**. *Kevin* through the CYTA office managed strategic and operational activities for the first four years while *Jan* was the Music Director for the first seven years.

Kevin and Jan never seemed to have enough to do. The **CYTA TEAM** were also heavily involved in Black Stump getting off the ground and for several years after.

The format of the festival involved the majority of the music being presented on the main stage. Several smaller stages were placed around the venue. Speakers generally Christian evangelists spoke at the festival.

Black Stump was a camping music festival over three days. It operated on the first weekend in October, from 1985 till 2014. The October weekend is a long weekend in NSW. The festival was not held in 1987 due to there being a two-year plan to establish an ongoing festival in a permanent location. The festival was also not held in

Going places - CYTA

1995 and 2010 due to concerns with the ongoing financial viability of the venture and in 2001 after the Sydney Olympics occurred and many of the possible attendees were exhausted from Olympic involvement in the cultural program.

> **A side note:** *The name Black Stump was coined by **Ivor Lewis** who was Youth Director at Gymea Baptist at the time. Kevin while involved with Black Stump, (which he referred to as Beyond the Black Stump) concentrated on what could be achieved through the festival.*

The **CYTA TEAM** played a great part as volunteers at the Black Stump Festivals in which **CYTA** was involved, carrying out tasks such as traffic movement, assisting in setting up camps and catering as well as the many features required for the conduct of this great outdoor event. Once **CYTA** was no longer involved the festival seemed to change direction and became more like a "secular music festival" possibly losing some of its evangelical Christian zeal.

Going places - CYTA

> **A side note:** You could never tell when the skills and knowledge of a **TEAM MEMBER** would come in handy. A copyright problem arose in regard to the use of a boomerang in the signage for Black Stump. Kevin was able to call upon the services of a former **TEAM MEMBER**, *Mark Standen* who at the time of writing is a partner with the one of the top Australian Law firms, Minter Ellison, listed on the business's website as a specialist in mergers and acquisitions. Mark fixed the problem. Mark was a handy former **TEAM MEMBER** to have on your side.

Reflections on changes of the life of *Mike McCarthy,* an *attendee* at *Black Stump* during the period it was managed by **CYTA**.

> *"As a rebellious young man with a police record for petty crime, I landed on Australia's shores early in 1989. Born in Scotland, the oldest of seven children from a good Catholic family, my parents were hard working. Poor decisions had led me into deeper trouble.*
>
> *In a desperate effort to escape, to move beyond this seemingly inevitable life of ruin, in 1989 I sold my motorbike and bought a plane ticket to Sydney. Staying in a backpackers and couch surfing, I did some busking and casual work, spending the proceeds on alcohol. With little hope of ongoing work, I took a job with a company selling Encyclopaedias door-to-door (it was the pre-Google era!).*

Going places - CYTA

It was a mostly fruitless endeavour, apart from the fact that I met an attractive blonde Aussie girl. **Julie** *shared with me that she was a Christian, and I began to read the New Testament… determined to prove to her it was unreliable and untrue. She also invited me to a Music Festival – I loved Music Festivals and had enjoyed many in prior years, under the influence of excess alcohol and drugs. Somehow the notion of it being a "Christian" festival failed to register. So, in October of 1989 I found myself in a massive paddock at Cataract Park, south of Sydney, alongside several thousand young people. In a variety of venues, influential Christian musicians, artists and keynote speakers discussed faith the arts and the revelation of the truth of Jesus. Keynote speakers like Rev. John Smith and seminars by musicians like John Dickson, led me to a spiritual awakening that weekend. Around 11am on 1st October 1989, in front of the mainstage at Black stump Festival, I responded to God, surrendering to Jesus Christ as the Lord of my life and I have never looked back.*

Since that day, I have gone on to study Bachelor and Masters' degrees – in the ongoing pursuit of understanding the change God made in my life on that day, to make the most of the opportunity. I have been a staff MEMBER of a large suburban church, planted churches and taught church planters, aiming to see the Kingdom advance. I have been leading in Church life for

> *over 25 years, all as an outcome of that historic day in a field south of Sydney. Most significantly, I married the attractive blonde Aussie girl, and we celebrate 30 years of marriage this year. We have two beautiful daughters, young women who are leaders in church life, in their own right. I am thankful to God for all that I have and wonder sometimes, would it ever have happened, if there had not been an event like Black Stump Festival?"*

Musicians, musical groups and artists appearing over the life of Black Stump during and beyond **CYTA**'s involvement included the Queensland Christian band the *Newsboys, Priority Paid*, the internationally known Christian singer **Rebecca St James** and **David Butts** from the children's band the **Hooley Dooleys**. **Tim Harding** from **Hi-5** also appeared at Black Stump.

Sarah Blasko appeared at Black Stump. By the time she appeared she appeared she was recognised as a successful high profile singer/ songwriter in the wider music scene. **Butterfly Boucher** and **Paul Colman** whose career is discussed in the chapter dealing with the Australia Christian Music Festival were also artists to appear at Black Stump. **Tim Costello** the then CEO of World Vision Australia was one of the key note speakers that spoke at Black Stump.

This was a venture started by CYTA but never owned by CYTA. This like other later ventures of the organisation showed the slowly changing role of CYTA. The ministry was changing from an initiator who followed through and

Going places - CYTA

owned a venture to one that initiated a venture and passed it on to others.

Part Six – The initiators, the stayers

32. The Decision to finish it up

The end of CYTA, though it lingers on

The Christian Youth Travel Association was a creation of its time for its time. This was a time when both young men and women began to travel abroad as well as a variety of locations in Australia as an expected part of their lives. This was unlike many people from previous generations who never left Australia or were transported to foreign shores as part of a war effort. Though the young people of the 1950's to the 1980's expected to travel many chose to travel with like-minded people as part of a group.

Today the intrepid traveller journeys with friends or goes alone to unknown places but many young people in the 1960's and beyond did not have the confidence to make such journeys. They wanted to travel in a safe way, to undertake an adventure in a group, touring to new locations, in the company of people, of a similar age and interests.

Many young women especially but also young men (and their parents), whether Christian or not, wanted the reassurance that they were in a group in a safe environment where they would meet people, often for a little while and in some cases make enduring friendships.

The **CYTA TEAM** working with and on the **CYT** tours was an avenue that allowed young people to meet a wider group of people. As almost all of the tours involved camping, the prices were in the reach of young working adults, or were within the reach of supportive parents.

A new era dawned. Travel for young people became the norm. More young people had a university education. New jobs arose that previously did not exist, which carried large salaries and allowed young people to travel overseas and use their skills in a variety of countries and locations. Young women especially saw no barrier to travel on their own or in a group of two or three.

The nature of the Christian church was also changing with an emphasis on personal experience and reward central to many newly created churches. The societal message of "You can do anything, be anything" carried along Christians as it did for other young people during the years from the mid-eighties onward.

The change in socio-economic status of young people created a climate of competition in an ever increasing number of airlines. This occurred as there was a declining interest in coach travel. Organised group travel of a Christian and non-Christian nature diminished and so did the need for **CYTA**. After around 50 years of Christian based activities, the holiday travel, the travel to an event as well as the Christian music all of which, **CYTA** had largely pioneered were no longer needed and with that came the end of **ACMS**. The tours began by CYTA were no longer financially viable.

It took some years till the final closure of all arms of **CYTA** in April, 2014. Jan sums up some of the feeling of the end times as the life of **CYTA** was slowly coming to its end.

> "As the composition of the Board changed so did the dynamics of the working of the Board. Without the original Directors on the Board, it was easier to accept that the end was here.
>
> What would it take as a sign from God to end **CYTA**?
>
> If we got an offer to buy the Lodge, surely that would be a sign- we got an offer.."

Kevin:

> "All the things we did with **CYTA** especially at the LODGE were mostly for young adults at the time when **CYTA** existed. Times changed."

Jan goes on:

> "Every year, we asked ourselves, should we do another snow tour season? Do we believe that God would have us run another **AUSTRALIAN CHRISTIAN MUSIC SEMINAR**? Each year we started with a clean sheet of paper."

The tours have ended, the musical halls are quiet. However, **CYTA** still lingers on. Small groups of **TEAM MEMBERS** keep in touch with each other, via the **CYTA** Facebook page and by gathering together in small groups.

Some of the MEMBERs of one overland tour still get together from time to time. Small groups of former **TEAM MEMBER**s now as friends get together on occasion. Some former **CYTA TEAM MEMBER**s are in

Going places - CYTA

long-time friendships and are the best of friends. End of year functions, (I might add without a musical), still occur. There are regular visits with Kevin and Jan.
TEAM MEMBER *Ros Alibone* attends a Bible Study run by **Jan** on many Thursday nights held at the Craik's home. ***Dione Shoeman*** one of the authors of this book, who provided invaluable assistance particularly to Kevin in recording and provided information and valuable input in editing of this manuscript also attends the *Bible* study.

Kevin has been sorting out and will continue to sort tour folders. These will be returned by mail to the tour staff where addresses are known. There is still work to be done, nine years after the "final siren" sounded

In February 2021 a group of men organised by former **TEAM MEMBER, *John Grinsell*** cleaned out Kevin's lockup. Many treasures were found. The old blue jumper knitted by Jan that Kevin wore often at the **LODGE** and in fact everywhere he went. There were photos from tours, many of the **LODGE** and of course of the **TEAM MEMBERS** that came and went over time who served Christ through **CYTA**. The clean out was meant to be a time of throwing out, but many "treasures" were taken back to Jan and Kevin's town house for future sorting.

Amongst the treasures discovered was a fifteen year old box of chocolates. Kevin tells a great story (this one is a post **CYTA** story) of how at auction he bought a large number of "slightly out of date" chocolates from a failed warehouse for $200 which, he and his daughter Meredith (Susie) sold through their respective churches for a total of $4500. The proceeds were donated to

Christian charities. It is a great story and would lose much in the telling here. If you have access to the **CYTA** Facebook page you can see Kevin telling this story.

Barbara Wimble (Née Moore) is one of many **TEAM MEMBERS**, remembers the influence of Kevin and Jan on her life

> "Jan and Kevin 'lived their love of God' and encouraged us all in our service for Him. Jan particularly inspired me with her creativeness in so many ways."

Astrid Karlsson who we know as *Evie* on seeing the pictures of Kevin and the "**TEAM**" men cleaning out Kevin's lock up commented

> "This is pure delight to hear and see Kev!!! One of my all-time favourite guys, thank you (and Jan) for all you mean to me. "

Kevin today still remains always committed to taking up every opportunity to talk about and support the *Kingdom of Jesus Christ,* Kevin Craik is a good man, a man of faith, an innovator who along with his wife, Jan Craik served *Jesus Christ* through the establishment and growth of **CYTA**. When "a crowd too big to count" as described in Revelation 7 gather around the throne of God it is likely we won't be able to see Kevin or Jan. They should be down the front close to the Throne of God.

> A side note: **Kevin** and later **Jan** were recognised for their services to youth with each receiving an **Order of Australia medal (OAM)**

32. Kevin and Jan
Reflections

The story of **CYTA** is incomplete if we don't tell something of the untold story of Kevin Craik the man, the father as well as Christian entrepreneur. This is a small insight into Kevin's and Jan's life, coping with pressure of having a family, working, and the impact of managing a growing successful organisation.

As **CYTA** grew, Kevin gave up a career/job with the then Post Master General's office (now Telstra) along with the accompanying permanency of government employment and benefits to work full time for the **CYTA** organisation in 1978.

Kevin was working every spare moment, almost full time for **CYTA** before he officially took up the position of full-time Managing Director. Jan stood with Kevin as the only female director of **CYTA**. Jan was not just a support to Kevin but an active participant in forming and building the organisation. She also did much of the work on preparing menus for tours, but right from early on Jan was involved in administration work for **CYTA**, as well as providing training to tour staff. Jan has been and still is a support and counsellor for the female **MEMBERS** of the former **CYTA TEAM**.

Before we move to an interview that Kevin did with assistance of Jan did for this history, let's get the thoughts of their oldest child **Darren Craik** of his growing up in the world of **CYTA** amongst the life work of his parents.

Going places - CYTA

*"When Dad asked me to write a few words about my memories of growing up with **CYTA**, I said to him that it would be more like a short story and not just a foot note.*

*My **CYTA** life started at a very early age, born in August 1969 and in the snow by September 1969. That set the tone and theme for most of my childhood. Not just the son of Kevin and Jan, I was part of a bigger family which was the **CYTA** family.*

My earliest memories are that of my sister and I being bundled into the old lime green HT Holden station wagon CKC 002 for the 4 plus hour drive to Cooma, where we spent our weekends, long weekends and school holidays at the LODGE. Some kids grow up with holiday homes or caravans. My sister and I had a 14acre holiday paradise, where the only limits placed on us were 'be back for dinner'.

During the warmer months, there were so many activities we could amuse ourselves with and 'stay out of trouble', such as:

- *· Riding bikes around the paths and roads terrorising pedestrians and dodging the occasional coach or car coming along the back dirt road.*

- · Building cubby houses and playing wargames in Sherwood Forest.

- · Fire cracker night over the June long weekend and being tasked with helping to build the bonfire (cheap labour), then spending the night lighting crackers and staring at the stars and marvelling at how many there were compared to what we could see in the city.

- · Playing pool or table tennis in the rec. room.

- · Watching people drop coins through the timber flooring near the drink machine and working out a way of getting underneath the floor to find an assortment of things lost forever through the hardwood slats of the veranda decking. Let's just say it kept us supplied with cans of Pepsi for a few weeks each time.

- · The massive water fights on the last day of a work weekend and me running across the old kitchen roof trying to escape an onslaught and falling through the asbestos roof and almost through to the kitchen.

- · If we weren't planning to go down to the Bidgee River for a swim and a jump off the bridge, we would cool off by going for a swim in the town's water reservoir up near the lookout.

- *Spending hours belting the ball around in circles on the numerous totem tennis poles and breaking our necks on the pogo sticks.*

- *Running and jumping into the huge pile of cushions in the lounge – that was the best!*

Then there was winter which as you know was all about the snow. Getting up at 4 or 5am to get dressed, with the first breath you took when you walked out the room into the frozen frosted dawn and doing the mad dash from either C, Y, T, A blocks to get into the breakfast line and the warmth of the main building.

*After breakfast there was the dash back to your room to grab what you needed for the day, then onto the coach for the 1hr drive to Jindabyne where we would stop and pay the park fees and grab a quick snack before heading to Smiggin Hole for a day's skiing. We would return at lunch time where there would be hot soup and on occasion hot dogs cooked on gas cookers right next to the coach. Then back to the slopes for another few hours, before climbing back onto the coach for the return trip snooze before arriving back at the **LODGE**.*

I will leave it there as there are some activities that, as they say, 'what happens on tour, stays on tour'.

Going places - CYTA

*Whilst there were a lot of people that called the **LODGE** home for parts of the year, there were those that were lucky to call that place home for many years. The Shakespeare family, the Bolton family, Robyn Harris and the most lovable man giant, the one and only Kev Pool, who was a memorable character not only for his love of life but also for the love for those around him. When I was a small child he would tower over us and fake tripping over and yelling out:*

"Look out, we'll all be killed" where I and other small children would scatter, screaming in delight.

*I could keep writing about the **LODGE** forever, but **CYTA** was bigger than that. A big part of **CYTA** was the **CYTA TEAM**. A bunch of madcaps, crazy, interesting, dedicated people you could ever know, and it was my duty as a kid to run amuck and annoy them as much as I could. It was from this bunch of 'crazies' that **TOUR LEADER**s were nurtured and developed to guide and lead tours to a growing number of destinations both national and international.*

I will never forget the days going to Campbells at South Strathfield/Belfield and loading up the one tonner with bulk food products. We would then fill up our garage at Homebush with all the purchases that would eventually get divvied up according to the menus on a tour and according to the itinerary along with what would be needed for the tour from tents to tables and cookers. Trying to ride my skateboard up and down the home driveway was impossible on the weekends that the distribution of the shopping was being performed. I was grateful when it was moved to the Everton Road Strathfield office, and I could get my whole driveway back.

The Strathfield office metamorphosed soon over a few years to the long stay premises at Homebush. This was a building that contained a lot of memories, Thursday night **TEAM** *meetings and Uncle Kev's Pancakes not to mention it had a nice, ramped driveway which could be skated on in all weather.*

My proudest memory, however, was the day in 1985 that we had to drag my father Kevin Craik along to Government House in Sydney to see him accept his OAM medal for service to Australian Youth. That being said, I am very proud of both my parents for what they achieved.

There were other aspects of the **CYTA** *world that I was dragged along to oops I meant to say happily coerced to attend, but a story for others to tell."*

Darren is married to Michelle (Née Carter). They have two boys, Julian and Connor. The family lives in Queensland.

Going places - CYTA

Not to be out done **Meredith (aka. Susie) Dimarco** (Née **Craik**) has given her take on growing up as a **CYTA** kid.

> "Growing up as a **CYTA** kid I am fortunate to have wonderful memories of growing up with the **LODGE** at Cooma as our playground, and I must say when I think of the **LODGE** I think of beautiful long hot summer days, freezing cold crispy winters and all the time we spent there with our friends. But when I really think about what has affected me the most it's the growing up alongside a group of amazing people doing wonderful acts of service and having so much fun at the same time learning of God in the **TEAM**. It showed me that not only could Christianity be faith in action, but it could be fun and it could be even more effective with friends, working together as a "**TEAM**". It showed me what it meant to look out for others ahead of yourself and commit yourself fully to whatever you do, and what an amazing plan for life that is.
>
> My parents modelled leadership in a way that constantly built others up by constantly affirmed their strengths, developing their weaknesses, and helped them to learn new things. They learnt skills that would equip them in many ways in a future that they couldn't possibly have dreamed of.
>
> Future leaders, teachers, pastors, caterers, communicators, and organisers were nurtured,

Going places - CYTA

developing so many abilities that have now been used greatly in God's Kingdom. One of my favourite memories of my childhood were the Training Weekends, where my brother and I would be whisked away to some bush, farm or beach camping ground, along with up to 80 or 90 other young people, to learn the essential skills required to successfully run a **CYTA** tour. Here they (and we) were taught skills as diverse as: how to safely turn on a generator, safety in the use and storage of L.P. Gas, de-pressurise a pressure cooker, cut tomatoes with minimal wastage, *store lettuce for maximum crispness, cook a tasty roast dinner for 35 on a single gas ring, pick a safe camp spot away from bull-ants, emus, echidnas and sudden water courses, set-up hand hygiene "Sadie", pack an under-coach for efficient access, run a devotion with impact and have immense fun all at the same time! Little did I know that the skills I gained almost by osmosis would become second nature and immensely useful later in life. Even food served on orange plastic plates in the desert need to look enticing, colourful and well-presented! This was taught to me by Linda Webb when I had the opportunity of assisting her on a Central Australian Tour.*

The **LODGE** *was not just an amazing setting for summers and skiing, but it was a home for the* **AUSTALIAN CHRISTIAN MUSIC SEMINAR** *which was a great time for me as a child and teenager, but also an immense time of spiritual* *learning of what it means being the body of Christ together. We learnt that worship didn't need to just be a "hymn sandwich" in church, but that it could (and should!) be so much more. Our days were filled with singing in the Kids Choir with Sister Eleanor, listening to the lunch-time concerts, swimming in the rapids at the Murrumbidgee River, walking down to Monaro High for the evening programme (batting off enormous Christmas beetles) and then finishing off the day with pancakes and apple cider at the Insomniacs Supper Club. Music Seminars were so much fun, and the friendships developed there are precious to this day. Who knew that the tips and tricks learnt way back then would suddenly be useful when a pandemic struck from nowhere, and we had to spontaneously learn to live-stream worship or sing to a full church with no one else permitted to sing! Equipping that we didn't know we would ever need!*

*Concerts, Black Stump, Kiah Ridge Work Weekends… there was always something to look forward to. Mum and Dad worked 7 days a week in the lead-up to big events, but they always did it cheerfully and with excitement, passionate about whatever lay ahead. One moment it was sitting in a circle around Evie, singing songs for a TV special, the next moment it was having competitions to see how quickly we could set up 10 tents and pump up 20 air mattresses! Being a **CYTA** kid meant life was never dull, there was always the next*

> "adventure", and whatever it entailed there would be good friends there to share the experience. I feel very blessed to have been able to be involved in such a deep way, and it is lovely to hear how so many of the kids around me back then, feel the same way now as my brother Darren and I do. We are deeply grateful for our Mum and Dad, Jan and Kevin, for the tireless servant-hearted modelling they gave us, and the beautiful extended family that "The Directors", staff both in Sydney and at Cooma and "**TEAM**" became in our lives."

From (**Susie**) **Craik**, now **Meredith Dimarco**

Meredith and her husband **Santino** have three children. **The** oldest is **James** who is married to **Karla** the middle child is **Alessandra** who is married to **Liam**. The youngest child is **Laura**.

An Interview with Kevin and Jan for this book

What motivated you Kevin, to create an organisation that served the young people of Australia and what sustained your interest in CYTA for the more than fifty years?

> "The ongoing drive to present the message of Christ crucified for our redemption and His raising from the dead. I suffered with ADHD in my early years, and got into some mischief *but came to faith at 16 and was always active in my faith, not only devoting time to the development of* **CYTA** *but also to the NSW Baptist Youth*

Fellowship (BYF) and later on as a member in the NSW Baptist Church – Department for Youth and Christian Education.

I was active from the 1950's through to the 1990's. I am disappointed today that I am an invalid and unable to be as active as I was in Christian ministry and presenting the message of Jesus Christ."

Kevin, tell us about your family? Your parents lived at Burwood for some time, but what happened before that and how did your parents and your two brothers respond to having a work table in the lounge room in the family home as a de facto CYTA office?

"The family home I grew up in was at Marrickville. My family was fully supportive of all forms of ministry. I worked off a small table in the lounge area. My mother was used to my father having Christian material around the house. My father was involved in various areas of ministry including being the Superintendent of the Sunday school at Marrickville Baptist Church. He was also the Captain of the local Boys Brigade Company.

*My two brothers **John** and **D**a**vid** were supportive of **CYTA**. John was an active **BOARD MEMBER**. David was indispensable in the legal and accounting work. David at the time was completing his accounting and law degrees,* *studying at night. He replaced John on the **CYTA** Board after John's departure."*

*Jan came into the picture in 1962. When we married in 1966 we bought the family home at Marrickville being our first home as a married couple. My parents moved into rented accommodation after the Marrickville home was sold. The move to the unit in Burwood by my parents occurred when **my brothers and I purchased the unit for our parents**.*"

At this stage **Kevin** talks of **Jan**

*"They say behind every man is a great woman. This was true of Jan. She was not only integral to the development of **CYTA** she was also good at her job as a nurse educator, she was asked by Graham Drayton to go to various regional school districts to provide training to senior staff in relation to biological education as it related to maturing teenagers."*

Kevin, what about the snow? What made you fall in love with the snow on those early trips? Were either of you surprised at the popularity of the snow tours?

"It was less a love of the snow and more the desire to provide a safe environment for Christians to travel to and enjoy the snow. The snow was somewhere which was generally not open to Christians. I wanted to have tours to the snow that provided a safe environment in which

to travel and allow Christians to enjoy their time in the snow.

There was no surprise as to the popularity of the Snow Tours. No one else was doing these sorts of tours at the time. Now most all travel organisations have tours that cater to Christian groups. There was disappointment when we ran our last snow our in 1998. The world had changed as has the travel industry. Young people had more money and more choices."

What was your vision for the organisation?

"There was no vision or plan. Everything grew like topsy. The organisation grew and changed in response to opportunities that arose and which the **CYTA** Board believed they were led to take up through the leading of the Holy Spirit.

I was seen at that stage by others to have leadership abilities by others and was urged to lead. My entrepreneurial abilities were channelled into **CYTA** while also being involved in BYF and Boards of the NSW Baptist Church. I was motivated and enthused by what could be achieved by God through my efforts and the very many people with whom I worked. It was all about bringing young people to Christ ".

When did you think of expanding the list of tours beyond the snow and how did you choose the locations?

> "Almost straight away we considered tours to other locations. What worked at the snow could be replicated and modified to work on other travel tours and in other locations. Graham Drayton took our first non-snow tour (discussed in the tours section). We went overseas to various locations including to the Philippines for the Baptist Youth Conference. The goal was affordable tours which Christians could enjoy and where non-Christians who travelled on **CYTA** tours would hear the Gospel."

Kevin you have mentioned in our conversations that some people on the TEAM regarded you as a second father. Others saw you as a role model, yet others as a mentor. How do you respond to those thoughts?

> "I was humbled that so many men, (and women), held me in such regard. However, others would disagree with the suggestions included in the question."

A side note: The following arre comments on Kevin's skills. **Penny Johnson** said of Kevin: "Kevin was one of my first managers. He was a man committed to getting the job done and worked hard with a little or a lot. He loved to see the results of his labours - particularly enjoyment and smiling faces from those returning from a tour. He loved to encourage people to learn new skills and stretch themselves and invested in many volunteers spanning many years." **Jim Gibson** said of Kevin: "Kevin is a creative, entrepreneurial organiser of events and finder of resources with superlative skills in getting large

Going places - CYTA

> community events to happen. I was his Pastor for some time."

Kevin, who proposed you for the OAM? What did you know about the process?

> "The process for such an award is that you must be nominated for the award and that the nominator must come up with four people who can confirm the facts provided to the committee who manages the awards. The information of these four people is fully investigated. Recommendations are made based on the information secured as to whether or not an award should be granted.
>
> The process is a secret one, though I suspect that I may know one of the people involved in the nomination. The recipient is asked if they will accept nomination. All must be kept secret till the award is made, if an award is made. The only person I told of the nomination was Jan."
>
> In 2017 my brother John Craik also gained a commonwealth award – Member (AM) IN THE GENERAL DIVISION OF THE ORDER OF AUSTRALIA for significant service to the community through Christian Prisoner Fellowship groups and services to the Insurance Sector.
>
> Jan was awarded her OAM for services to youth.

How did you feel when you were awarded the medal for "distinguished service of a high degree to Australia or to humanity at large"?

> *"I was awarded the honour for services to youth. At the time I received the award it was only one of 160 medals awarded. In last set of awards (2021) there were 1200 OAM'S. I felt greatly honoured and humbled. I was one of a small number, though my achievements were only possible through the work of the great people that I worked with.*

Congratulations to Jan who was awarded an OAM some years after Keven. Jan was asked about her recollections of becoming part of CYTA and the impact of the ministry on her life. She decided to put her response down on paper, but found it difficult to find a starting point. The following is her thoughts.

> *I've found it hard to put on paper my thoughts regarding **CYTA**. Where do I begin? I married Kevin because he was a man with a purpose – just like my Dad. I knowingly married into **CYTA**, which at the time of our wedding was taking on the form of a great adventure. With our close friends we became **DIRECTORS** of the ministry that swept us along for so many years.*
>
> *From the beginning we saw the potential of the tours to be an opportunity to talk with other young people about Jesus. A couple of weeks sitting in a coach together provided a place for many conversations, which brought about changed lives.*
>
> *Of course there was a cost. Kev held down a full-time job as well managing **CYTA**. I often found*

myself alone with the children, **Darren** and "**Susie**" on many a weekend and night. It was painful. I missed Kev so much. When he went to the **LODGE** for a weekend – which of course was quite often- Sunday afternoons were agonisingly looming.

I remember clearly one afternoon, Darren who was a toddler at the time had me open our bedroom curtains so he could watch and wait for Daddy to come home in the coach. It was more likely for him to see "Uncle" Cliffy, the driver - but wait there was Daddy as well.

The "plusses" far outweighed the cost. When God has placed you or me in such a position where pain is involved, HE provides strength and resilience and many good experiences as a reward.

What I benefited from was having a husband who had confidence in me to do many things I had never dreamed of doing. Concert M.C., hosting tours, developing menus for the tours (with much help from **Colleen Barrington**, **Robyn Harris** and **Carole Reece**, thank you), organising and managing the music seminar each January, organising the stages and managing the main program at Black Stump every October long weekend (thanks to **Julie Barnaby**) along with many other activities. Kev encouraged me to stretch my abilities in all directions. What a Blessing.

A question for both of you: Why the interest in music? How did music and travel go together?

> "We started with music at the **LODGE**, for which you (Howard) auditioned and recruited bands for some years as well as local concerts you ran in Sydney and elsewhere. Brain Willersdorf (See the preachers section) told us that if we wanted to bring in the biggest Christian Act in the world at that time it was Andraé Crouch and the Disciples covered in the music section.)

> The first Christian band was booked into the Opera Hose. We had two nights we wanted to fill. Securing those dates took perseverance and patience with regular phone calls to the founding manager of the Opera House. As I said earlier this was another activity of **CYTA** an organisation that grew like topsy"

How did the music tours turn into the Australian Christian Music Foundation?

Jan begins:

> "I attended a music seminar at Estes Park in the United States and was able to bring home firsthand information on how a Christian Music Seminar would/could work. The **CYTA** Board had discussed the possibility of a seminar."

Kevin continues:

> "However, it was the challenge by Fletch Wiley to us that we should do something for music that started the planning for a seminar. During

> summer the Lodge was generally empty. We wanted to have a revenue-generating activity at the **LODGE** in summer. We had tried summer camps which attracted no interest so why not try a music seminar.
>
> The Board also agreed that a committee apart from the **CYTA** Board should manage the seminar, of which you in the first two seminars along with, Jan and I were members of the committee, with you Howard and others with **Fred Grice** as Chairperson. (Refer to the **AUSTRALIAN CHRISTIAN MUSIC SEMINAR** Chapters)
>
> As is recorded elsewhere **(AUSTALIAN CHRISTIAN MUSIC SEMINAR),** Jan was the music director for the seminar and started with a blank sheet every year. Each year started off with fresh thinking.
>
> The seminars lost money but this was offset by the money paid for accommodation at the Lodge.

Kevin mentioned the leadership Jan has shown as a worship leader for many years in their local Baptist Church. He went on to say:

> "Not having enough on her plate with being a worship leader, under the direction of four pastors, she produced and coordinated three full scale musicals some of which travelled to two country as well as interstate presentations."

What if any might be your single biggest regret? Kevin responds.

> "In hindsight we should never have sold the Homebush Centre. Though I was always conscious of neighbourhood complaints, we never had a complaint. We never had council permission to turn the street outside the premises into a bus stop. The centre had an office area, accommodation upstairs. The area inside of the centre could be converted into a **TEAM** area, an area to set up equipment for tours and a car park for **TEAM MEMBER** cars while **TEAM MEMBERS** were on weekend tours. The Silverwater centre served a purpose but did not offer the flexibility that we had at Homebush.
>
> The other regret was not being able to make Kiah Ridge functioning. Funding the development of the camp from an overdraft when interest rates were so high was not sustainable."

A side note: At this point I offer Kevin the observation that Kiah Ridge could be seen as being started by **CYTA**, and completed and carried on by the NSW Baptist Churches, an observation recorded in the chapter on Kiah Ridge. **CYTA** became an initiator but not necessarily a finisher in many of its later endeavours.

Kevin continues.

Going places - CYTA

> *"We did sell the property with considerable substantial income generating existing bookings. The property has moved on from the early days and is a location which is used to bring people to Christ. When on the Board I did vote for the appointment of the current manager and he is doing a good job including setting up Kiah Ridge for future development."*

Love to behold. I have sat in Kevin's and Jan's house and listened to the journey of **CYTA**, which is their journey. I asked Jan to write some information about her time on the Board, requesting she write about her strength as a person, you know "I am woman". (This is mentioned briefly in an earlier section.)

Jan was around in the era of "I am woman". She worked and looked after a family. She initially said she couldn't write about herself and turned to Kevin, who then waxed lyrical about his wife. He spoke of her faithfulness in fulfilling all manner of tasks.

Kevin reflected on Jan's selfless approach of giving time to **CYTA**. How proud he is of his wife, of what she has achieved, the new tasks she took on especially the musical events. Knowledge which Jan gained on planning, developing and managing events, she shared with other organisations and used in mounting musical events for other organisations.

What Kevin said about his wife was love to behold. I saw a tender moment in the lives of this couple. There was more than "three points" but every point demonstrated his ongoing love affair with his wife.

> *A Side Note:* In case you may not know or have forgotten, Kevin opened almost every address to the **TEAM** by saying, **"Just two points"**. There were always at least ten or eleven

The public and private always the same

Many famed and followed people in the public space present one persona in public and another in private. When things are going wrong in the private lives of people in the public eye, and become known to the public, such people are often seen in a different light by the public. Sometimes the public sees them as being different people to what they had previously conceived.

Jan and Kevin are not. What they are in public they are more of in private. **CYTA** was not just a tour organisation, not even just a mission field but a work of love. Kevin and Jan's love for the **TEAM**, the love they showed through the employment they created for casual staff and contractors and the love they had for their loyal permanent staff. Most of all their love for each other and their love for *God*

After you have read this history, you might wherever you are, consider giving three cheers for the couple who positively affected many lives – Jan and Kevin Craik.

Going places - CYTA

Part Seven - My Chapters - The author

Going places - CYTA

35. The man, the timing, the mission

This chapter is what I have read at the launch of this or what I would have read of there was a launch of this book.

I know, as someone chronicling a history that it is not for me to make much of my personal observations or provide comment on, or commentary on what is written. However, the timing of the emergence of CYTA is in line with a world-wide Christian revival – **Jesus Movement – Revolution** that occurred outside the established churches. *God's* timing and choice of people is immaculate.

This chapter places **CYTA** within the "*Jesus Revolution*" revival in 1960's and 1979's and as aprt of the history of Christianity.

I realised for the first time this week, the week I am writing this chapter in May 2023 (more than two years after we started the journey that is this book) that when it came to the establishment of CYTA that *God's* timing and the choice of leader that God's judgement is impeccable. Remember that *God's* timing and choice of leaders is always impeccable.

The time in which CYTA was established was a time in the 1960's when the lives of believers and non-believers were changing. It was a time when many people began to doubt the value of the organised church and new forces were changing or possibly manipulating the teachings of *Jesus* to fit self-designed outcomes.

Going places - CYTA

It was a time when what is called the philosophy of Modernism cast doubts upon the veracity of anything that claimed to be about truth. Over time the world moved from Modernism to Post Modernism. Post modernism carried with it an implied destruction of the organised church. The philosopher Friedrich-Nietzsche extended his original view that each person decides and should decide what is truth according to their personal beliefs, to saying there is no one truth. No absolute truth, which is at variance form the Christian message.

Churches at the time CYTA commenced often were empty or near empty, in many locations in Sydney and elsewhere in the world. I remember attending a church along with **Malcom Power** (someone who was also a **CYTA TEAM MEMBER**), that had been built on a merger of two reasonably healthy churches but churches still with problems.

As the 1960s progressed there was diminishing attendance in that church. The church suffered from what I now would call a spiritual deadness. The morning congregation of attendees reduced every year during the 1960's into the 1970's. The evening congregation became almost non-existent to the point that the minister of the time decided to hold in place of the service, "**A Fireside Chat**" for the few people who attended evening church meetings. The meeting was held in his home.

In the rest of the world, during the sixties and seventies war was brewing and reached boiling point in ASIA. Edwin Star, wrote the song WAR The-Key Lyric line was

"War, huh, yeah

What is it good for?

Absolutely nothing"

A band named **The Grateful Dead** was growing in popularity. Eleanor Rigby was picking up rice at a church where the wedding had been while wondering what happened to all the lonely people.

There was a battle to be number one between the two biggest bands in the world at that time the Beach Boys and the Beatles who were rated five and one respectively by music commentary website Ledger in a listing of the ten best bands of all time.

The Beatles wrote that all you need is Love while Dr Timothy Leary, an American Psychologist wrote all you need is drugs.

Meanwhile with much going on in the world**, Chuck Smith** a Californian minster was looking at a near empty church he pastored. The church emphasised compliance with the government (and with the ideal of T.V. show "Superman" – the American way) and the need for each person to fit into a particular life style to be a good American.

> **A short note:** Smith's church was in California. A new revival began on a University campus in California in 2023.

Chuck Smith was introduced to an itinerant preacher who Smith thought on their first meeting had broken in into his house. His name was **Lonnie Frisbee** who changed Smith's church to the point that they needed bigger premises, and then again bigger premises. The result was the establishment of the **Calvary Chapel** churches.

Smith and Frisbee argued, not unusual in the *Jesus* movement and Frisbee founded his own church **the Vineyard Movement/Vineyard Churches. Greg Laurie** a young adult who was searching for truth was converted under the preaching of Smith and Frisbee. He left Smith's church and started **Harvest Crusades/Harvest Christian Fellowship**

The **Love Song Band** was a Christian band who played at Smith's original church. The leader of the band is credited as saying that on the night of their first appearance at Smith's church that he was attending church for the first time.

This was a Christian band which did not attend church. Like most bands the line-up changed over time. I met one of their prominent members, who went solo after leaving the band. His name is **Chuck Girard.** Before joining the Christian band he had been a membership of a one hit wonder "secular" band.

Girard kept me standing empty handed in front of around 400 people in Newcastle. I was wondering why he was late for his performance. He did turn up after around forty minutes and the reason for his lateness turned out to be a funny story.

Just as Smith thought that **Lonnie Frisbee** was creating a cult of personality, there were some Christian artists who may have been doing the same. One artist left me empty handed when he told me he would not go on stage in front of 5,500 people at Brookvale Oval unless the piano supplied for him was changed. He caused considerable friction on the day that went beyond his demands in regard to the piano. Not a funny story this time.

This *Jesus* movement was not about churches, certainly not existing churches, it was about *Christ*. The movement had its problems and controversies, and took on various forms in different countries. In Montreal there was the Montreal Miracle and other things were happening in Britain.

In Australia the *Jesus* revolution saw new organisations established. A group named **FUSION** provided an alternate approach to presenting the message of Christ than through an established church network.

Don Gillespie in Queensland and later in association with **Rhema Music** in Sydney (who were on their own journey to promote and record new Australian Christian artists) published a Christian music magazine **Keystone.**

There was the **House of the New World** that was established at Ryde. This appeared to me as a somewhat hippy style commune where people lived collectively. One of the members of the group worked in the **CYTA** office for some time. The House was sponsored by the NSW Baptist Church.

The Christian Band **Family**, who owned **Rhema Music**, reached number one the Australian Music Charts with a cover of a version of a song sung my Michel Jackson, courtesy of an embargo on playing American music on Australian radio. The song was called **Hallelujah Day.**

The *Jesus* movement inspired people into the 1980's and beyond. **John Dickson** has a degree in theology and a PHD. At the time of writing John Dickson presents a course on the "Historical *Jesus*" at the University of Sydney. The same John Dickson was the lead singer of the Christian rock band **"In the Silence"** through the late 1980s and early 90s. The band would play up to six shows a week. They played in pubs and clubs. In song introductions and between songs members of the band talked about their faith

Even after the year 2000 the media talked of the *Jesus* Movement of the sixties and seventies

NOVEMBER 28TH, 2019 03:11 PM and article appeared in a news service called **Eternity News**,

> "Kevin B Smith passed away recently, in Perth, at the age of 75, after a long illness. He was a champion in the Jesus Movement in the 1970s and 80s. He was a visionary, an innovator, and a revolutionary. He was passionate about following Jesus and about helping the **Jesus Movement** express a united voice. Kevin founded **On Being** magazine, one of the most important elements of the Jesus Movement in those days."

The *Jesus* movement in Australia just like the US and elsewhere was scattered and, had no central, and did not need, any central coordination. Nearly all of the actions taken and all the new organisations established did not emanate from churches. They were established

Going places - CYTA

outside of churches or broke away from established churches.

In 1956 a nineteen year old **Kevin Craik** not recognised as an adult in law at that time, took a trip to the snow with two mates. It was not yet about Christian tours but just some mates enjoying a trip to the snow.

This book, **Going Places CYTA** carries the details of the development **CHRISTIAN YOUTH TOURS (CYT)** not initially **CYTA**, which would come later with the first **CYT** snow tours beginning in 1962. A Christian movement, a Christian business, a ministry had begun that expanded quickly into other areas of travel other than snow tours. **CYTA** took thousands of predominantly young people across Australia and across the world. **CYTA** later pioneered the development of a contemporary Christian music ministry in Australia, which was my area of interest in regard to **CYTA**, not the tours.

If you want to know what happened and why, and hear about some of the wonderful life changing experiences for many thousands of people, you will need to buy and read this book. If you want to know how like other organisations and Christian people involved with the changing Christian landscape of the time (and really of all time and any point in time), including how **CYTA** was criticised, then you should buy this book. There are stories of catering, cooking and crashes but so much more.

I can say that I believe that *God* chose you, Kevin, to be involved in your own way in the *Jesus* Revolution, a momentous point in Christian history, with your lifelong partner, Jan. Jan has stated elsewhere in this book, that she married into **CYTA** into a life that I suspect that not every wife may have wanted to live. To me in retrospect you shared the prefect union.

This book is not the life story of Kevin and/or Jan their family, or the initial **DIRECTORS** or anyone else. It is the story I believe **of *God's* purpose for Kevin's life.**

God was right about the timing of the establishment of **CYTA** and the man to lead it. Kevin, I know in these days you feel frustrated from time to time that you can't be involved in Christian service as you were once. Issues of age and health, impinge on what you would like to do sometimes.

However, Kevin you have positively affected many people's lives not necessarily through direct contact but by providing the infrastructure, paid employment for many people and giving support to a team of voluntary workers. You created a ministry in a form of a business that was able to show people the world, that is *God*'s creation, and expose thousands of people to, or re-expose people to sound Biblical knowledge.

You stood behind people and supported them to achieve things for the *Kingdom* here on earth that they might not have otherwise achieved. Kevin, what a purpose *God* gave you in your life. What a life. I thought then and still think now that you had the best job in Australia and you did it well.

I was a great privilege for me to be involved with **CYTA** where I enhanced my Biblical knowledge, met a

Going places - CYTA

wonderful group of people in the CYTA Team, saw people come to Christ and picked up most of the very few practical skills I possess.

I have written elsewhere in this book that I won't see Kevin and Jan in heaven as described in the book of Revelation, as they will be down towards the front of the throng, while I will be near to the back. Also when you have read the book and realise the enormity of the work carried out by Kevin and Jan I have suggested you could stop where you are and give them three cheers. Let's do it now.

Now I get to ask you some questions and then everyone here and on-line can ask questions.

My questions:

What do you think is the most significant aspect of the book?

What don't you like about the book?

Questions anyone?

36. The message of the story of CYTA

Is there a message for YOU from this book?

If you have read this far, then **PLEASE** finish this chapter as there is one recurring theme you may have noticed in this book. Each person mentioned is someone working for and relying on *Jesus Christ*. Everything that **CYTA** did was to contribute to the building of *God's Kingdom* here on Earth.

In the *Bible* is the story of the parable of the sower. A farmer is broadcasting (throwing) seed onto the ground. Some seed fell on the path and was eaten by birds. Other seed fell in rocky places, with little soil and though the seed took root it soon was burnt by the sun. Some seed fell among thorns, which over grew the small seed plants that grew. Other seed fell on good soil and produced a crop, multiplying itself many times.

This parable of the four soils/the sower is really the story of how people respond in different ways to hearing about the word of *God*. The ministry of **CYTA** is not unlike this story (parable).

When the *Word of God* was presented to people on tour some were like rocky ground in that they did not want the word of God to apply to them. Others listened the *Word* took root but was soon subsumed by life. Other people had a life that inhibited growth like the thorns. The *Word* took root but as time went on other things seemed of more immediate importance and the word was choked out. The last group were those who already believed or came to belief. *God's Word* for these people became a reality a guiding light in their lives. All these instances were ever present among people who came into contact with *God* through the activities of **CYTA**

Which response applies to you?

If you are challenged by the faith of the many people working for the *Kingdom* through and with **CYTA**, then it is time to explore what was behind their actions. You might start by reading Mark or Luke's gospel (or maybe both) in the section of the Bible referred to as the New Testament.

The Bible is free online. There are many different versions just as there are different versions of many books printed over the centuries. The New International Version (NIV) is generally a great way to start reading.

If you still like the feel of paper, you will no doubt find a Bible in your local library. If it is out, then ask the librarian to get a copy from another library or have it reserved for you upon its return.

If you are new to church, or you are returning to church after a period of leave, then check out the list of local churches that is held by your local council and/or is on the council website.

Visit a few churches. Sunday is a good day to go church shopping. Keep visiting. It's a little like buying new clothes. You may visit a church and like clothes shopping it does not fit or suit you. Keep visiting churches until you feel sufficiently comfortable to make

Going places - CYTA

a choice of church suitable to you. Make sure the church you decide to attend is focussed on God's message and God's will for you.

You should be aware that Christians generally sign up for life but you don't have to sign for life at a particular church. You can change church as often as you need. It is good when you find one which fits your needs.

It might take a little research and a little effort to get hold of a copy of the Bible that suits you, or to find a suitable church. The result of your efforts is very likely to change your life.

CYTA no longer exists but *Jesus* still does.

He is free and available to those people who seek Him today.

Acknowledgements
Author
I want to say thank you to all those people who contributed to the writing of this book. Without the input of all the people quoted in the book, the book would not have a life. It would be no more than a dry history of what occurred in over more than fifty years. Your input helped make the book come alive.

I especially wish to thank *Jan* and *Kevin* for the forthright discussions I have had with them and the disclosure of information which constitutes the core of this book.

Also, to the many former **TEAM MEMBERS** and former **CYTA** staff that provided information and quotations on the **CYTA** Facebook page and especially to those people who sent material direct to me and to those who responded to Kevin's direct call.

Special thanks to *Chris Pieper Otten* for her wonderful chapter on the Victorian **TEAM** and to *Collen Barrington* for her contribution on the Queensland **TEAM**. Special thanks also to *Max Watson* and *James Mann* who every time they put up a post on the **CYTA** Facebook page stimulated a new discussion which led to an outstanding response from others much of which has been included in this book.

I would like to especially recognise *Robin Morris* who created and sustains **Teapot Ministries** as a mission to Women. Robin provided a strong message in her story of her time in **CYTA** and how it influenced her whole life

Going places - CYTA

Thanks to **Elva Harris** for her input into the book and for her contacts and addresses for distribution of information on the book.

Thanks to the readers/reviewers, **Linda Webb**, **Bev Carruthers** and **Elaine Aurel Smith** who cast their critical eyes over the manuscript and provided crucial and critical feedback on the draft manuscript. The knowledge and interest of each of them in the project was excellent. Thanks also to **Gary** and **Robin Morris** for their work in reviewing the book. My thanks to **Dione** for keeping Kevin up to the task and more particularly her support to him and of him and her excellent work in recording Kevin's thoughts and the editorial work she did.

My thanks to the love of my life, my wife **Julie** in agreeing for us to financially support this venture as well as her efforts in editing not just the early version of this manuscript but the many others I have written over the years. I count myself fortunate and blessed to be with her every day.

This has been a story of **God** at work through HIS **people.**

I would like to say that I am always looking for a good story to write about, especially memorable stories such as this one **"Going Places CYTA"**.

If you hear of a story that needs writing, then feel free to pass my name onto another person or their name onto me. Though I never want to tell a story again in which I had some involvement and the book should be finished to initial draft stage in six months and published within nine to twelve months of commencement

Kevin Craik Acknowledgments
Dione Schoeman chief encourager, supporter and active writer

South Africa is famous for its gold deposits, diamonds and the infamous jailing of Nelson Mandela. Australia has received many South Africans as immigrants to our country.

The book would have been all the more difficult to write and more belated had it not been for a lady by the name of Dione Schoeman who with her family arrived here from South Africa in 2003 and became "Dinky Di" Australians in 2005.

Dione has been a tower of strength to Kev and Jan, researching and writing up material, typing and retyping copy from interested **TEAM MEMBERS**, not to say the least deciphering Kev's handwriting. Tracing the **CYTA** Badge for Kev was a highlight! Dione has a heart of gold (also has a love of diamonds) and has given up time over a period of many years assisting 86 year old Kev. Many days have turned into very late evenings. Thank you very much for your help, Dione. You are a tower of strength and have the tenacity to always get the job done.

> **A side note:** As *Dione* prepared copy she continued to express her disappointment that she wasn't part of the **CYTA TEAM**. It has been at Dione's **PERSISTENCE**

> and **INSISTENCE** that Going Places has finally been written.

Howard Reid The author behind Going Places CYTA

Howard was a **CYTA TEAM MEMBER** from 1970 – 1977. No longer a **TEAM MEMBER** Howard, was involved in the Australian Music foundation/**AUSTALIAN CHRISTIAN MUSIC SEMINAR** till January 1980.

During his time as a **CYTA TEAM MEMBER,** he led numerous weekend snow tours and camping tours to the Barrier Reef and New Zealand, across the Nullarbor to Perth and to Tasmania

He was also involved in the music ministry of **CYTA**, playing an important part in coordinating the concerts that were programmed at that time. Howard was more interested in the music ministry of **CYTA** than the camping ministry. He recruited bands/artists for the Saturday night concerts at **CYTA LODGE** during the Snow season for more than three years.

He organised the weekend country concerts and concerts in Sydney and as well provided leadership for the tours of Andraé Crouch and concerts leading up to the Evie Tornqist tour. Howard was a member of the Australian Gospel Music Foundation, the forerunner to the **AUSTALIAN CHRISTIAN MUSIC SEMINAR.** He was also a **MEMBER** of the originating organising committee for the **AUSTALIAN CHRISTIAN MUSIC SEMINAR.**

Going places - CYTA

This is Howard's first book authoring the history of an organisation though it is his fourteenth book as an author/co-author.

Going places - CYTA

Authors note:

Howard Reid has authored/co-authored thirteen previous books. In addition, he has been involved in authoring television scripts, research reports and a wide variety of educational publications for both government and the private sector over a period of more than forty years. He had extensive an extensive in teaching in TAFE NSW, various Australian universities at undergraduate and graduate level as well as authoring and presenting numerous learning programs in the private sector. Howard has hosted several televisions series made with the Open Training and Education Network, some of which enjoyed a second screening on public television on the ABC.

This Book

Writing this book has been different to those books I have authored/co-authored previously. I have been pleased to be able to tell the story of the **CHRISTIAN YOUTH Travel ASSOCIATION (CYTA)**. It is a story in which I played a small part as a **TOUR MEMBER, TEAM MEMBER**, and **TOUR LEADER** and as a music coordinator. It is always exciting to start a new project but I am pleased and relieved this elongated project over some three years with some unpleasant side journeys is now complete for others to read

My greatest interest in **CYTA** was in the music ministry. My involvement especially in mounting local **CYTA** concerts, supplying bands for the snow season for several years as well limited contact with the

Going places - CYTA

international visitors and my small involvement at the start of the **AUSTRALIAN CHRISTIAN MUSIC SEMINARS** especially the first two seminars when I was on the organising committee, were at the time my greatest joys. I did enjoy the tours I led but music was an unstated ministry of my heart uncovered during my time in **CYTA**.

This trip back in time has brought back many happy memories but also times of great sadness, particularly of my "black" years from late in the year I turned 25 till late in the year I turned 29 when *God* gave me back my life that I had butchered.

I believe *God* watches us, protects us, (people could have died, but no one did on the New Zealand trip I have written about). *God* has expectations of each of us and speaks to us. I know *God* spoke to me four times in my "black" years which came out of a particular personal situation that started in **CYTA**. *God* gave me back my life after the dark period.

I am not a life planner. I am not sure why *God* leads me/us in certain directions, what plans *He* has for me/us and will never know.

Enjoy reading about the past. But remember the past is gone. There is today to thank *God* for and hopefully tomorrow, though eventually tomorrow will not come.

To **Kevin** and **Jan** especially but also to all former **CYTA TEAM MEMBER**s, friends of **CYTA**, all the staff, the coach captains and all those people who contributed to the wider mission field created by the existence of **CYTA**. This book is:

My gift to all of you

Going places - CYTA

Addendum

Going places - CYTA

1. Managers in order of appointment
Office Managers CYTA Sydney office
Ron Drayton

Steven Doran

Rod Hills for an interim period

Geoff Aurora

Office Manager Brisbane
Vic and Colleen Barrington – from 1976-1981

Office Manager Melbourne

Roger Vincent King

CYTA LODGE managers
Mervyn and Daisy Clare 1970-1975

Les and Ros Shakespeare 1975-1978

Kevin Pool Acting manager for a period in 1978

Bruce and Heather Bolton 1979-1993

Trevor and Lyn Blood 1993-1997

N.B. Pacific Hills Christian School purchased **CYTA LODGE** in June 1997.

2. Chaplains in order of appointment

Geoff Rowcroft

John Crowther

Garry Coleman

Steve Kearns

Going places - CYTA

3. Years Tours Commenced

1959/1962 School tours

1962 Tasmania

1965 Central Australia

1966 Fiji and Barrier Reef

167 Western Australia

1968 New Zealand

1968 Snowy Scheme Holidays, USA, Japan, Philippines, New Guinea and South Pacific Safari

1973 Israel, Himalayan Trek, Singapore and Thailand via Nepal

4. The Anne McDonald Bible College Scholarship Fund
Grants made to Students

1982-Jennifer Farrell Uniting Theological College $300

1983-Tracy Quinn Sydney Missionary and Bible College $450, Gary Mulquiney Moore College $450, Queen Lukins United Theological College $450

1984-Rodney Macready Morling Theological College $500, Heather Coombes Uniting Theological College $500

1985-Helen Richmond Uniting Theological College $500

1986-William Bassett Sydney Missionary and Bible College, $350 Phillip Scheul Morling Theological College, $350 Charles Green Moore Theological College $350

1987- Herry & Freda Kambuou Emmaus Bible College, $350 Peter Clegg Churches of Christ Theological College $350, Marilyn Hinton Churches of Christ Theological College $350

1988 -Marcus Amann Sydney Missionary and Bible College $500, Narelle Jones Tahlee Bible College $500

1989 - Stephen Kearns Churches of Christ Theological College $400, Peter Crawford Morling Theological College $400.00, Donna Johnson Emmaus Bible College $400.00

Going places - CYTA

1990-Alan Hood Morling Theological College $500, Maxwell Stewart Moore Theological College $500, Margery Gehrmann Moore Theological College $500

1991-Richard Howarth Churches of Christ Theological College $650.00 Richard Jenner Tahlee Bible College $650

1992-Neil Anderson Morling Theological College $550, Michelle Stewart Moore Theological College $550

1993-Richard Jones Sydney Missionary and Bible College $750

1994-Christian Corfu Emmaus Bible College $750

1995-Todd Rigby Aquilla College $750

1996-No applications received No grant made

1997-David Tidley Morling Theological College $650

1998/9-Geoff Gunton Sydney Missionary and Bible College $525

Value of Scholarships for 1982-1999 $14 775.00

2001 Wind up of fund:

 Morling College $8 300

Holy Trinity Anglican Church Panania Jubilee Fund

                                             $8 300

(Total $31,375)

These grants will keep on giving, far into the future.

4. Years of CYTA acting as sponsor for touring overseas music acts

Andraé Crouch 1973-75-76

Evie Tornqist - Karlsson 1976, 1977, 1978, and 1979 in conjunction with the Billy Graham Crusade

Ken Medema 1973, 1981, and ACMS

Sandi Patti 1982, 1987

Joni Eareckson Tada 1984

Steve Taylor 1985, 1987, and ACMS

Barry McGuire 1985, 1987

Kenny Marks 1986, also for Black Stump

Amy Grant Sydney Concert (assistance) 1983, 1984

5. Heather Andersen's A-Z List of "I've Been Everywhere" with CYTA

A – Alice Springs	N – New Zealand
B – Brisbane / Burnie	O – Overland
C – Cooma	P – Port Augusta
D – Darwin	Q – Queenstown
E – Eden	R – Richmond Tasmania
F – Fiji	S – Surfers Paradise and Sunshine Coast
G – Gold Coast	T – Tenant Creek
H – Hobart	U – Ulladulla
I – Inverell Gem hunting	V – Victoria
J – Jindabyne	W – Woomera – Wombeyan Caves
K – Kosciuszko	X – Xantippe (it is W.A.)
L – Lord Howe Island / Lightning Ridge	Y – Yarrangobilly Caves
M – Mt Isa	Z – Zeehan Tasmania

6. The A-Z of what CYTA means

(Heather Anderson, Kev's first Personal Assistant.)

Adventures	Every time you went on tour
Board **MEMBERS**	Whose vision and guidance for the growth of **CYTA** were inspirational
Camping trips	Loads of fun and most passengers cooperated by helping with camp chores
John Denver	Songs were popular and cassette tapes – then new – were nearly worn out when played on the coaches in the early '70s
Exercise	Blowing up air mattresses with foot pumps. We all had good leg muscles
Food	Glorious food on coach trips and at The **LODGE**. Boxes under each coach seat
Good times	**TOUR LEADERS** and **HOSTESSES** set the scene for successful holidays
Hygiene	To keep everyone healthy, we had a plastic bowl With DX to sanitise hands when on tour. This was nicknamed "Sadie The Cleaning Lady. A song by John (Johnnie) Farnham's newly released song in the '70s
Imagination	To keep everyone awake on long trips with quizzes and games
Jokes	Just having fun were sure to lift your spirits
Keenness	Rise early and set the tone for a new day
Lofty	An Aboriginal Tour Guide based on Ayers

Going places - CYTA

		Rock. We sent him letters with our arrival dates Lofty wrote on our letter by return- "ok".
M	Menus and	Lovingly prepared by Jan Craik and typed up by
M	Milk maids	Carole Reece. Up to 10 litres of powdered milk.
N	Nutritious meals	In my time, no-one had special diets
O	Opportunities	To learn new skills as a **TEAM** MEMBER
P	Pre-packing Passengers	Camp gear and food boxes that became special to us on each tour
Q	Quickness	Having a Plan B when unexpected things happened often
R	Reading	Bible passages and giving devotional talks each day prior to setting off on another travel day, around the campfire, cooking marshmallows
S	Sleep	Lack thereof. Sometimes surviving with shortened hours of sleep
T	Tea towel	The Washer People were greatly appreciated
U	Uniqueness	Of each person on tour and each tour
V	Values	Shared by our Christian **TOUR LEADER**S, wh impacted on lives of many **TOUR MEMBER**S
W	Willing Workers	Created a "**TEAM**" culture. Before, during and after
X	eXtra	Special moments which, 50+ years on, remembered
Y	Young at heart	Attitude helped in every challenge
Z	ZZZs...	Time of catch up on sleep after every tour/snow trip

Detailed Table of Contents

Part One – The Beginnings 11

1. 1956, Olympics, television and the inklings of CYTA 13
CYTA starts going places 13
A kindred spirit 24

Part Two – Buildings so much, manage 27

2. CYTA LODGE 29
3. SEASONS OF MINISTRY 41
   Everything changed - the LODGE was no more. 41
The Monaro Post November 28. 2019 at 5:43 PM ... 46
4. EVEN CYTA NEEDS AN OFFICE, STORAGE ... 51
Offices and training facilities 51
Storage of all that gear 59
5. OTHER VENTURES – NOTHING VENTURED, NO. GAIN 61
Kiah Ridge 61
Stories of coaches and other vehicles 66
   Not just property - A Hino Coach 66

Another Coach story- Not a coach owned by CYTA 67

The significance of the Leishman family to CYTA 68

Other vehicles 70

Part Three – The people who built CYTA 71

6. THE FIRST DIRECTORS, FAMILIES, COMMITMENTS 73

The Original DIRECTORS 73

The changing Board 83

The first change of a DIRECTOR 84

    From John Craik to Stuart Gow 84

Families of the original Directors 85

7. The TEAM, IT GROWS 87

The pre-TEAM 87

The TEAM – Beginnings and Growth 89

Training Nights 99

    Coming to the TEAM as a result of conversion 105

Wild Weekers 107

A time to leave the TEAM 108

One More Time, 22 April 2014 108

8. L'ABRI AND OTHER GIFTS 111

L'Abri 111
Other Gifts 114
    A pastor in training 114
9.   GROUPS, MINISTRIES, ACTIVTIES 115
Many Groups, ministries, activities 115
    On Eagles Wings (Men) 115
    World Vision Sponsorship 116
    Ex CYTA Friends Group 117
    Deportment Classes 119
    CYTA sports clubs and sponsorship 119
    Supporting Horizons Ministries 120
    Friends of CYTA 120
    Nissan is our car 121
    Church Promotions 122
    Fun and Frivolity 122
    Uncle Kevin's Pancakes 122
    End of Year Events 122
    The CYTA mums and dads 124
10.   YESTERDAY and TODAY 125
A great story to finish this chapter 131
11. TODAY AND TOMORROW 135
The Next Generation 135
    CYTA contributes to other ministries 146

12. TEAM EXPANSION – MELBOURNE AND BRISBANE 148
Melbourne 148
Brisbane 158
13. DEATH, FAITH, THE TEAM 160
Death in youth - Anne Macdonald 160
    Anne McDonald Fund 162
Paul Webb - A death of a Christian man 165
Death and a life well lived - Kim Forsyth 166
14. TEAM, WORK AND TRAINING WEEKENDS 170
Work Weekends 170
Family reunion work weekends 176
Training Weekends 177
15. THE PEOPLE OF CYTA LODGE 182
16. OFFICE, ADMINISTARTION TEAM 196
17. THE CHAPLAINS BEHIND THE TEAM 207
The significance of Chaplains 207
The first Chaplain - Geoff Rowcroft 207
John Crowther – Number 2 208
Garrett (Garry) Coleman 210
    Could he be called the Rev Head? 210
Steve Kearns the last chaplain 214
Were there some temporary chaplains? 218
    Fun and food - Word of Life 218

18. A SAFE PLACE TO DATE 221
Here comes the bride 221
Disappointment and hurt 231
    Dating with *God* the ultimate relationship 232
19. SOME OF THE KEY-NOTE SPEAKERS INCLUDED 235
20. KEVIN RECOGNISES 245

Part Four – The Tours   265

21. THE OTHER TOURS OF CYTA 269
22. THE TOURS - THE GOOD, UNUSUAL AND THE UGLY 277
The purpose of the tours 277
    The unusual from the tours 277
    A visit to the Shining Light Hospital Pothra Nepal 278
    Now to the Pacific 280
    How dare the King of Tonga disrupt a CYTA tour? 280
    Mystery Tours 281
23. THE TEAM IS ON TOUR 283
    A tour to New Zealand 283
    New Zealand yet again more good than bad . 287
    Barrier Reef - the good and the unexpected .. 289
    Barrier Reef - the bad but all good in the end 290

To Perth and back with an unusual request.. 293
The good and the unusual................................ 294
Central Australia – the middle of nowhere 295
Lofty.. 296
Fiji not all it's cracked up to be........................ 298
Tours – short comments on assorted tours 299
The good the bad, and the unusual................. 299
Serious problems 301
Tour Reflections from the Desk of Kevin Craik 301
A roll over.. 301
Almost a drop in the ocean 301
A view from the bridge................................... 301
But the ticket says.. 302
"*Yes I am staying at the YMCA.*" 303
Hoppy to the rescue 304
A sad sight.. 307
Surprise, Surprise 305
Two coincidences of timing 306
Coincidence One- Kevin catches Geof changing gear.. 306
Coincidence Two - Near at hand.................... 306
24. SNOW WEEKENDS.. 309
25. GRAND EUROPE TOURS.............................. 317
Overland 75 the trip that is still going 317

The Tour of '76 326
Another oft discussed trip in 1981 329

Part Five - The Music 333

26. CYTA MUSIC – THE INTERNATIONALS 335
Opera House Opening 335
27. CYTA MUSIC - THE LOCALS 345
The beginnings and the locals 345
Concerts, tours of Local Artists 346
True Colours the Voice 347
Sunday Sing 347
First Concert 347
Short tours by local artists 348
The night band members catch a felon 350
Talent in the TEAM 352
Concerts and Costs 352
28. AUSTRALIAN CHRISTIAN MUSIC SEMNAR (ACMS) 355
Foundation to Seminar 355
A Children's program at ACMS 360
Notes of thanks from ACMS 363
29. ACMS - FEATURED ARTISTS AND SPEAKERS
.... 365
30. RESPONSE TO AND IMPACT OF ACMS 373
Food sleep and music 373

Not just music 375
The Formation of the Christian Dance Fellowship 375
   A side note: Mary's tale of a moving seat 376
Impact in Worship 377
The Witness 377
Waratah Girls' Choir 379
Impact on Attendees 381
   Random Reflections of attendees 384
Future? 386
   Was it worth it? 387
31. "TRUE COLOURS" AND "THE VOICE" 388
The move to create new ministries 388
31. BEYOND THE BLACK STUMP 395

Part Six - The initiators, the stayers 403

32. THE DECISION TO FINISH up 405
The end of CYTA though it lingers on 408
33. KEVIN AND JAN 411
Reflections 411
An Interview with Kevin and Jan for this book 419
   The public and private always the same 431

Part Seven – My Chapters – The author 433

35. THE MAN, THE TIMING, THE MISSION 435
36. THE MESSAGE OF THE STORY OF CYTA 444
Is there a message for you from this book 419
Which response applies to you? 445
ACKNOWLEDGEMENTS 447
Author Acknowledgements 447
Kevin Craik Acknowledgements 449
Dione Schoeman chief encourager, supporter and active writer 449
Howard Reid The author behind Going Places CYTA 450
Authors note: 453
This Book 453

Addendum 457

1. Managers in order of appointment 458
Office Managers CYTA Sydney office 458
Office Manager Brisbane 458
CYTA LODGE managers 458
2. Chaplains in order of appointment 459
3. Years Tours Commenced 460
4. The Anne McDonald Bible College Scholarship Fund 461

Grants made to Students 461
5. Years of CYTA, acting as sponsor for overseas music 463
6. Heather Andersen's A-Z List of "I've Been Everywhere" with CYTA 464
7. The A-Z of what CYTA means 464
Detailed list of content 464

www.ingramcontent.com/pod-product-compliance
Lightning Source LLC
Chambersburg PA
CBHW071951290426
44109CB00018B/1991